Father Lacombe

Also by James G. MacGregor

Blankets and Beads (1949)
The Land of Twelve-Foot Davis (1953)
Behold the Shining Mountains (1954)
North-West of Sixteen (1958)
Pack Saddles to Tête Jaune Cache (1962)
Edmonton Trader (1963)
Peter Fidler (1966)
Edmonton: A History (1967)
Vilni Zemli: The Ukrainian Settlement of Alberta (1969)
The Klondike Rush Through Edmonton (1970)
A History of Alberta (1972)
Overland by the Yellowhead (1974)
Paddle Wheels to Bucket-Wheels on the Athabasca (1974)

James G. MacGregor

Father Lacombe

Hurtig Publishers
Edmonton

Hurtig Publishers
10560 105 Street
Edmonton, Alberta

ISBN 0-88830-091-3

Printed and bound in Canada
by John Deyell Company

Contents

Acknowledgments

For anyone seeking more than a casual insight into the life of Father Lacombe, access to *Les Missions de la Congrégation des Missionaires Oblats de Marie-Immaculée* and the *Archives de la maison provinciale des Oblats à Saint-Joachim* is essential. Fortunately through the friendship and kindness of Rev. Father Eméric O. Drouin, O.M.I. of the *Archives Oblats*, Edmonton, I have enjoyed that privilege. Since I started delving into these mines of information on the early history of the prairies, their documents, letters and diaries have been deposited in the Provincial Archives of Alberta. As usual the staff there have been most kind to me.

In following the adventures of Father Lacombe I have been fortunate in being able to compare the points of view expressed in the three published biographies of Father Lacombe — those by Katherine Hughes, Rev. Father Paul Breton and *par une Sr. de la Providence.*

Once again I have had the usual helpful assistance from the Glenbow-Alberta Institute, the Cameron Library and the Centennial Library in Edmonton, the Dominion Archives in Ottawa and the provincial archives of Manitoba and of Saskatchewan, while Mrs. La Rose of the Edmonton City Archives stretched forth her hand to give me most timely help.

With her habitual kindness Mrs. Shirlee A. Smith, now archivist of the Hudson's Bay Company Archives for the Manitoba Provincial Archives, has allowed me to quote brief passages from some of the volumes of the Hudson's Bay Record

Society and from the Fort Edmonton journals. The extracts used herewith are published with her permission.

I am particularly grateful to the Honourable Horst A. Schmid's Department of Culture, Youth and Recreation for a grant which helped defray my expenses in visiting the Public Archives in Ottawa and also the archives of Saskatchewan and Manitoba.

I cannot forget the kindness of the Reverend Father Gérard Théorêt, Paroisse St. Sulpice, Quebec, who when I visited him took a generous and helpful interest in my project and gave me pictures of his interesting old church to which Father Lacombe had returned so often.

To Claire Kirkland I am also greatly in debt for her kindness in translating many a passage in various documents in the Oblate Archives when my rudimentary knowledge of French started me stumbling.

The photographs used in the book have come from the following sources, to all of which I am very much indebted: Glenbow-Alberta Institute, Provincial Archives of Alberta, Provincial Archives of Victoria, B.C., the Hudson's Bay Company, the St. Albert Historical Society and the Reverend Father Théorêt.

Introduction

When Albert Lacombe was born in Quebec in 1827, western Canada was a far-off wilderness. When in 1849 he first came out as a newly ordained priest he found it to consist of a small settlement, where Winnipeg and St. Boniface are now, at the fringe of a thousand miles of parklands in which there were half a dozen sod-roofed Protestant and Catholic missions and a handful of Hudson's Bay Company posts.

When he died in 1916, the 1,600,000 inhabitants of that wilderness had divided it into three provinces, each of which boasted a number of cities of which Winnipeg with its 150,000 people was the largest. Not only had he witnessed that transition from empty wilderness to economic wonderland, but for sixty-seven years he had played a leading and sometimes vital part in its success. For nearly twenty years, from his crude headquarters at Lac Ste. Anne or St. Albert, he had devoted his life almost exclusively to those with native blood: to the Métis for whom he had a special affection and to his wandering Assiniboine, Blackfoot and Cree neophytes.

During the ten years following he filled many roles: beggar and diplomat for his bishop, colonizer, parish priest at the new village of Winnipeg and confessor to rowdy gangs on Canadian Pacific Railway construction. Returning again to Alberta, hoping to shepherd the Blackfoot into the new agricultural day that was dawning, he kept peace between their angry leaders and the CPR. During the North-West Rebellion his influence did much to keep the mighty Blackfoot Confederacy from

9

wiping the West's slate clean of white men. And during all that time he moved about as parish priest in the new NWMP towns of Fort Macleod and Calgary, and was soon involved in starting one of the first of Canada's Indian Industrial Schools for the Blackfoot.

About that time the vexing question of sectarian schools raised its head and for a few years as ambassador for his bishop, and indeed for the Catholic hierarchy, the old Indian missionary directed his many talents into political channels. He enjoyed astonishing success, becoming the friend and sometimes confidant of three or four of Canada's prime ministers, and at one stage he tried his hand at making and unmaking a federal cabinet. On the schools issue Lacombe ultimately suffered defeat at the hands of his compatriot and fellow religionist, Wilfrid Laurier, yet he still retained deep and vibrant friendships with most of Canada's senior politicians.

Always busy with charitable works, he played a leading part in the encouragement of *Quebecois* settlement on the prairies. Observing that the morale of the Métis was being eaten away by encroaching white civilization, he organized the St. Paul des Métis colony to help them help themselves. Finally, in his eighties, he brought into being the Lacombe Home for the Poor. All along he had a hand in every pioneer advance.

With his experience of decades of hunger and hardship spent in Indian camps came a deep understanding of prairie Indians, and he became an expert on matters affecting them. Following his day to day experiences in some detail offers us an opportunity to utilize his knowledge to reconstruct a period in the history of the West about which all too little has been written — that period from 1850 to 1870 — and that is part of the purpose of this book.

Adventures — hunts, epidemics, wars and rumours of wars — had crowded into his earlier years. Benevolence, wisdom and political sagacity crowned his later years. In his youth he had galloped frantically to the rescue of his beleaguered Métis in their decisive battle with the Sioux. A few years later, during an attack upon a Blackfoot camp, he had rushed to make peace and had been hit by a Cree bullet. Year after year he attended the victims of epidemics, ministering to the living and burying the dead. Year after year, sometimes waist-deep in snow and often going for days without a morsel to eat, he had ranged the prairies. Through these adventures he had grown in stature with white men and Indians alike. As the years sped by anniversaries followed on each other's heels: his seventieth birthday, fifty years as a priest; his eightieth birthday, and sixty years as a priest. And each one found him ever more benign and more beloved by his many associates and ever rising in public acclaim as the Old Chief of the West, until before his death in 1916 he had become a legend in his own lifetime. Finally, when his earthly days had ended, all Canada paused to pay homage to his memory.

Prior to his death some sixty years ago Katherine Hughes wrote her excellent *Father Lacombe: The Black-Robe Voyageur*. In the present work there is little about the man himself to add to her account. It does, however, attempt to tell the great man's story to a current generation of readers from the slightly different point of view of a Protestant admirer. Moreover, it is hoped that it presents a closer look at the conditions of life on the western prairies during the fifties, sixties and seventies of the nineteenth century against which to view the heroic priest's intense activity and courage. If in addition, here and there between the lines, it presents some of the wild magnificence of the parkland landscape as Father Lacombe saw it, the cause of the parklands will be well served. If through it, of a summer evening after a brief shower when down by a creek the mists start to rise, an occasional reader should glimpse shadowy tepees or hear the moan of a smallpox victim, the author will not have written in vain.

CHAPTER ONE

Preparation

On a February day in 1827, when dull clouds blanketed the
rich, flat land of the parish of St. Sulpice and turned the mile-
wide expanse of the St. Lawrence River to a sullen grey, Albert
Lacombe was born. That gloom was not reflected in the home
of his habitant parents, Albert and Agathe, for the arrival of
this robust first-born boy dispelled the dejection of some
months' standing over the death of his infant sister and filled
the house with sunshine.

As Albert and Agathe gloated and friendly neighbours came
to rejoice, all held high hopes for his future. In time he would
surely help his powerful father clear more stumps and go with
his mother back along the strip farm to the maple sugar bush.
In time he might have an opportunity, denied Albert and
Agathe, of going to school. In time — who knew? — the Virgin
might look favourably on their devotion and sacrifice and ex-
alt him to the high calling of a priest. For a sturdy lad reared
in the hard working, wholesome environment of Father Viau's
parish, all things might be possible.

In St. Sulpice parish, with its humble yet cozy and sometimes commodious log homes, its plain but nourishing farm
fare and its dawn to dusk toil by a gregarious society, many
things were possible. For its parishioners were daring, intelligent and witty fathers, and devoted, tidy and thrifty mothers
and grandmothers. Having been reared in that society, regardless of whether he remained to farm or to lumber in the nearby woods, or even went farther afield into the *pays d'en haut*,

far off to the west to paddle canoes or trade with the Indians, Albert, like his forebears, would measure up as a man.

For generations they had been sturdy men meeting the hardships of pioneering in new and harsh lands. For some decades the Lacombes had been domiciled in St. Eustache parish along La Rivière des Mille Isles, a branch of the St. Lawrence west of Ile Jesus and the island of Montreal. Then Augustin Lacombe, son of Pierre and Marguerite Chretien, had moved downstream some thirty-five miles to the parish of St. Sulpice where in 1824 his son Albert had married Agathe Duhamel.

Even when Augustin had come to live in St. Sulpice it was already an old settlement, having joined in the celebration of its first mass in 1706. And many a tale its old ones had to tell of their forebears' hardships and heroism, of the adventures encountered as the settlers sought their livelihood from the fish of the St. Lawrence in front of their homes, or from the game of the woods behind their river lots, or from the little fields they had hacked out of their hardwood forests. Some stories told of warding off the lumbering bears which denned in the nearby woods. Indeed, the first burials entered in the St. Sulpice records were those of two children mauled by bears. Every family in the community had its tale of capture or death during the Indian raids of the pioneer days. None, however, was of more interest than that told by Albert Lacombe's grandparents.

One day shortly after the lands of the parish of St. Sulpice had been claimed and everyone was toiling to enlarge the little patches of cleared acres, all the adults of the Beaupré family were working at the edge of the forest with their guns leaning against nearby trees. The two younger children had been left with Marie Louise, their sixteen-year-old sister. She had been told to keep them near the house and to give the alarm if she saw any Indians prowling around. At any time the dreaded Iroquois might raid the settlement.

What happened no one ever knew, but when the group returned from their clearing it was to find the younger children howling in fear; their elder sister had vanished. As the news spread, all the neighbours asserted that no Iroquois had been encountered in the woods or seen on the river. It was true that two or three canoes paddled by Ojibways had been noticed, but they were friendly Indians and therefore were not under suspicion. In any event, the girl had disappeared and as the days extended into weeks and months she was presumed dead.

One of her uncles, however, was a trader whose ventures took him far into the *pays d'en haut*, allowing him to return to St. Sulpice only at intervals of two or three years. One evening near Sault Ste. Marie, some five years after the girl's disappearance and some seven hundred miles along the main water route leading west from Montreal, this uncle pulled his canoe up the pebbly beach to spend the night trading with a camp of Ojibways. Before long he noticed that one of the Indian women nursing a baby was watching every move he made. Two or three times their glances met before he became aware that she was a white girl and before he suddenly recognized her as his niece. Being careful not to let the rest of the camp observe his interest in her, he nevertheless managed to talk to her and to arrange that in the dark he would steal her away.

On their long trip home to St. Sulpice she told him the details of her capture and her sojourn with the Ojibways. Once she had ceased struggling and they could trust her not to try to run away, the Indians had treated her well and in due course a young man chose her for his wife. But for the fact of her captivity and the wandering life of an Indian band she had fared reasonably well and had borne her husband two children.

Great indeed was the excitement and rejoicing upon her return to St. Sulpice with her two infants. A year or so later, in 1767, she married Pierre Duhamel, who raised the two children as his own. They became respected members of the parish and one of them was to become young Albert Lacombe's grandmother. From her came his inheritance of Ojibway or Saulteaux blood.

Long after this incident the woods gradually became tamed, the fields grew larger and by the time the baby Albert's father was a young man, the parish had become a comfortable, thriving community. By 1823 the settlers had felt prosperous enough to build the fine stone church which still rears its steeple proudly to watch over the mighty river and to assert its benign authority over the surrounding flat fields. During his long life,

Albert Lacombe had many a reason to count himself fortunate that he was descended from such stock, that he had been born into the affection of a French Canadian home and reared in the security of a parish along the St. Lawrence.

The family did all the work about the home and the farm and as Albert grew up he laboured long hours beside his father out in the sunny fields. When winter came with its heavy snowfall, the work load was reduced to the chores necessary to tend the livestock. It was then that young Albert, the first-born son, worked in the shop with his father fashioning all the tools and utensils needed about the farm or home. In doing so he developed the skilful hands of the craftsman. Everything used was home-carded, homespun or homemade. All the food was home-grown and while it produced a limited and at times a somewhat coarse fare, nevertheless, all his life Albert could look back fondly to the delightful meals prepared by Madame Lacombe's loving hands.

Outside the home, the road winding along the north bank of the St. Lawrence was dotted with neighbours' houses, each within shouting distance of another and thus forming a comfortable community in a comforting society. While the road along the river ran all the way from Montreal to Quebec City, the habitants' vision rarely extended beyond the limits of the parish. Its development and much of its progress had been achieved by the tireless clergy who in turn were guided by higher ecclesiastical authority. The curés with their intimate knowledge of their parishioners not only did all the lay clerical work but were always the leaders in their communities.

As Albert Lacombe was growing up many of the older folk could remember back to the days of the collapse of the French regime in 1760. After the final capitulation of the French in that year the Catholic church was the only formal organization that remained to deal with the British administration. As such, the incoming rulers relied on it as the go-between to the people, and the habitants knew it to be the only institution which could plead their cause with the new authorities. As such, the church's influence increased and during the next half-century acquired a political importance it had never possessed previously. In that capacity it had been forced to assume the role of protector of both the Roman Catholic faith and of the French Canadians who were caught in the midst of an otherwise Protestant North America.

During that era the church's higher officials fought with patience, diplomacy and strength to maintain the civil and religious rights of their flock. Falling in line here and there they established a mutual dependence between the new administration and their church, a dependence which resulted in the tradition of loyalty to the British crown that for so long was one of the dominant attitudes of the Catholic church.

Furthermore, due to their diplomacy and tact, church officials were able to wrest control of the system of education from the uncertain hands of the British civil authorities. Thereafter, at great cost in energy and money, the clergy began developing its system of Catholic schools which were later to play such a vital part in the lives of the habitants. In the heroic struggles which the church had put up on their behalf lay added reasons which endeared the curés to their parishioners. More than ever before the parish priest became the pastor of his flock; he became their revered and beloved leader.

And no parish had a priest more respected and loved than Father Viau who during Albert Lacombe's youth ruled his St. Sulpice flock with a firm but gentle hand. It was he who watched the Lacombe family increase until in all Agathe had borne eight children. Of the six which arrived while Albert was growing up, the only boy, Gaspard, and two of the girls eventually settled down far from their home parish. In due course this moderate sized family of devoted children shared in the hard work of Albert *père*'s fertile farm.

But all was not incessant toil and Albert enjoyed the coziness of the family hearth and the conviviality of the socially minded community. Around the fireplace the talk sometimes turned to speculation about the fortunes of his father's uncle, Joseph, who many years before had left the security of Quebec and gone out to the prairies of the far, far West. From time to time for a few years his family heard snatches of news about him and how he had become a voyageur travelling in the remote hinterland of the Athabasca and Saskatchewan rivers. Then when Albert was about ten Uncle Joseph had come back to St. Sulpice for a visit and had told the boy that he had married a Cree girl and had a few children. That visit was the last time anyone in the family ever saw him.

In having a relative who had gone out into the West the Lacombe family was not alone. Most people in St. Sulpice parish had someone who came home at long intervals to tell of adventures in that vast land so many hundreds of leagues away — so many weeks of continuous travel away.

All of these tales of adventure made their impression on Albert. Though the community, all of one race and all of one religion, was so self-contained, nevertheless the waters of the mighty St. Lawrence lapped at the feet of its fields. Many a time, like all the lads, he had strolled across the two or three hundred yards separating his home from the river's edge and, standing on its relatively low bank, had gazed out across its mighty flood.

Down it sailed ships headed for Trois Rivières and for Quebec City 125 miles away, and beyond that, beyond the Atlantic Ocean, thousands of miles away lay France. Up the river some twenty-five miles went other craft bound for the vast city of Montreal with its bustling population of 50,000 and its bishop's palace. Beyond that, incredibly far away, lay the West and the *pays d'en haut*. As Albert watched and talked with the other boys many a dream of adventure flitted through his mind.

As Albert *père* realized, part of the fulfilment of dreams lay in education. Ordinarily, as the oldest son and at the time the only son, Albert's role would be to succeed his father on the farm and to leave the outside world with its many tricks and complications to others less fortunate. Nevertheless, despite the fact that the boy's help was needed on the farm, his father was willing to make the sacrifice which allowed his son to attend school, a sacrifice to which Agathe gladly acquiesced. Recognizing the boy's ability, she had her own secret ambitions for him.

Since there was no school in St. Sulpice, she cheered him on his way each morning when for three years he set out on his three-mile walk to the school in the neighbouring parish of Lavaltrie. There his intelligence and ambition soon mastered the art of reading and writing and made him eager to seize the knowledge held out to his keen mind. Every night his mother was a glad accomplice as he told her of the new ideas that his schooling was putting within his grasp. Agathe, however, was not the only one who held out high hopes for young Albert, for Father Viau had been watching the boy.

Beloved by all, Father Viau, a corpulent little man and grey around the temples, knew the secrets and the hopes of everyone in his parish. Quick to castigate sin or irreverence, ever ready to encourage the heedful and never failing to prod the slothful, he guided his flock with an unwavering hand. Though his life had its share of the vexing problems borne by all priests, nevertheless it was a comfortable existence and had its enjoyable aspects. Certainly as he drove his pot-bellied horse and his rickety buggy, he was always welcomed with smiles and joy whenever he stopped before any door.

No one welcomed him with more cheerful goodwill than Albert and Agathe Lacombe or with deeper respect than their son, young Albert. A bond was forming between the curé and this sturdy lad with the dark skin and jet black hair, who in reminiscence of the Indian strain in his blood the father in kindly jest called *"mon petit sauvage."* When late in the summer of 1840 the good father called to talk to the parents of the thirteen-year-old boy it was to suggest that if they agreed to Albert furthering his education at the college in nearby L'Assomption, the curé would see that he and the church would find the money to pay for his schooling. That early in Albert's life the father had discerned in him the qualities which, carefully nurtured and guided, might fit him to be a priest.

Nothing could have pleased the boy more. That night during a session of prayers much longer than usual and for many days thereafter the family offered thanks for the good fortune that had fallen to their lot. Their thanksgiving, however, had its fringe of anguish.

Albert, the boy of thirteen, eager to embark on his studies, nevertheless dreaded the approaching day when he must make the almost final break which would leave behind the tenderness and warmth of the family home. Bursts of anticipation alternated with bouts of inner anguish which he tried to conceal from his father and mother. On their part, they too were counting the diminishing days that lay between them and the morning when they must set out to deliver their son into strange hands and in effect cast him forever into the outer world. When, finally, that morning came, Albert *père* hitched the team to the wagon and the family climbed aboard for the two-hour trip to town.

On one or two previous occasions young Albert had made this eight-mile trip to L'Assomption. It was a pleasant little village with widely spaced homes and stores strung along its typical, tree-shaded habitant main street. Much of its charm lay in its almost total enclosure by the windings of L'Assomption River, which on its way south from the Laurentian hills had hesitated before losing itself in the St. Lawrence River. In its hesitation it had taken an abrupt turn and for about two miles flowed east through the flat farm lands before making a hairpin bend and doubling back west to envelope a long peninsula which was never more than half a mile wide. The hamlet's main street, running east and west, bisected that point of land.

On the street called the boulevard *L'Ange Gardien*, L'Assomption College had been built. Although at the time of Albert's entry the school was only eight years old, it had already acquired an enviable reputation and young scholars from many a Quebec parish were eager to attend its classes. To them it offered the Catholic curriculum of the day, designed to turn out highly competent scholars of whom the best fitted would go on to holy orders.

A couple of blocks south of its relatively new stone building the river flowed west. To the north, about the same distance, lay the cemetery with its northern edge washed by the river on its easterly swing. Beside the cemetery and on the far side of the stream lay the college's vegetable gardens and its extensive fields. To these fields the institution looked for much of its support and to its husky young scholars it looked for the labour to till and harvest the crops. In this way, helping to support themselves, the young men worked off much of their exuberant energy.

Within the college's walls every boy partook of meals derived mainly from the produce of the fields he tilled. Many a time, like all the other boys, Albert Lacombe contrasted longingly the plain fare of the college table with his memories of the fragrances which wafted from his mother's kitchen. Many a time too when doing his own laundry the student looked back nostalgically to the home which had provided all the services a boy needed but had never really noticed before.

But the boys had little time to waste on nostalgia. Their days, starting with an early breakfast, followed by attendance at mass, flowed by in a round of classes. For seven years, Latin, Greek, French and philosophy alternated with syntax, rhetoric, literature and versification and led to frequent oral and written examinations. Black-robed but generally kind instructors dominated their lives and demanded strict observance of regulations and strict adherence to the code of conduct that was to make gentlemen and indeed scholarly gentlemen of them all. At all times an air of solemn dignity and an atmosphere of piety and devotion pervaded the halls and classrooms. But if the fathers were strict, they were invariably just and impartial to all.

In their hands Albert, like his associates, came to realize the value of discipline. Under their guidance he developed the almost mystic love he and his fellows had for each other — the tender regard for a fellow doing his best, the complete forgiveness for one who fell short that was to characterize them in later life. Building on the good material of a husky farm boy, the wise heads of the institution added to it a generous helping of book learning, a deep sense of piety and the ready obedience to discipline that produced the calibre of a man that they could foresee in Albert Lacombe. As well as forming a lifelong attachment to most of his fellow scholars who later on were to rise to important positions on the Canadian scene, he carried from the college a lively sense of gratitude to his instructors. Nearly half a century later he was to write: "This dear L'Assomption House, in spite of distance and years, remains one of my precious souvenirs. Never will I be able to forget this dear home of learning and virtue."

Occasionally, however, on short holidays, Albert was able to return to bask in the homely luxuriousness enjoyed under the parental roof. Then, taking his place within the hallowed walls of the church of St. Sulpice, he listened to Father Viau and afterwards at the *presbytère* enjoyed long chats with his revered mentor. Once in a while the good father, driving over to L'Assomption, tied his horse to the college hitching rack, went in to see how Albert was doing and came away proud of his protégé.

Similarly, the rector of the college, pleased with Albert's progress and knowing of the boy's desire to go on to the priesthood, eventually put him in charge of a junior class. There, instructing younger students — one of whom was J. N. Ritchot — Albert sharpened his own grasp of his studies. His ability, application and pleasing personality were rapidly hauling him up the ladder of preferment. After the passage of seven immensely rewarding years, he was given the chance of continuing his studies in Archbishop Bourget's palace in Montreal.

There he was in a new world. For Montreal was not only the largest city in the Canadas but their commercial capital. It was a far cry from the rural parish of St. Sulpice or the classical college of L'Assomption.

But the farm bred boy had little time to investigate its allure. He was far too caught up in the stirring changes which were agitating Quebec's religious life and which not only resounded through the palace but indeed had their inspiration there. In a large measure they emanated from the dedicated, disciplined brain of Bishop Ignace Bourget. For about the time Albert Lacombe had started his studies at L'Assomption the saintly priest had entered upon his labours as bishop of Montreal by throwing his weight into the struggle against the liberal and anti-clerical spirit of the preceding era. His ultramontane outlook had already revivified the clergy and had gone far to infuse a new and growing nationalistic spirit into Quebec. In France, Catholic circles, enduring a wave of anti-clericalism, were experiencing difficulties and under Bourget's inspiration, French Canadians began to look upon themselves as charged with the divine mission of ensuring that Quebec should become France's successor as the prominent Catholic nation. Moreover, Bishop Bourget was one of the leaders who gave every encouragement to the few priests of the Oblate order who had recently come from France to serve in Quebec.

When he was appointed an undersecretary to Canon Pare, Albert Lacombe quickly became a part of this challenging crusade. At the same time, of course, he pursued his theological studies under the tutelage of Monsignor Prince, the coadjutor bishop. One of his fellow students who became a lifelong friend was Edouard Fabre, destined to become archbishop of Montreal. Father Viau's *petit sauvage* (a nickname which had been carried into the palace) was fortunate in his contact with this scion of a highly honoured family and from him learned much of a way of life and a philosophy rarely glimpsed by a farm boy.

From the constant flow of priests who came from their far-flung rural parishes and stayed a few days to consult their bishop, he also learned much. They were good men, usually congenial, genuinely pious and always concerned for their parishioners. For the most part they led comfortable lives, but in spite of his love for his former curé Father Viau, Albert often looked at them and hesitated. From a stripling of more than average height he had grown into a robust man. Moreover, although he may not have realized it, he was developing itchy feet that might soon tire of the rounds and the bounds of a circumscribed parish.

Bishop Bourget and the rest of his mentors, ever guiding and ever watching, wondered too. For in the great cause of Catholicism they needed strong men. Of the many who appeared to be called to its ranks, few could be chosen and the heavy responsibility of choosing lay in their hands. Observing his devotion, sensing his strength and encouraging his gropings towards the goals of their mystic high calling, they waited for some sign of the challenge against which Albert Lacombe would pit his strength and to which he would dedicate his life.

That challenge came during the winter of 1848 when Father Georges Belcourt, a missionary from the hamlet of Pembina on the frontier of the far western plains, came to Montreal seeking alms for his work amongst the Indians. A tall, rugged, brusque man, he brought the fresh air of the endless prairies into the palace and with it tales of battling Saulteaux and Sioux, as he pleaded for help — money and men — to carry the cross to these pagan people. His tales were of thundering buffalo herds, of alternating feast and famine in Indian lodges, of suffering thirst in the scorching summer heat and of hardship and death in bitter winter blizzards. His talk was of great rivers coursing through vast plains, the Missouri, the Athabasca and the Saskatchewan. He numbered on his fingers the tiny chapels planted along them three hundred miles apart where black-robed missionaries armed with little but their bare hands fought to bring peace and hope to warring tribes. Whether in the palace's parlour, at table or in chapel, he pleaded for men fit to pick up the gauntlet he flung at them.

Though many of his young listeners were stirred, none was more ready to take up the challenge than Albert Lacombe. And when one Sunday night the rugged missionary preached in the old Cathedral Basilica of Mary, Queen of the World and St. James the Greater, throwing out his challenge, Albert came away bemused and nearly speechless as for certain he glimpsed his mission in the world. When in later life he recalled that sermon he was to say: "I was struck to the heart. An interior voice called to me and I replied 'Behold, I am here; send me.' "

Next morning he pleaded with his bishop to let him go. But the older man, perhaps merely testing him but also sadly aware that wild enthusiasm is often a sign of weakness and uncertainty, advised him to delay his decision, to think it over and to pray to seek God's will.

Canon Pare and Canon Mercier likewise counseled delay. So did the aging Abbé Viau. By this time he was an invalid in a nearby home but as he looked at his *petit sauvage* and thought of earlier days in St. Sulpice and remembered his one-time comfortable *presbytère,* he urged the young man to follow in his steps and seek the security of a parish.

But he could not heed their kindly advice and, as he admitted in his old age, he even thought of giving up his clerical career if he could not fight the church's battles on its faraway front. "I wanted to make every sacrifice, or none at all. That was my nature." As the spring with its scent of adventure swept over Montreal, he became restless. Finally, after many a plea, the good bishop, feeling that he had tested Albert enough, told him to prepare to take his sacred vows. After his ordination he would be allowed to go to the far West.

In his elation he ran to tell Abbé Viau, who, glad to see that the seed he had planted in the mind of a young boy had borne such magnificent fruit, gave him his blessing.

On June 13, 1849, in the old college of St. Hyacinthe, in a solemn ceremony witnessed by hundreds, he was raised to the priesthood. That day sixty priests stood in line to bless him, to lay a hand on his head and then to salute him as their brother and their equal. Whether his mother Agathe and his father were there, we do not know, but after the ceremony he again sought out his beloved mentor.

But when he reached the hospice the Abbé Viau was dead. Gently they broke the news to the sorrowing youth that the very hour of his ordination his dear friend's soul had sought repose with his Maker. Writing many years later, Father Lacombe described how he wept unreservedly beside the body and how Abbé Viau seemed to say "I have finished the course. Take my place as priest, for I have helped to make you what you are today."

If, however, this great sorrow was to temper his elation, the passing of weeks helped to mellow him. Nearly two months were to go by before he could leave for the West. Some of that time was spent in eager contemplation of his approaching adventure, but most of it was devoted to prayer. Finally, however, the evening before his departure was to be marked by the outstanding episode of his career and by a humility he had never previously experienced.

For that evening in the palace chapel after appropriate prayers and in the presence of his peers and so many of his betters, Bishop Bourget called him to the altar and bid him stand before the tabernacle. Well he knew that they were about to bid him godspeed in his career in the manner followed by the Seminary of Foreign Missions at Paris. On previous occasions he had watched it but now when it was about to happen to him he was caught up in an anguish of disbelief that he could be worthy of such tribute. Before him in solemn and benign array stood the flower of the Diocese of Montreal, Archbishop Bourget, canons and priests. And now as he stood humble and filled with almost suffocating emotion, the venerable archbishop kneeled and kissed his feet. "How beautiful upon the mountains are the feet of him that bringeth good tidings and that preacheth peace. . . ." Then one by one, canons and curés in a reverent and never to be forgotten procession approached, kneeled and also kissed his feet.

He gradually came to realize that it was not Albert Lacombe that these men honoured, not the farm boy from St. Sulpice, but the recently raised ambassador of Christ that they were sending out to carry the divine message to the ends of the wilderness and to the pagan Indians. Father Viau had found him a bright boy, many of these men had taught him and honed his disciplined mind and now they honoured the priest they had made of him. For they knew what so few people ever learn, that good deeds and great sacrifices come only from believing hearts. And in that moment if never before, even through his embarrassment — perhaps because of it — he could perceive the spiritual world and in a rapt trance merged with it. With a clarity he had never known before, he beheld a rough-hewn cross, and Christ and the tears of the Virgin Mary. Forever these were to be his driving forces and his verities.

To conclude the service the bishop reminded him of the sacrifice he had imposed on himself. "My dear brother, we cannot go with you on your journey, but you will be accompanied by our prayers. . . . Go to those nations still seated in darkness and ignorance. . . . Go and make them children of God."

Then coming closer, he concluded solemnly: "My son, never forget your holy and precious calling. . . . *If God is with you, who can be against you.*"

On the morrow Albert Lacombe was to step forth on his long road.

CHAPTER TWO

Provencher's
Pioneer Missions

Nine years before Albert had come to form part of the happy
Lacombe household, three intrepid Roman Catholic priests had
left Montreal to carry the light of the cross to the western wilderness. Six years earlier still, at modern day Winnipeg, a few
of Lord Selkirk's settlers had clambered up the river bank to
start the first agricultural colony on the prairies — the Red
River Settlement. With them had come the Reverend Charles
Bourke, the first man of the cloth to set foot on Canada's
prairies. He had done so in an irregular manner without the
blessing or permission of his Irish bishop of Killala and his
service at Red River smacked so much of other anomalies that
he soon returned to Ireland.

For a few years misfortune which was to embitter relations
between the Métis and the white newcomers dogged Selkirk's
settlement. By 1818, however, Lord Selkirk had arranged with
Bishop Joseph Octave Plessis of Quebec that the first trio of
pioneering French Canadian priests should be sent to the settlement. At Selkirk's suggestion, Sir John Coape Sherbrooke,
governor-in-chief at Quebec, granted the church a seigniory
embracing an area of twenty square miles on the east side of
the Red River near the mouth of the Seine, as well as an area
of some twenty acres on the west side. On July 16, 1818, the
three priests, Joseph Norbert Provencher, Severe Joseph Nicolas
Dumoulin and Guillaume Etienne Edge, stepped ashore to size
up the settlement and to get their first look at the illimitable,
grassy prairies extending west from the river.

Of the three, all of whom had been somewhat reluctant to obey the bishop's orders to pioneer in the West, the powerful six-foot-four Provencher was to prove the most enduring. The psychological wrench of foregoing a gratifying and possibly even humdrum parish amidst the contentment of Quebec's settled and comfortable countryside and plunging into the stark uncouthness of the frontier was not a light one. Some of their successors, indeed, were to find that wrench too much to endure and soon returned to *la belle province*.

Provencher, resolutely determined to make the best of the situation, wrote his superior, saying: "This is indeed a fine country, the river is large. It has a border of oaks, elms, poplars, aspens, etc. Beyond this fringe of woods extend prairies as far as the eye can reach. . . . The soil seems excellent."

It was to be a month or so before he dared to write expressing his opinion of his flock, the overwhelming majority of whom were Métis. When he did, he regretted that "their commerce with the whites, instead of advancing them towards civilization, has served only to drive them away therefrom." Father Provencher had come face to face with a problem which for a century and a half was to test the tact, skill and humanity of a devoted line of his successors.

The Red River Settlement and the outpost of Pembina to which the priests had come to minister had a combined population of about a thousand souls. Some sixty-five of them were de Meuron soldiers, a remnant of the Swiss mercenary regiment that served under the British during the War of 1812, and nominally Roman Catholic and there were about twice that number of Canadiens who were practising Catholics. Then there were 225 Scottish settlers, mainly Protestant, and the balance, over five hundred, were Métis and practically all pagan.

The settlement was an uneasy mingling of civilization and barbarism. So too were its mainstay, the Métis, who for all their brilliance and intelligence, all their vivacity and colour, were an uncertain and unsettled mixture. For several generations their conflict, the contact of ancient French and English culture with primitive barbarism, was to be the central core of western Canada's history. Even before Provencher's time, the Métis had found themselves having to choose between following their maternal ancestors' wandering footsteps or settling down to their paternal ancestors' discipline of plough or pen. With the connivance of the North West Company they had already chosen the short-term easy course and most of them had reverted to a nomadic existence.

In using them as tools and combatants to fight the Hudson's Bay Company, the Nor'westers had fanned their discontents and their group consciousness into a belief in their destiny as a "New Nation." In that role, two years before Provencher's arrival, they had fought the Nor'westers' battle of Seven Oaks. Nothing could have given them a better demonstration of their power as a military force. Their half-century as a major factor in the West's history had begun.

Realizing this, Lord Selkirk tried to win them around to the view that the Red River colony was not a threat to their existence but was a sanctuary. In doing so, he invited Roman Catholic priests to come to Red River to serve them and to help relieve some of the uneasy tension that threatened the settlement's harmony.

The first priests arrived during the early uncertain years of the Red River colony, before agriculture had been given time to succeed and when settlers and Métis alike were dependent on hunting buffalo. By their bravery when confronting the Sioux and their expertise in the hunt, the Métis saved the settlement, and for many years the farming folk and those of native stock were interdependent. But while the settlement was their headquarters, nomadic hunting and trapping were their livelihood. Their great hunts made them politically and militarily the strongest force in the West. But even though they lived on river lots and paid lip service to farming, their hunts, temporarily poising them between white men and red, eventually bound them to the open prairie.

These, then, were the people with whom Father Provencher and his priests had to deal in a harsh milieu inconceivable to them when they had been parish priests in Quebec. In short order, with the courage only devotion could sustain, they set about their task. First they built a combined house and chapel fifty feet by thirty feet. Shortly afterwards Father Provencher sent Fathers Dumoulin and Edge to start another mission at Pembina.

On All Saints Day, November 1, 1818, the West's first church was dedicated to St. Boniface and songs of worship rose to its crude rafters. To it came the baptized Canadiens rejoicing in renewing their contact with religion, as well as de Meurons to whose Germanic patron saint the church had been dedicated and a few Catholics from amongst the Selkirk settlers. To it also came some Métis titillated by the ritual and curious about this religious magic of which they had heard their old folk speak.

To it came Jean-Baptiste Lagimodière and that day two of his children, Jean-Baptiste and Reine, were baptized, and a daughter, Marguerite, married to a de Meuron.

In Jean-Baptiste Lagimodière Father Provencher came into contact with one of the West's outstanding French adventurers, a man whose wife, Marie-Anne, had in 1808 been delivered of the first all-white child born in wedlock in the Canadian West. Not only was he a well-established citizen, but because of his wide wanderings across the breadth of the prairies he was in a position to tell Father Provencher about the country and its Indians.

Several tribes, numbering perhaps fifty thousand individuals, lived their free lives on the prairies or in the forested areas extending from the Red River to the Rocky Mountains and bounded by the Eskimo in the far North. They were an interesting aggregation, with Kootenays and Sarcees near the mountains seven hundred miles straight west, the mighty Blackfoot next to them on the open, grassy plains and the large Cree tribe north of them extending east as far as Hudson Bay. North of them again were a variety of tribes, Chipewyan, Slave, Sikanni, Yellowknives and Dogribs, while in the parkland between Red River and the Blackfoot lived the large tribe of Assiniboines. As might be expected, four-fifths of all these lived on that portion of the West which, later on, white men were to describe as arable. Some Crees lived within trading distance of the Hudson's Bay Company's post in the Red River Settlement and so did some Assiniboines who dealt there and from time to time joined the Métis in protecting the Red River colony from the dreaded American Indians, the Sioux.

Learning all the time, working on his church, holding services, baptizing many children and a few adults, Father Provencher passed his first cold winter at the edge of the plains.

When March 1819 came he set out to visit the fur-trade posts along the Souris River and went as far as Peter Fidler's post near the junction of the Assiniboine and Qu'Appelle rivers some two hundred miles west of St. Boniface. There the old trader told him of the immensity of the million square miles which we call western Canada.

Its main features were well known to the traders who, utilizing the services of Quebec voyageurs, had three main canoe routes to its remote fringes. From Lake Winnipeg the 1,100-mile-long Saskatchewan River gave them access to the western prairies and the mountains. Along it lay some of the traders' main posts, Cumberland House, Fort Carlton and, far into the West, Edmonton House. Branching off to the north from Cumberland House was another route which ultimately took the voyageurs down the Mackenzie River to the edge of the Arctic ice floes well over two thousand miles by canoe from the Red River Settlement. On the way they passed Fort Chipewyan on Lake Athabasca and other posts on Great Slave Lake and farther north. Still another route which set off west from Fort Chipewyan ascended the Peace River for nine hundred miles to its headwaters in contemporary British Columbia and then by other mountain-girt rivers provided a route to the Oregon coast. Along the Peace River lay Fort Dunvegan and Fort St. John.

Now Provencher could begin to see what a vast field, what a tremendous task and what a glorious opportunity lay before the Catholic church. Moreover, in strapping on his snowshoes and running behind his team of dogs on his round trip, he had taken the first steps towards penetrating this vast land. He had broken the trail others were to follow. His four-hundred-mile jaunt was but the forerunner of the thousands of snowshoe trips which, God willing, his brothers would take and the millions of miles his successors would plod through the unbroken snows of this wilderness. But he had made a start.

In spite of Father Provencher's spirited overture, some twenty years were to elapse before he had enough recruits to establish a mission on Canadian soil west of present-day Manitoba. In the meantime, with unflagging zeal, he tended his flock and watched the Red River Settlement evolve. Some developments, such as the arrival of the Reverend John West in 1820, were discouraging. For West, though another worker in the vast untended wilderness vineyard, came representing the rival Anglican faith. One of the encouraging events was the end of the fur-trade rivalry when in 1821 the North West Company and the Hudson's Bay Company amalgamated and between white man and white man at least peace returned to the prairies.

In May 1822 Provencher was consecrated bishop of Juliopolis with his headquarters at St. Boniface. Since his mission was so far removed from Quebec, it was a practical move to set up another diocese in the West. It covered an area larger than Europe and, as well as including a colony of Métis and other settlers, it contained some fifty thousand Indians — fifty thousand possible converts. Magnificent as the prospect was, facing up to it would certainly have dismayed a less devoted bishop. For to cope with it his total ordained following consisted of one priest — one priest only — Father Destroismaisons.

As the years rolled by, his efforts were rewarded until by 1830 he had two outlying missions — Pembina and White Horse Plains. From time to time he was able to recruit some priests from Quebec but, like himself, they found their work unpleasant and the results of their efforts discouraging. Unlike him, they soon returned to Lower Canada. One exception was Father Georges Antoine Belcourt, a priest of active habits, intelligence and enterprise, who came out in 1831. Even he had been reluctant to come and had been filled with what Father Morice, an historically minded priest, was to call the "dread with which all Canadian secular priests looked upon the Red River Settlement."

Nevertheless, the little spot of white civilization straddling the Red River continued to progress materially and spiritually. In 1834 the Hudson's Bay Company completed Upper Fort Garry, the settlement's first major stone building. Three years later, but across the river, Bishop Provencher finished his stone cathedral, the "Church of the Turrets Twain."

In 1838, yielding to the pleas of some French settlers at the Pacific coast, he sent two priests to Oregon. One of them was Father Demers and the other was Father Blanchet who had invented a Catholic ladder whereby he tried to explain Christianity to the Indians. This ladder was a scroll illustrating Bible and church history by a series of pictures one above the other like the steps of a ladder and leading the eye from the creation to the final ascent to heaven. These two priests accompanied a Hudson's Bay Company brigade up the Saskatchewan River to Fort Edmonton, and, crossing the mountains near Jasper, went on to the lower Columbia River. On their way they provided some spiritual consolation to the Hudson's Bay Company's employees and engagés. Their trip established them as the first missionaries of any faith to visit Alberta.

In 1840 Father Belcourt, who spent most of his time at Pembina, held services at Duck Bay on Lake Winnipegosis, and in 1842 Father Jean Edouard Darveau established a mission there and found himself competing with the Reverend Abraham Cowley of the Anglican Church Missionary Society. From there in 1844 Darveau went on to preach at Le Pas where the rival church was represented by a native convert by the name of Henry Budd, who was acting as teacher and catechist. Unfortunately while serving there Darveau was drowned. Some mystery surrounded his death and rumours persisted that Henry Budd had been involved indirectly, though knowingly, in the tragedy. The animosity between the two faiths made it possible for sincere men to believe these rumours, which indeed may well have been true.

The same month that marked Darveau's death also saw the arrival of the first nuns at St. Boniface. Bishop Provencher had persuaded the Sisters of Charity of Montreal to come to the aid of his flock. The first of these "Grey Nuns" entered upon their unselfish work when on June 21, 1844, they stepped ashore at St. Boniface. There were four of them, the superior, Sister Valade, and three other brave women, Sisters Lagrave, Coutlée and Lafrance.

Bishop Provencher's arduous labours were bearing fruit. Some semblance of religious order had come to the Red River Settlement where in 1843 the population had been slightly over five thousand souls of whom fifty-five percent were Roman Catholics. Out of 870 families, 571 had been Métis, 152 French Canadian, 110 Scots of various sorts and 22 English, with the rest of several nationalities.

While he had been consolidating his base, Bishop Provencher had also been able to reach out to the far West. In both 1838 and 1841 Chief Factor John Rowand of Fort Edmonton had written the bishop asking that a priest be sent out to serve the relatively small number of Métis who were living there. Due to the courage of Father Jean-Baptiste Thibault, a devoted young Quebec priest who had come to serve at St. Boniface in 1833, Bishop Provencher's endeavours were able to leap the 600-mile gap from Le Pas to Fort Edmonton. Thibault left St. Boniface on April 20, 1842, travelling with Hudson's Bay Company personnel and reached Fort Carlton on the North Saskatchewan River on May 27. After spending a few days there he rode west along the sketchy trail until he reached Fort Edmonton on June 19. There he found Chief Factor Rowand, as well as a "Canadian or half-breed population including women and children" of about eighty souls. While there he became the first Roman Catholic priest to meet a band of Blackfoot. After visiting the Hudson's Bay Company's fishery station at Lac Ste. Anne and baptizing 353 children during his four-month sojourn in the West, he returned to St. Boniface.

There he was able to report on the conditions in the Saskatchewan River country. And one condition of paramount importance was that still a third religious organization had entered Bishop Provencher's far-flung diocese. For the Wesleyans had also been looking up the long line of communication to the far West. In 1840 the Reverend James Evans, their superintendent and the man who had invented the Cree syllabics, had established his headquarters at Norway House near the north end of Lake Winnipeg. In October that year the Reverend Robert Terrill Rundle had reached Fort Edmonton to become the first missionary to reside in Alberta. Subsequently, James Evans had paid him a visit and then on his departure made a reconnaissance trip to Fort Dunvegan and thence down the Peace River. He had reached Fort Chipewyan two days before Christmas 1841 to become the first itinerant missionary to enter the Mackenzie River watershed. Moreover, during the time that Thibault had been at Fort Edmonton, John Rowand had started men building a house to accommodate the Reverend Mr. Rundle.

Now it was not only the need of the far-flung Indian tribes of the western prairies that claimed Bishop Provencher's attention. Now the competition from other denominations whetted his interest. That, of course, merely gave a new emphasis to his already desperate need for more help and particularly more priests, a need to which he had consistently turned his attention with earnest effort but discouragingly little success.

Being unable to recruit enough priests from Quebec, he had carried his quest to Rome when in 1841 he visited the holy city. There he strove to interest some religious order in his problem and in the course of the next year or two his efforts resulted in having one of the outstanding orders take up the burden of his cause. While he was in the midst of supplicating them to come to help, he explained his reasoning:

> "Secular priests will make slow progress; there is no unity in their views, without mentioning the fact that they put their hands to the plough only for a short time, which they always find too long."

Fortunately the order to which he appealed was already domiciled in Lower Canada. That group to which western Canada must ever be grateful was the Congregation of the Oblates — the Oblates of Mary Immaculate — the O.M.I.

Founded in 1816 at Aix in the south of France by Monsignor Ch. J. E. de Mazenod, bishop of Marseilles, they were the first missionary order to come to Quebec after its cession to England. By profession the Oblates were missionaries to the poor, and indeed who could have been poorer than the Indians of the West. During the few short years they had been in Quebec they had established an enviable record for the fervour of their preaching and an astounding one for the spiritual rewards their efforts earned them. Though not even Bishop Provencher could have envisaged the successes that would crown their efforts amongst the Indians and Eskimos of northwestern Canada, the Oblates by their organization, vows and sacrifices were destined to establish the greatest record of service of any missionaries of any faith.

On August 25, 1845, the first sign of the approaching Oblates' canoe cheered the priests at St. Boniface. When it landed, the Reverend Casimer Aubert, O.M.I., and Brother Alexander

Antonin Taché stepped from it. The first of the Oblates had reached western Canada, the first of a long line of missionary priests which, making rapid strides, was to carry the Oblate cross to the foot of the mountains on the Pacific coast and even to the shores of the Arctic Ocean. For the next seventeen years all of the very few secular priests who came to serve in the St. Boniface diocese soon joined the Oblate order.

Already a brother in the order, Taché, a youth of twenty-two in whose veins flowed the blood of Lavérendrye, set the example. On October 22, 1845, he was raised to the priesthood and on the following day pronounced his vows as an Oblate.

Three more Oblates, one of whom was Brother Henri Faraud, arrived the next year and two more in 1848. Many others were to follow. A large percentage of these had left refined homes in France and Belgium to face the unknown rigours of serving their native charges under incredibly harsh circumstances in the West and the North.

Two years before the first of the Oblates arrived at St. Boniface, however, Father Thibault had returned to the assault at Fort Edmonton and in 1844 he and Father Bourassa started building the mission at Lac Ste. Anne. He may or may not have been aware that his presence in that region was worrying Sir George Simpson, governor-in-chief of the Hudson's Bay Company territories, who wrote asking the bishop not to let Thibault engage in trade "except for provisions." Then he went on to say that Thibault was to "avoid as far as in him lies that collision of creeds which is as unnecessary in so wide a country as it is inexpedient among so ignorant a race."

In this wide country, passing from band to band and taking Father Blanchet's Catholic ladder with him, Father Thibault visited Lac La Biche and Cold Lake and by 1844 was holding services at Ile-à-la-Crosse. While he was doing so, Father Bourassa also moved about and in 1846 went to Lesser Slave Lake and the Peace River country.

That same year on one of his visits to the fort Father Thibault met Father De Smet, a Jesuit priest who had wandered north from St. Louis on the Mississippi River. That year, too, Fathers Laflêche and Taché established the mission at Ile-à-la-Crosse and a year later went on to hold services at Reindeer Lake and at Fort Chipewyan. In a vigorous three-year burst of activity the priests had visited Indian bands scattered from Lac Ste. Anne to Reindeer Lake.

With the men at his disposal, Bishop Provencher had achieved remarkable results. The mission at Pembina, which was just south of the international border, had been taken out of his hands and transferred to the American diocese of Dubuque. In a way, that had been a help to him because there were times when he and Father Belcourt had not seen eye to eye. Looking to the West, however, where he had men like Fathers Thibault, Bourassa and Taché, he could visualize a thin red line across the map of its vast wilderness. As yet that line was but a hopeful tendril, but he knew that from it in due course a mighty trunk would spring. All he needed to make it grow was men.

Fortunately at that very time in Bishop Bourget's Montreal palace young Albert Lacombe was dreaming of the day when his superiors would allow him to set his face towards the West.

CHAPTER THREE

Métis and Buffalo Hunts

At Montreal on the first August morning in 1849 young Albert Lacombe, now Father Lacombe, boarded the train for the West. He rode it as far as it went — to Lachine. Then a few minutes later, with the sun on his back, he gazed forward over the rail of a steamboat heading west. At last, as he had so often dreamed he would, he was setting out for a mission on the prairies over two thousand miles away. Attired in his spotless soutane, the dark, fresh-faced lad appeared remarkably young to be a fullfledged priest.

If his fellow passengers could have known the anguish of his departure from Montreal they would have felt confirmed in that opinion. For, regardless of how glamourous his adventure looked, he was in effect leaving home for the first time and, although he had studied everything he could lay his hands on, he was entirely lacking in experience of the rough world beyond his schools' gates. Hitherto, whether at St. Sulpice, L'Assomption or in the bishop's palace, he had led a student's sheltered life, always surrounded by his French-speaking and Catholic compatriots. He had read and heard of sin and backsliding and hatred, but up to this point they had been largely matters of hearsay.

Then, abruptly, while the steamer was still in sight of Lachine, he came face to face with all of these. Most of the passengers and crew had come from another world — a world where they took every opportunity to display their hatred of his religion and race and to jeer at his cassock which they sneeringly called a petticoat. A slap across his face would have caused him less pain than this sudden, blinding flash of the intensity of intolerance.

Though this intolerance marred his enjoyment of the trip, he nevertheless went to bed late and rose early. Sleep was not allowed to rob him of a moment of the joy of travelling or of the scenery. Throughout his long life the sheer thrill of being on the move to visit new places or revisit familiar ones contributed much to his well-being. So did scenery, and over the years his diaries were to contain brief but pertinent comments about hills, valleys and vistas and about the weather. As a born traveller weather was important to him. Rain, snow, or excessive wind detracted from the pleasure of his journeys, but page after page of his diaries begin with his appreciation of good weather — *beau temps!*

The trip along Lake Ontario and the voyage west from Buffalo thrilled the itchy-footed adventurer. At the west end of Lake Erie he left the bulk of his fellow passengers, not only without regret but with positive relief. From there, mainly by stage, he bumped along a further four hundred miles west to Dubuque, where he reported to the bishop in charge of the diocese in which he was to serve. The warmth of Bishop Lauras's welcome and the fact that once more he was among compatriots went far to heal his memories of the rough accommodation for travellers along this recently settled route and the crudeness of his fellow passengers. At Dubuque he preached his first sermon.

There, too, he caught his first sight of the Mississippi River. For his twelve-day steamboat trip up that stream to St. Paul, Bishop Lauras suggested that he refrain from wearing his cassock. Perhaps that helped, but however attired, increasingly as he progressed into the frontier, he found the folk more ready to accept the stranger regardless of race or religion. In speaking of his great pleasure in ascending the Mississippi on a steamboat he was later to declare, "I began to breathe freely at last; I felt myself a new man."

When the boat warped up to the rough dock at St. Paul, all the inhabitants of the river bank settlement of some thirty log shacks came down to meet it. Amongst them was Father

Ravoux who exulted as he led Lacombe to his eighteen-foot square combined log chapel and sometime residence. At last the newly ordained priest could see with his own eyes the conditions under which pioneer missionaries lived. They came as no surprise; they were about what he had expected them to be.

He had to admit, however, that his sleeping arrangements that night were unorthodox. Father Ravoux explained that he had to leave for another charge but that the new arrival was to make himself at home until the brigade of carts came in from Father Belcourt's Pembina mission. As Katherine Hughes in *Father Lacombe: The Black-Robe Voyageur* told the story, the young man acquiesced but rather naturally asked where he was to sleep.

"Why, here," said the older priest, pointing to a long narrow box. "That box has blankets inside. Just open it up."

"But that's a coffin!" Father Lacombe cried, shuddering as his sensitive nature recoiled at the thought.

"Yes," agreed the other in the most matter of fact way. "A half-breed died in the woods the other day and I helped to make his coffin. It was too short, and we had to make another. I kept this one. It is very useful; I only had blankets before."

While waiting to continue his trip towards the northwest, the young priest talked to trappers and frontiersmen, improved his limping command of English and learned about the country which lay along the route he was soon to travel. St. Paul's prospects were impressive. Recently it had become the jumping-off place for those bound for the Red River Settlement along a trail capable of bearing Red River carts. During the last few years, partly at the instigation of Father Belcourt of Pembina, the Métis and some independent traders from the British territory adjacent to Fort Garry had been using it to avoid selling their furs and buffalo hides to the Hudson's Bay Company. Because it was the logical route along which to carry on commerce with the Red River Settlement, everyone, except that company's employees, looked to the day when the trail would be improved. The route by which the Hudson's Bay Company brought in its goods — the water route originating at York Factory on Hudson Bay and approaching Fort Garry from the north along Lake Winnipeg — was a costly one. The next few years after Father Lacombe's stay at St. Paul were to see a trebling of the traffic along the cart trail and a corresponding growth in the village of St. Paul.

Every day of his month-long stay in St. Paul made Father Lacombe more eager to set out along the trail north. Finally Father Belcourt's two-wheeled ox-drawn wooden carts arrived, were loaded with their goods and started squealing their way home again. The brigade was driven or tended by two Canadian freemen, a Métis and an Indian, and for the first time Father Lacombe was thrown into the exclusive company of these natives of the Canadian prairies. For the first time too, he began to sort them out in his mind. A freeman, he found, was one who had been an employee of the Hudson's Bay Company and when his term of service had expired had elected not to renew his contract but to live and trade independently of the company.

A Métis, of course, he knew to be one of mixed blood, usually of French descent on the paternal side but whose mother was wholly or partly Indian. As for the Indian, he was one of the very people the young man had come so far to serve. He was predisposed towards liking these two members of the party; they were the first two of his parishioners he had met.

During the trip which for over six weeks threw the priest and his four new acquaintances together, they proved worthy of his trust. They turned out to be competent and cheerful companions even on the dreary, rainy days when, time after time, they had to put their shoulders to the wheels of the carts to get them through mud holes and over swollen creeks and marshy spots. Many a time when every cart stuck fast they had to carry the goods out to firm land and then, with the ox pulling and the men pushing, shove it out of the sucking mud, load it up and go back to get another cart through the quagmire. Under such conditions the cheerful men showed up well, and by the time Father Lacombe arrived at Pembina the bond of six weeks' continuous toil and hardship had made them all fast friends.

Although the trip had started amidst the magnificence of September's autumn colours, it did not end until November's snow ushered the wayfarers into Pembina. The journey had taken him over a hundred days to travel from Montreal to Pembina and on every day of his trip he had learned something new. He was no longer a greenhorn.

He found that Pembina was a rather indifferent village on the west bank of the Red River and, of course, at the edge of the open prairies. There, several Métis families chose to live and to pay lip service to some small garden plots. Their main food supply came from ranging the rolling prairies to the west in pursuit of the plentiful buffalo herds. Originally an offshoot of the Red River Settlement, Pembina had turned out to lie just south of the 49th parallel and was therefore in the United States. In 1824, after the boundary had been established, most of its Métis had moved away; some to the Red River Settlement, but the majority of them, led by Cuthbert Grant, started a new settlement on the Assiniboine River about twelve miles above Fort Garry. It was on White Horse Plain and was known as Grantown until the Saint-François-Xavier mission became established on Grant's land. During Father Lacombe's sojourn at Pembina, Father Belcourt was able to increase the frequency of his services for the seventy families at Saint-François-Xavier while the young recruit stayed home to serve the smaller number at Pembina.

After spending some weeks at Pembina, he and Father Belcourt went to St. Boniface to pay their respects to Bishop Provencher. The visit may have lacked some warmth because Father Belcourt's dislike of the Hudson's Bay Company had caused the bishop some embarrassment. Father Lacombe, however, was impressed when he met the rugged old six-foot-four bishop. He was also impressed with the task that he had accomplished and listened eagerly to his account of the few far-flung missions which looked to him for support: Lac Ste. Anne, far up the Saskatchewan River, Ile-à-la-Crosse near the headwaters of the Churchill River, and a few others.

Within a few days of their return to Pembina, Father Belcourt, shouting to his dogs, set off for a trip of several weeks' duration to make the rounds of distant Indian bands and the younger man was left to carry on alone. He spent the winter in a cosy fashion, having plenty of dry meat, pemmican and occasionally some fresh meat, and on the score of comfort had little of which to complain. On the score of companionship he also fared well; the Métis had come to like him and the few Saulteaux who came in were apparently devout. Having a great deal of time on his hands, he spent much of it studying the Saulteaux tongue. In this he found the rough grammar and dictionary Father Belcourt had devised a wonderful help and also discovered what his tutors at L'Assomption College had suspected, that he had a ready ear for picking up new languages. Nevertheless, though he was at a prairie mission where there was so much to learn and where so much was new to him, he passed a rather uneventful winter.

Spring with its crocuses and its new grasses soon changed that state of affairs. For the time of the great buffalo hunt was approaching. All winter the Métis had talked of little else, all winter he had longed for the day when with luck he too might take part in its thrilling adventures. And now, while the local Métis planted their little gardens, a few small groups of their compatriots came in every day. Finally the large contingent from St. Boniface straggled in and camped beside their carts. By the time the erstwhile quiet village was ringed by some eleven hundred carts the humdrum winter had been succeeded by hectic activity. Dogs barked everywhere, children played about, men repaired their carts and looked to the harness, and women, sitting around a hundred campfires, laughed merrily.

A week or so before the expedition was ready to set out, Father Lacombe's broadaxe glanced and cut his right foot so badly that he had to hobble about on crutches. Consequently, Father Belcourt decided that he would accompany the cavalcade himself and leave the younger man to tend the mission.

A priest's presence had become vital to the hunt. Not only did it give some sort of official sanction to it, but from the church's angle it enabled the father to keep in religious touch with a great mass of Métis, many of whom he rarely saw on any other occasion. On the trip he could teach the older folk, instruct the young ones, baptize the new arrivals and in the event of accident or death he could help or give the last rites.

At this point, however, as it was to do on so many occasions during his long life, Father Lacombe's empathy with the Métis paid good dividends. They liked and respected Father Belcourt's sometime severe countenance and were always glad of his company, but their affection for the young missionary was of a deeper, personal kind. They knew of his disappointment at not accompanying them and appealed to Father Belcourt to let him go with them. They brushed aside his foot's incapacity by promising that until he could ride a horse they would take him along in a cart. Father Belcourt, touched by their sincerity, deferred to their wishes, stayed home, and allowed the younger man to go.

Never in all his long life was Father Lacombe to embark upon a more thrilling adventure. He had heard all winter of the hunt's long march over the free prairies, of its wild gallops amongst the flying tails of the fleeing herds and its frequent skirmishes with hostile Sioux. Without ever having experienced them, he knew the details of the hunt's many practices and its strict discipline. Now, out into the summer prairies he was to go as a welcome guest with these the most skilful of all hunters, the most deadly warriors, yet the kindliest, most generous-hearted people of the plains. And he was to ride as their respected guest. Not just one, but many winters of boredom would have been little to pay for this privilege.

Next morning, in mid June 1850, when this host of hunters and their dependants — some thirteen hundred souls in all — set out, Father Lacombe, confined to his cart, gazed around in amazement. Individual hunters, whose main concern was with their favourite two or three buffalo-running horses, led their groups off west. As the whole party of eleven hundred carts fanned out laterally and straggled along in a ragged column some three or four miles long, pandemonium broke loose over the flower-dotted prairie. The crowd's only unanimity was that all were happy and all were headed west paralleling the valley of the Pembina River.

Their scouts had told them that on this first leg of their trip they had nothing to fear from their implacable enemies the Sioux. Consequently they rambled along until a few days later they made their rendezvous with the White Horse Plain contingent at some spot on the Pembina River near the point of its intersection with the 49th parallel. From there, after the formal organization of the hunt took place, the Pembina party set out west coursing leisurely over the billowing prairies on the real start of its weeks-long foray.

Somewhere in the Turtle Mountains he experienced the

wild thrill of his first significant buffalo kill. A couple of scouts signalling with flags reported a great herd to be grazing beyond the next ridge. Intense excitement ran through the marching horde. That was not allowed to disrupt its discipline, however, and after a short advance the entourage halted. The women formed the carts into a circle and placed all the draft animals inside it. Amidst much happy laughter and chatter they erected their tepees outside the circle.

Meanwhile, the men jumped on their prized buffalo runners and all, including Father Lacombe, forgetting his bandaged foot, rode pell-mell for the top of the ridge ahead. There they paused and there Father Lacombe got his first view of the immense herd below, grazing in their thousands, a black mass stretching far towards the horizon. Though even the horses shared their excitement and pawed the ground, the strict routine of the hunt was observed. Quietly the mounted men formed in a line abreast, poised on the brink of the ridge and waited with bowed heads as Father Lacombe recited an act of contrition. For some might not return from this foray alive.

Then they were off — Father Lacombe among them — galloping madly down the slope on the first of his many buffalo hunts.

Many men have left descriptions of a buffalo hunt but none of them recalled its thrills, excitements and its tragedies more vividly than Father Lacombe. As several hundred mounted Métis charged into the midst of the herd dealing death with every shot, he rode among them exulting as the joy and indeed the lust of the slaughter took possession of him.

"What a scene!" he was to exclaim, "what confusion!"

But it was over in twenty minutes of hard riding and fierce excitement. Tired and sweating, the men and their lathered horses returned across the stretch now strewn with dead and dying buffalo. Each hunter, having thrown some marker beside the animals he had brought down, was able to claim his own victims. By the time the men swept back over the field of carnage the women had driven their carts up from the tepees and begun the process of butchering. Along the route of the run lay eight hundred carcasses.

The last of the evening light found everyone back at the circle of tepees, the men sitting around the campfire reliving the thrills of their wild chase, the women and children rejoicing at carts piled high with fresh meat. The coyotes and wolves, satiating themselves with the offal, had taken possession of the scene of the killings.

The following day Father Lacombe led hundreds of the Métis to the top of Turtle Mountain where he erected and blessed a large cross.

Meanwhile the women who had been far too busy to climb the hill had been curing the meat and dressing the hides. Most of the flesh was cut into thin strips and dried in the sun or over a slow fire. When dry, it would be bundled into tightly bound packages weighing some sixty pounds, which could be carried along and finally made into pemmican if desired. Drying the meat took three or four days — days when the women worked and the men sat around gossiping, but days filled with feasting and the smell of meat roasting at the fires.

During those days Father Lacombe was almost as busy as the women. In the happy camaraderie of the camp he started each morning with mass, during which his Métis were most attentive and devout. During the day, interspersed with his duties as physician and counsellor, he held catechism classes for the children. Then in the evening he would ring his bell to summon his Métis to sing hymns and pray.

When it came time for the group to move along in search of more herds, it once more observed its rigid discipline and progressed warily over the widespread sage-scented plains. Never had Father Lacombe enjoyed any pleasure to compare with this almost fancy-free wandering through flower-filled valleys where antelope as fleet as cloud shadows fled before them. Never could he forget the magnificent views from hilltop after hilltop as they revealed wide vistas or a trickling stream down below making its way through its fringe of woods or willows.

Several weeks later the hunters returned to Pembina, bringing home tons of dried meat and pemmican. Not only would it feed them throughout the winter, but much of their surplus could be sold to the traders. All his long life detailed memories of this hunt of 1850, his first and therefore his most enjoyable, remained fresh in Father Lacombe's mind.

His next hunt, that of 1851, however, brought a brush with the Sioux that established a landmark in the history of his

Métis people. It left Pembina on June 16, 1851, and once more straggled across to the familiar rendezvous several miles up the river where it met the Saint-François-Xavier group. This northern party's 250 people, driving two hundred carts, were headed by sixty-seven hunters, and were led by Jean Baptiste Falcon, the son of the bard of the Métis, Pierre Falcon, and were under Father L. F. Richer Laflêche's watchful eye. For a day or so while the Métis folk visited among themselves, Fathers Lacombe and Laflêche took full advantage of every opportunity to enjoy each other's company.

At this point, where practically all the prairie Métis met in one huge camp spread loosely along the river's valley, the serious business of the hunt started. As they had done in previous years, the leaders of the northern party met with those from Pembina and it was decided to move south and west along a fairly definite route but as two separate parties in parallel columns some twenty miles apart. At all times, scouts ranging between the two groups were to maintain contact. The Sioux, who undoubtedly would be met somewhere ahead, were known to be in a dangerous mood and had vowed to stop this intrusion of Métis hunters into their territory.

That settled, the real organization of the foray began. Each of the two parties elected the captain of its own hunt: Jean Baptiste Falcon from the White Horse Plain and Jean Baptiste Wilkie of the much larger Pembina party. Each captain then chose ten subsidiary captains and each of these picked ten soldiers who were to report to him as camp guards and scouts. With the captain the ten sub-captains formed their party's council. For many years the hunts had been organized in this way, but although all present knew all the rules, it was invariably the practice for the council to enunciate the laws of the hunt afresh — laws upon which their safety in the lands of their enemy depended. In contrast to the lack of organization the Indians brought to their warfare, the discipline of the Métis had been an infusion from their white inheritance and in most battles proved to be victorious. Once these laws had been approved in council no one dared break them.

As Father Lacombe listened, Jean Baptiste Wilkie stood up and asked for the group's acquiescence in these laws. Everyone indicated acceptance and in effect Wilkie declared: "If any one of you does not approve these laws then leave the camp now. Once we set out tomorrow no one will be free to act independently or to separate from us." Every old hunter in the group knew full well that anyone breaking these laws or wandering off separately could bring disaster to the whole hunt. Each old-timer could recall occasions when it had been necessary to discipline such a straggler and sometimes that discipline meant death.

Next morning when Father Lacombe's Métis set out, the happy-go-lucky meandering of the previous few days had been transformed into an orderly procession. Ahead of the whole body rode the guide who directed their march, at times halting it and again ordering it to proceed. Ahead of him and on either flank other mounted scouts kept watch for bands of either Sioux or buffalo. The captain rode in the midst of the two or four orderly columns of carts, and acting on information brought in by the scouts was ready at any moment to order them to stop and to take up a defensive position or to get ready to run a herd of buffalo which had been sighted.

For some days both parties headed west in columns a few miles apart but, as they approached Turtle Mountain, Father Lacombe's large group veered off in a southerly direction. For the next few days they ran several small bands of buffalo and once the captain called a halt and corralled the carts into a defensive position while they parleyed with a small party of Sioux. Within a few moments they chased these enemies away and hastened to send a message to warn the Saint-François-Xavier group.

So, hunting and camping and wandering over the endless rose-dotted prairie, the middle of July found them in the vicinity of modern Minot, North Dakota, and finally they camped on the Missouri Coteau near the famous *Maison du Chien* — Dogden Butte — some thirty miles southeast of Minot. From the higher land the scouts reported seeing another immense herd of buffalo and because they were eager to approach them, Father Lacombe allowed the group to travel on Sunday, July 13. Once more while they were on the march another small band of Sioux tried unsuccessfully to pick off some stragglers. Thus far what news reached them from the small Saint-François-Xavier group had been reassuring.

But that northern column was also in risky territory and on the evening of Saturday, July 12, somewhere on the Missouri Coteau not far from Minot its scouts reported a camp of Sioux. The most desperate battle that the Métis ever had with Indians was about to begin.

Immediately the northern convoy was put into its usual posture of defence while scouts went out to reconnoitre. What they found astounded them. They sent back word that they had seen an encampment of 2,500 Sioux warriors! Undoubtedly their estimate was considerably exaggerated but even half that number of the fiercest fighters of the plains was enough to threaten complete annihilation of this small Métis band.

Hostilities started with the Sioux capturing the five scouts. Two of these, however, with a mad daring characteristic of the Métis, whipped up their horses and in spite of a hail of Sioux bullets reached the hunters' camp unscathed. When they dashed in with an eyewitness estimate of the overwhelming might of the Sioux forces, Jean Baptiste Falcon and Father Laflèche, counting all boys over twelve years old, found that they had seventy-seven men who could handle a gun. With their priest encouraging them, these braced themselves to face attack from hundreds of Sioux warriors. Their chances of survival lay in their discipline.

They had already ranged their carts in a circle, wheel to wheel, with the poles usually carried along to make meat-drying racks jammed through between the spokes. They piled everything else they had under the carts to fill the gaps in their barricade. Inside the circle they tethered the cart ponies and oxen. These were their means of locomotion over the plains; if they were killed the party would perish almost automatically. The women and children dug trenches under the carts while the men dug firing pits in a circle surrounding it and well out in front of the barricade. From these they hoped to make it so hot for the Sioux that they would never break through this outer ring and get at the barricade. These preparations took up the balance of the afternoon and evening and when dark fell they sent messages south to Father Lacombe's group asking for help.

Next morning as insects began to buzz in the waving grass, here and there over the bright prairie landscape meadowlarks proclaimed that the day looked propitious. The sheer joy of their songs fell on unreceptive ears as the besieged Métis, watching all points of the compass, steeled themselves for what was to come.

Father Laflêche "exhorted and confessed all those who presented themselves" and then celebrated mass and gave the last sacrament. Almost immediately, appearing suddenly and riding up the slope towards the beleaguered hunters came hundreds of Sioux warriors. Then, at a signal, they stopped.

Through a gap which was quickly opened and as quickly closed after them, thirty Métis horsemen rode out to parley, to take presents to the Sioux and to ask them to go away in peace. But the Sioux waved away the presents and scorned the peace. They had come to crush the camp and now began to press forward.

The Métis galloped back to their barricade, shoved their horses through its gap and ran out to their ring of pits. Some Sioux charged, hoping to overwhelm the barricade, but the Métis' fire daunted them. Here and there some warriors tumbled off their horses, some dead, some to writhe for an hour or so. Except for a wounded ox or two, the Métis suffered no casualties. The painted warriors paused.

But they came on again, surrounding the camp, never charging in a body but making sudden mounted sallies, or creeping forward on their bellies and sniping. Elan, dash and courage they displayed as now and then, a warrior at a time, or in groups of five or six, they charged, only to be tumbled from their horses by the fire from the gun pits. Never once, however, throughout all the long day did they do the only thing which would have crushed the camp — charge in a concerted body.

For hours sporadic assault after assault broke before the guns fired from the pits. Plainly visible within the ring of carts, Father Laflêche, clad in his surplice and gripping his crucifix, not only encouraged the defenders but mystified the attackers. As the day lengthened their awe at his magic increased until with a thunder storm impending and after six hours' fruitless fighting they withdrew, saying: "The French have a Manitou with them. . . . It is impossible to kill them."

After the Sioux retired the Métis emerged from their holes and their barricade. Out in the surrounding field they had seen eight of their enemies lying dead and had watched as their foes departed, carrying away many wounded men. Early in the fray two of their three scouts, held overnight by the Sioux, had escaped. Punctured by three bullet holes and bristling with sixty-seven arrows sticking out of it lay the body of the other one. Except for that scout, none of the Métis had been killed, but twelve horses and four oxen lay dead or had to be shot.

So ended the first day's encounter. Somewhere off to the south the Métis messengers may already have reached Father Lacombe's camp and maybe help was on the way. Near at hand the Sioux camp still simmered. Till late in the evening Father Laflêche and Jean Baptiste Falcon debated their next move. On the morrow should they once more stand and fight, or could they execute one of the most difficult of all war operations — retreat with an overwhelming force behind them? They decided to retreat.

Next morning their carts set out south once more in the usual precautionary four columns. From the caravan they sent out three mounted parties each about a mile away; one ahead and one on each flank. A fourth party was to remain until it too was a mile away. All of them were charged with the duty of signalling the approach of any Sioux, and in that event, they were to use the time honoured signal of two horsemen galloping past each other on a butte.

When the caravan had crawled ahead about three miles, they saw the signal on the slope of the valley behind them. The enemy were once more on their way. Knowing that surely Father Lacombe's large party must be rushing to their compatriots' aid, the Sioux had decided to crack this little nut of a ring of carts and scoop up its contents before that help arrived.

Once more the Métis hurried their carts into the barricade formation. Once more they dug their gun pits, but this time at a greater distance from the carts. Yesterday they had been too near to prevent the loss of some of their indispensable transport stock.

For five hours the battle raged around them. The Sioux,

howling and charging, fired scores of volleys and hundreds of arrows. And then once more, as a summer storm darkened the sky, the Sioux called it quits.

In a final and perhaps magnanimous gesture to a foe which had defied their utmost efforts, an unarmed chief rode up alone and raising an arm with empty palm extended towards them made the sign of peace. But the Métis were in no mood for gallantry or friendliness and threatened to shoot. Daring them long enough to shout the message that the Sioux had stopped fighting, he declared that the Sioux would never again attack the Métis.

But to emphasize their chagrin at the Métis' snub, they came back once more howling a last defiance. The whole war party, hundreds of them, painted and feather-bedecked, galloped in single file once around the ring of carts and pits and fired one last tremendous volley. Then as the first heavy drops of the sudden prairie storm fell they sped over the nearby ridge and vanished.

During the ensuing almost unbelievable silence, the cramped Métis climbed out of their pits and hurried over to the carts to count what they were certain would be the heavy casualties from the last wild fusillade. Once more the gods of the prairies and *Le Bon Dieu* had been merciful. Only three people had been wounded and slightly at that. The Sioux losses had been about the same as on the previous day. The growling grizzly bear of the Sioux had pounced on the Métis weasel and had fallen back licking its wounds.

Then through the pelting rain the sound of galloping horses announced the arrival of the forerunners of Father Lacombe's party. Early that morning the priest and Jean Baptiste Wilkie had sent them off with word that the main force was following at the best speed it could make. When its 318 hunters arrived, they were accompanied by an equal number of Saulteaux warriors who had come rushing up eager to get in on the kill. All of them were astounded at the terrific battle the seventy-seven Saint-François-Xavier fighters had put up, a defensive fight that had been such a great victory. Some of the Pembina party and of course the Saulteaux were anxious to chase and chastise the Sioux, but the two priests talked them out of doing so. They pointed out that the small Saint-François-Xavier party had won an almost miraculous victory, their enemies' pride had been sadly humbled and now that they had nothing to fear from the Sioux, the very practice of mercy towards them would emphasize their victory.

Indeed, never again would they have much to fear from the Sioux or any other tribe. Even though as the years went by and they had to travel ever farther west after the receding buffalo and thus encroached again and again upon the lands of other Indian bands, no tribe was ever again able to match their fearful prowess as fighters. The great battle of the Grand Coteau which Father Laflêche experienced and of which Father Lacombe saw the results had settled that. The Métis realized that they were indeed masters of the plains.

Alas, though they were at the zenith of their career as the Métis nation, that great victory worked against them. At some point, as Bishop Provencher and his priests knew, they would have to make the hard choice between the glamourous but fleeting pleasure of the hunt and the steadfast virtues of a sedentary, agricultural existence. This success tipped the scales towards a thirty-year continuation of the thrills of the chase and the freedom of wandering over the prairies' endless landscape. And as the scales tipped more and more in that direction the Métis slipped faster and faster down the slope of their destiny.

But, as Father Lacombe and his devoted Métis roamed the prairies for several weeks after that victory, few could have guessed that long before his life was over their fate would have sucked them into its bottomless vortex. At Pembina he saw them at the height of their glory. Laughing, happy, obliging, generous and hospitable and especially devout in his presence they carried him home in triumph. How could he help but admire these people, with their tremendous ability on the plains and on the hunt and with their ready acceptance of his advice or admonition.

In any event, he did admire them, and, indeed, love them. By that time he had come to know a hundred of them as respected friends and individuals. Though he might not see them again for twenty years, he would recognize them immediately and rejoice. Frequently in after years he was to write: "How good these Métis of the plains were, these fervent Christians, these fine, fine people, these people with the hearts of gold."

During his two summer-long hunts he had enjoyed more adventure than all of his St. Sulpice boyhood friends had ever dreamed of and during his two winters at Pembina he had relished the unparalleled respect and devotion of his Métis parishioners. And yet something was lacking; his itchy feet, or was it his trace of Indian blood, kept nagging him to move on. He had been a conscientious priest and, as a scholar during his ample spare time he had made remarkable progress in learning the Saulteaux language. Nevertheless, what he had been doing had become routine and lacked the challenge he had expected. Father Belcourt, otherwise most satisfied with his engaging personality and his performance, had sensed his yearning for more responsibility. Although he felt disappointed, he agreed that in the fall of 1851 the best thing for Father Lacombe to do would be to return to Montreal for a while. There, prayer and the passage of time would surely set his feet on essentially the same course.

CHAPTER FOUR

Fort Edmonton
1852

By the spring of 1852, a matter of months since he had left Pembina, Father Lacombe was on his way back to the West. For a time after leaving the prairies for Montreal he had enjoyed the luxury of consorting with many of his fellow priests in the bishop's palace. After a brief visit to St. Sulpice and a few days' indulgence amidst all the delicacies of his mother's cuisine, he went to talk over his problem with his mentors at L'Assomption.

Then through a winter of prayer and uncertainty as assistant to the venerable Abbé Gagnon at Berthierville, he came to the conclusion that his dedication needed further bolstering. He felt he must have the sustaining influence of the devotion and discipline which only a strong religious order could inspire in him and impose on him. Knowing the high reputation which the Oblates of Mary Immaculate had built up during their brief sojourn in Quebec, he felt that the demands which that order made upon its votaries would provide him with a vital spark still lacking in his makeup.

While he was in the midst of these meditations Bishop Alexander Antonin Taché, an Oblate from the farthest wilds of the West, some eight hundred miles beyond St. Boniface, came to Sorel to plead for men and money for his missions. Father Lacombe crossed the river to hear him, and the fortunate meeting of these two men both in their twenties resulted in him volunteering for the West again and the bishop promising to accept him as a candidate for the Oblate order. Destiny had thrown together Albert Lacombe the farm boy and Bishop Taché the scholar and patrician. Together they had joined hands to travel the long, hard road — the road which was to lead both to a lifetime of service to Canada and to recognition as two of Canada's great men.

Bishop Taché had arrived at St. Boniface in the summer of 1845. There his merit soon came to the fore and five years later he had been named bishop of Arath and coadjutor to Bishop Provencher at St. Boniface. In this capacity he was to make an outstanding contribution to the West. The Oblates of Mary Immaculate were on the march.

On May 4, 1852, that march led two Oblates, Bishop Taché and Father Henri Grollier, as well as the novice Father Lacombe, to set out for the West. They were to use public transport, presumably steamers, as far as Sault Ste. Marie. From there they had planned to secure accommodation in the Hudson's Bay Company's express canoes as far as St. Boniface.

That company regarded missionaries of any persuasion as a mixed blessing. Its officials in London looked on religion and education as means of training the people in their territories to an orderly way of life and as bound to assist the company in ruling its fretful realm. Undoubtedly the company's directors had leanings towards the Anglican church but, since at least half the people in the Red River Settlement were French Canadian and Catholic, they also tried to help the Roman Catholic church. As far back as 1825 the Hudson's Bay Company's Northern Council had passed a resolution which provided an annual stipend of £50 to the mission and that "an allowance of Luxuries [tea, sugar, wine and the like] be annually furnished for its use from the Depot." The preamble to that resolution had read:

"Great benefit being experienced from the benevolent and indefatigable exertions of the Catholic Mission at Red River in the welfare and moral and Religious instruction of its numerous followers, and it being observed with much satisfaction that the influence of the Mission under the direction of the Right Revd. the Bishop of Juliopolis [Provencher] has been uniformly directed to the best interests of the Settlement and of the country at large, it is [resolved]."

In 1835 the stipend was increased to £100 a year. Moreover, whenever it was possible to do so without overloading its transport service, missionaries of any faith travelling around the country were allowed to use its facilities.

As missionaries of competing faiths began to set up shop here and there throughout the company's domain, it had some qualms about furthering their competition. On one occasion in 1850 when Bishop Provencher consulted the company about sending a missionary to the shores of Hudson Bay the company secretary declined to assist on the grounds that "the collision of hostile creeds, which could not fail to result from the adoption of such a measure, would be injurious both to the spiritual and temporal interests of the natives."

The resulting correspondence brought out the fact that the company intended to endow "the bishopric of Rupert's Land, for a greater extension throughout the country of the missionary system adopted by the Church of England." While the Roman Catholic authorities naturally resented the unfairness of this action, it was undoubtedly a logical step for a British company — one whose nation was predisposed towards its own established church — to take in a British colony.

Perhaps it would have been some comfort to the Catholic fathers had they known that Eden Colvile, the associate governor of Rupert's Land stationed at York Factory, looked favourably on their endeavours. When writing to Sir George Simpson, the company's North American governor, on July 14, 1851, he said:

> "I am sorry to hear that there is so much prejudice against Catholic missionaries, as I feel bound to say that in my opinion, they are much better fitted for missionaries in this country, than members of the English Church — from their self denial, and the way they accommodate themselves to the circumstances of the country. . . ."

Further along in his letter he was critical of the Church of England missionaries who "must have in the first place a wife, and in the second place about two boat loads of goods, provisions and luxuries." He compared this to the "moderate way in which the Catholic missionaries conduct their affairs."

While Sir George Simpson carried out the company's London policies of helping all missionaries, he did so reluctantly. Providing space for their goods and persons in the company's canoes was only one of his problems. The other was a bit more complicated and involved the growing number of Métis in the West.

Although their numbers continually increased, the company could hire only so many of them as voyageurs and freighters. They paid only lip service to agriculture and showed no real signs of preparing for a future in which farming might become their main means of support. As a result, many of them turned to fur trading on their own account and thus as soon as fur markets opened up across the United States boundary they became the company's competition.

As George Simpson could have forecast and as the Red River Métis found out a few years later, that business of free trading was not all a one-way street with the Métis the good guys and the company the villain. The Métis had insisted on free trade and rejoiced that by winning it officially in 1849 they had humbled the Hudson's Bay Company. When they did so, however, they weakened its hold over the northwest. Then, when the evil days of 1869 came and they found themselves confronting the Canadian Party and looking to the company for support and found it lacking in the power they themselves had restricted, they relented. But then it was too late.

In any event, in the Red River Settlement by 1850 free trade open to the Métis was a fact of life which the company had to endure. Moreover, as various missionaries started new establishments farther west their policy would be to form new Métis colonies around their missions and the company had little taste for the possibility of having its Red River experience repeated.

It was then Simpson's fear of these Métis colonies springing up around the missions that made him reluctant to encourage missionaries, either Catholic or Protestant. That his fears were not imaginary is borne out by subsequent company correspondence. For instance, John Rowand, writing to him in 1847, complained that even that early in Lac Ste. Anne's life the half-breeds were trading and taking furs to Fort Garry to sell. Indeed, as Rowand wrote to his fellow trader Richard Hardisty in 1853, "every half-breed is a trader who laughs at the Company's Charter."

In spite of this reluctance, Simpson had arranged passage for Bishop Taché and Father Lacombe as far as St. Boniface. Unfortunately they failed to arrive at Sault Ste. Marie in time. As a result, they had to detour by way of Detroit, Chicago and St. Paul. There they stayed at the bishop's palace with Rev. Father Ireland and relaxed briefly before their caravan started along the arduous trail to St. Boniface. Of that trip Father Lacombe was to write:

"Our caravan was made up of carts drawn by oxen and horses. We have much baggage: tents, food, tools, etc. Our men, good Métis whom I have already learned to know. They are truly our people. Mgr. Taché and I love and esteem them. With the gaiety and good will they dispel the tediousness of this difficult and dangerous voyage made so by the heavy rains of the season, and the floods which had overflowed the Mississippi and the Red River valleys. The road was dreadful. It was disheartening, and, often at night, as we made camp we could see the smoke of the fire of the last camp we had made. Servants, priests, bishop, all floundered daily in the mud. . . . Dear Métis people, these Memoirs will oft' recall your name and recollections of you with whom I so often travelled over the vast prairie desert, and, through dense forests, as well as over our wide lakes and endless rivers."

Finally on June 27, after having been fifty-four days en route from Montreal, the little party arrived at St. Boniface. "How happy we were to kneel at Mgr. Provencher's feet, he who received us with such charity and goodness!"

Before Father Lacombe left Montreal Bishop Taché had assured him that he was to spend at least several months at St. Boniface where he was to make his noviciate as an Oblate. During that period he had planned to learn the constitution and receive training in the discipline of the Oblate order. After that he had hoped to be sent out to some mission in the vast northwest field.

God, however, had other plans and before his first twenty-four hours at St. Boniface had elapsed he found himself being catapulted out into the far West. Bishop Provencher was at his wit's end for men. A few days before Father Lacombe's arrival, Father Thibault had come in from his Lac Ste. Anne mission utterly worn out. To make matters worse, he had announced that Father Bourassa, his companion at his faraway station, had made up his mind to leave there a year later. At this heaven-sent juncture, husky young Father Lacombe had arrived. When Bishop Provencher suggested to the recent recruit that he fill in either at Fort Edmonton or Lac Ste. Anne, the young man hesitated until he was assured that he could carry on with his noviciate at the same time.

Within a few days he was on the move again. To get to his Lac Ste. Anne mission, or for Bishop Taché to reach his headquarters at Ile-à-la-Crosse, it was necessary for them to make their way north across Lake Winnipeg until they intersected the main trade route running east and west across western Canada. That route, the one by which the Hudson's Bay Company brought in its supplies and shipped out its furs — the Trans-Canada Highway of the time — started at York Factory on Hudson Bay and, by ascending rivers like the Nelson, reached the important depot of Norway House near the northern end of the huge lake. From there it crossed that lake to the mouth of the Saskatchewan River and ascended that stream some seven hundred miles to Fort Edmonton.

Norway House was also the point where the long water route originating in Montreal and passing through Lake Superior, Lake of the Woods and Lake Winnipeg, made connection with the main one. To reach their stations from the Red River Settlement, therefore, both Bishop Taché and Father Lacombe had to board some Hudson's Bay Company's craft to take them north across Lake Winnipeg to Norway House where they would effect a junction with the York Factory-Fort Edmonton route. At various points along that western half of the highway other routes branched off to the north or south. Of these, the most important was the one which veered off at Cumberland House and by way of Ile-à-la-Crosse gave access to the posts on the Athabasca and Mackenzie rivers. Bishop Taché and Father Grollier were to take that one.

Their leave-taking from their confreres at St. Boniface

early in July was a most affecting one. As Father Lacombe wrote:

> "As the bells announced the painful separation, on the shores of the Red River could be seen the two Bishops, greatly moved. At the feet of this venerable old man could be seen the two young missionaries, the Sisters of Charity, and the people. It was a heart breaking scene. Mgr. Taché too knelt at Bishop Provencher's feet requesting his blessing. This request occasioned these prophetic words: 'It is not the custom that one Bishop bless another, but as this is our last meeting, and I shall not see you again, I bless you once more here below, in awaiting our meeting anew in heaven.' These two great Bishops were never to meet again this side of the grave. Eleven months later, the holy Bishop of Saint Boniface was to quit this earth for a better world."

At Norway House Father Lacombe became a guest in Chief Factor John Rowand's brigade which was to ascend the Saskatchewan River to Fort Edmonton. Fortunately Rowand's rapid appraisal of the new priest was a favourable one. On his part, the young father, considerably overawed by Rowand's heartiness, could nevertheless see through some of the outward bluster and get at the warm, kindly disposed man under it all. Although, of course, neither could realize it, this meeting on a July day in 1852 had brought together an old man who had dominated the life of the West for the first half of the century and a young priest who was to be its best known figure during the last half.

At the time, John Rowand was a hard-bitten man of sixty-five whose whole working life had been spent between Lake Winnipeg and the Rocky Mountains. The son of a Scottish assistant surgeon in the Montreal General Hospital and a French Canadian mother, as a Catholic he had received some education at the Sulpician College in Montreal.

As a lad he had come west to work along the Saskatchewan River for the North West Company. Some twenty years later, as head of the Hudson's Bay Company's whole Saskatchewan District, he had made Fort Edmonton his headquarters. By the time he died a couple of years after he and Father Lacombe became acquainted, he had built up that post so much that it became the most important one in the prairies. From it he ruled the plains of modern Alberta and Saskatchewan and handled furs trapped in all the area between the Peace River in the north and Idaho and Wyoming in the south.

Father Lacombe was fortunate in falling into the hands of John Rowand, the outstanding expert on the Indians of the prairies and particularly fortunate that Rowand took a liking to him. In this young priest the burly old autocrat must have recognized more than usual possibilities. Many a young man's career has been made or marred by some domineering old man's quick assessment. Father Lacombe was lucky.

Throughout his long life the father was often to speak fondly of John Rowand. Amongst the rugged trader's good qualities was his overwhelming loyalty to his company. As Father Lacombe's memoirs record: "This man like most of those holding similar positions is an example of the Company's spirit and government. They work but for the Company. One day, Mr. Rowand, then my good friend, said seriously: 'The Company is like the Church which recognizes but God and the Pope. With us there is but God and the Company.' "

The year the priest and the paunchy trader met, John Rowand, conforming to a practice decades old, had left Fort Edmonton with his brigade of boats loaded with furs as soon as the ice went out — some time early in April. He had delivered them to York Factory on Hudson Bay and was returning with several boatloads of trade goods when about the end of July Father Lacombe became his passenger for the long trip up the Saskatchewan River to Fort Edmonton. At last Father Lacombe, in whose veins flowed the blood of adventurous voyageurs, was to travel for weeks on end by boat, and to witness the terrible toil the boatmen endured. "Our caravan was made up of ten barges [York boats] with a crew of nine men each. . . . These crews . . . had the courage to undertake this voyage which took from five to six months to complete, usually from May to September. . . . One might say that the way of life of these men, during the summer months, was as hard as that of the African slave. . . . At night they camped on the river bank. There, crushed with fatigue, and constantly tormented by the terrible mosquitoes, they were obliged to prepare their miserable meal of pemmican and dry meat with river water as their drink."

This then was how passengers and freight made their tedious way along the fur traders' route to Fort Edmonton, the main route to the West. Taking advantage of that route, Father Lacombe left St. Boniface on July 8, paused a while at Norway House and reached Fort Edmonton on September 19, a trip lasting about ten weeks. To his old companion John Rowand, who had made the trip over a score of times, the journey was merely a boring necessity. To the young priest, in spite of its minor discomforts, it was a romantic adventure, marred only by his concern for the boatmen's mishaps and inhuman toil.

As Father Lacombe observed it, no toil could be more frustrating, disheartening or laborious than tracking the boats up the rapid water. All of the crewmen of each boat put on their harness and, spaced out at ten-foot intervals, fastened themselves to a line and started inching their boat up the river. The actual pulling was the least difficult part of the work. Keeping their footing along slippery banks, over sharp rocks or through scrub willows, or floundering along knee deep in miry beaches was what exhausted the trackers. Moreover, doing this day after day in the lashing rain or the burning sun from daylight to dark — 3 A.M. to 9 P.M. — with brief stops for meals, was enough to tax the hardiest soul.

Never had the young priest seen such travail and his warm heart went out to the voyageurs to the extent that on behalf of one of them who was ill but carrying on he tried to induce John Rowand to give the man a rest. Rowand was flabbergasted by this unheard of leniency and scolded the priest for being impertinent enough to approach him in such a case. In Rowand's defence, it may be said that if he had permitted himself to relax the man's labours, he would soon have been overwhelmed by all his trackers trying to take advantage of a man they would consider a weak boss.

"But the man is ill," pleaded the priest, "and has been ill for a week."

"Bah!" said the rugged Rowand. "He's alright. Any man who is not dead after three days' sickness is not sick at all."

In spite of the fact that most of the way he and Rowand and the other passengers had to walk along in the mud, the young man enjoyed the whole trip. Towards the end of each day he looked forward eagerly to the warmth of their campfires. Then the bourgeois' tents were usually pitched in some small clump of pine trees amidst an assortment of packs and boxes. As the men settled down after their meal and enjoyed their pipes they could see the boats drawn up against the forested bank ahead and the fires of the various crews. At their backs night sounds emerged from the dense forest, while overhead, the moon and stars added their spell of magic to this very temporary resting place.

For days the party ascended the winding Saskatchewan River where, as they rounded each bend, it ever revealed a new and beautiful, but too often monotonously similar, vista of the broad channel flowing between banks clad in endless green forest. Finally as they neared the company's Fort Carlton they emerged into country similar to that which young Lacombe had known around Pembina. At last, after passing well north of the prairies for a month, they had finally emerged into the more open parkland. Everyone's pulse quickened for they had returned to the home of the vast buffalo herds. Here too, however, was also the home of the warlike plains Indians. From here on the brigade would have to post guards at night.

Fort Carlton was the most easterly post under John Rowand's jurisdiction. From here sometimes the traders took horses and rode the four hundred miles to Fort Edmonton. During the last few years a trail across the prairies from Fort Garry to Fort Carlton and on west had come into use. As early as 1841 George Simpson, using some carts and having all the facilities of his great company behind him and thus able to obtain occasional relays of horses, reached Fort Carlton and hurried on to Edmonton. He was the first man ever to travel from the Red River Settlement to Fort Edmonton with carts and he made the trip in the nearly incredible time of twenty-two days. A year later Father Thibault had also taken that trail, leaving St. Boniface on April 20 "with one man to guide me across the prairies that I had to traverse. I was on one horse and the other carried my baggage." On June 19, two months less one day after he had left St. Boniface, he reached Fort Edmonton.

In spite of the existence of this crude trail from Fort Carlton to Fort Edmonton, Father Lacombe's party continued up the river by boat until they reached Fort Pitt. Like Fort Carlton and Fort Edmonton, this establishment was known as a pemmican post. While it also traded for furs, its main value to the company was that it purchased dried meat and pemmican from the plains Indians. These foods were to be sent down the Saskatchewan River to Le Pas, Cumberland House and Norway House to feed the hungry voyageurs who, slaving away from dawn to dusk, were far too busy to hunt for their own food.

As a passenger in the York boats fighting their way up the river and living on the pemmican these posts gathered, Father Lacombe had lots of time to learn the logistics of the fur trade and it; transportation system. With John Rowand at his side, he came to realize that Fort Edmonton was the headquarters for all the vast region we know as the prairies of the Province of Saskatchewan and the whole of the present Province of Alberta. He also learned that generally speaking the North Saskatchewan River was the boundary line between the boreal forest north of it and the parklands and prairies.

Along both sides of that river as far west as Fort Edmonton the Crees claimed an immense territory. The traders at Forts Carlton, Pitt and Edmonton recognized two different branches of this tribe; the Woods Crees north of the river extending east from Lesser Slave Lake as far as Hudson Bay, and the Plains Crees, who with their sometime allies the Assiniboines, ranged far into the prairies. There they came in conflict with the Sarcees and with the Blackfoot Confederacy divided into its three related tribes, the Bloods, Piegans and Blackfoot.

John Rowand was a fount of information and, as the long days of the tedious voyage passed, the young missionary, thirsting for knowledge, came to have a fair conception of the habits of the various tribes and the conditions under which they lived. As Rowand interpreted the Indians' lives he put an end to any illusions the newcomer may have had about the natives leading an idle, romantic life. It was true that they appeared to be free to roam the magnificent, unspoiled wilderness at will, but in fact their ceaseless journeyings were just part of the very hard work of hunting on the one hand and avoiding or attacking their enemies on the other.

The tribes north of the Saskatchewan River, the woods Indians, who were mainly Crees, lived a peaceful life. Even though they were thinly scattered over a vast expanse of forest and averaged perhaps one soul for every thirty square miles, they and their dogs endured a somewhat precarious existence living on fish and the large mammals of the forest. At times they congregated at large lakes so as to dry fish or to freeze them for their winter supply. At other times, family by family, they spread out into remote corners of the forest to hunt. They enjoyed a magnificent and beautiful land of pine and poplar forest, of willow-fringed streams and balm-ringed lakes, but even there at times starvation wiped out a whole family. Very often it was only the presence of the nearest Hudson's Bay Company post that prevented several other such tragedies. Since they had benefited greatly by the white man's trade goods and presence, they were almost invariably friendly and cooperative with the traders.

Since the inauguration of the fur trade, conditions on the rolling parklands and undulating prairies had placed the Indians south of the North Saskatchewan River in an entirely different and, from the traders' point of view, an extremely difficult position. They too wanted some of the white man's goods but because they enjoyed and ruled a more productive land, they found it not worth their while to go to any great lengths to get them. For in the vast herds of buffalo which they were sure to find grazing over the next hilltop or down the next valley they had an almost certain and plentiful food supply. Independent, truculent and touchy of temper, nearly as ready to strike the traders as to slay their numerous native enemies, they led the white man a never-ending and harassing dance.

But they had their own harassments and in turn and at every step harried their neighbours. Though for more than two generations the interloping traders had counseled peace between tribe and tribe and had tried to keep the plains Indians from each other's throats, they kept up their unceasing, though not very deadly, warfare. Usually that intermittent warfare found the Plains Crees and the Assiniboines, the more northerly tribes, allied in their attacks upon the great Blackfoot Confederacy. And when the members of any band were not out actively looking for a fight, they worked long, hard hours trying to avoid it by constant scouting and guard duty.

Like white man's warfare, theirs had been forced on the tribes by economic reasons, by invasions of each other's hunting territory or by reasons inherent in their codes of honour. In their codes which were no less complicated and unreasoning than the white man's, stealing horses was a particularly honourable pursuit. Throughout all the years that the white men had known the prairie Indians this pastime had caused the traders the utmost vexation and had led to fight after fight between the native bands.

Because the plains Indians' warfare was sporadic, it was a rare battle indeed that took more than a dozen lives. Fortunately for the Indians, warfare on the scale practiced even in that era by white men was inconceivable. The very looseness of their organization saw to that. In their domestic affairs where public opinion was the dominating factor, the natives maintained a relaxed constraint that met their needs. In their warfare each man was largely a law unto himself. Centuries of civilization had drummed cooperation into white men; these centuries had also taught them the virtue of patience and the value of deferring the revenge of the moment or the immediate gratification of pleasure to obtain some larger reward later on. But these ideas were foreign to the Indians' individualistic and ultrademocratic nature. The average Indian was generous, brave, daring and infinitely patient in the chase, but in warfare he was his own boss and rarely submitted to prolonged discipline.

Similarly on the religious front, except for some fraternal mystic societies and except for the annual thirst or sun dances, there was little formal religious organization. The Indians were inherently religious as was evident enough on the occasions of these dances. They were times for the fulfilment of vows and for the more religiously inclined to fast, make sacrifices and to inflict torture upon themselves. All these were demanded by the faith of their fathers which required them to make prayers and incantations to the spirit world. White men, who were themselves divided by conflicting doctrines, called them pagan, but in fact they, like the white men, did believe in some power greater than themselves.

These, then, were the people the missionaries came to woo from their ancestral gods to new forms of worship. These were the people for whose sake Father Lacombe had made the long trip from St. Boniface and these were the conditions under which they lived. Thinking over all this plethora of information, Father Lacombe still had time for moments of solitude and reflection while he "considered the dizzy rapidity of the Kisiskatchiwan (swift running water) River, against which we struggled all day long. I gazed upon the hills, some covered with trees, others just rock, all of which deprived us of a view of the plains. I dreamed of the future, made plans, and built castles of air.

"Finally, on the afternoon of September 19, we arrived at Fort Edmonton, where the crew was awaited with impatience. Métis, mostly women, and Indians, covered the shore and the hillsides to cheer our arrival. The English flag with the honourable Company's coat of arms, floated over one of the bastions. The cannon and gunfire announced to all that we had tobacco, munitions, and booty for another year. I hurried to shake hands with each of the Christians making up that crowd, for, that day, they became my children and parishioners. There are moments and circumstances ever to be remembered in the life of a missionary when he reaches the land of his apostolate."

CHAPTER FIVE

Learning the Lay of the Land
1852–54

The Fort Edmonton to which the young priest had come was an impressive stronghold. With its high palisades and frowning bastions, its martial appearance fitted its dominating site some two hundred feet above the landing place. Within the walls, looking down on the encompassing sentinels' gallery with its iron cannons and towering above the massive bolt-studded gates, stood the Big House. Known as Rowand's Folly and showing signs of nearly twenty years' existence, it was the biggest single structure west of Lake Winnipeg.

After enduring weeks of unbroken solitude ascending the repetitive but magnificent vistas of the Saskatchewan River's forest-locked shores, Father Lacombe found this well-ordered establishment a most welcome change. As usual, he found his Métis folk deferential and glad to greet him. The fact that he knew many of their relatives in Pembina and in the Red River Settlement added to his popularity. Fortunately he had impressed John Rowand, and having gotten off to a good start with him found that the gruff old factor was going to set aside a house within the palisades for his private use. Rowand expected the young father, like other missionaries before him, to eat in the company's mess-room in the four-storey Big House.

Just as the rugged comfort of that house, which combined within its walls offices, warehouse and dormitory space, had overawed the Indians and impressed all travellers, it also excited Father Lacombe's interest. In a similar manner it had affected the artist Paul Kane who, five years earlier along with Father Thibault and the Methodist, the Reverend Mr. Rundle, had partaken of Christmas dinner in it. Of that occasion he wrote:

> "The dining-hall in which we assembled was the largest room in the fort, probably about fifty by twenty-five feet, well warmed by large fires, which are scarcely ever allowed to go out. The walls and ceilings are boarded, as plastering is not used, there being no limestone within reach, but the boards are painted in a style of the most startling barbaric gaudiness, and the ceiling filled with centre-pieces of fantastic gilt scrolls, making altogether a saloon which no white man would enter for the first time without a start, and which the Indians always looked upon with awe and wonder."

Feeling fortunate indeed to live in such an establishment, Father Lacombe also rendered repeated thanks that now, after some years of uncertainty, he was to be virtually independent and free to apply his untested talents and his devotion to the high cause he had espoused. Here the only limits on his crusade to win Indian souls to Christ were his own industry and his initiative, and he felt no qualms on the score of either. Here indeed he was in the very heart of the untamed Indian territory.

North, south, east or west for hundreds of miles, but all within the Hudson's Bay Company's so-called Saskatchewan District, of which Fort Edmonton was its headquarters, roamed some sixteen thousand Indians. Eight tribes in addition to some 280 Métis sought their happiness in the surrounding forests or prairies and their numbers had been estimated by a census reported by Sir George Simpson in 1841 as follows:

Saskatchewan District

tribes	tents	souls
Crees	500	3,500
Assiniboines	580	4,060

Blackfoot	300	2,100
Piegans	350	2,450
Blood Indians	250	1,750
Sarcees	50	350
Gros Ventres	300	2,100
Saulteaux	20	140
Half-breeds	40	280
Totals	2,390	16,730

As rapidly as he could, Father Lacombe planned to get in touch with them; first, when they came in to trade, and later on their home ground.

He had come to realize that Fort Edmonton was the most important post in western Canada. From it his new found friend John Rowand, like a corpulent spider sitting in the centre of his web, kept in touch with a quarter of a continent. It lay, moreover, on the trans-Canada route, the great cross-continent route on which travellers coming up the Saskatchewan River changed from boats to pack horses to make the eighty-mile portage to Fort Assiniboine whence, sometimes by water and sometimes on horseback, they ascended the Athabasca River, crossed the mountains at Jasper and then descended the Columbia River to the Pacific Ocean.

Following part of that very route, Father Lacombe had landed at Fort Edmonton with one of the brigades. Immediately on his arrival he was to see the bustle that invariably followed when the annual fall brigade came in. Even as he had walked up the slope to the fort gates the Hudson's Bay Company employees had started carrying the goods into the storeroom or spreading them out to dry. Within a day or so a large part of the goods had been repacked and loaded on nearly eighty pack horses for the trip to Fort Assiniboine. Some of these goods were to remain there, some were to go westward up the Athabasca River, while about half of the total were to descend that stream for a few miles and then start out towards Lesser Slave Lake and the Peace River country. All this activity Father Lacombe found most interesting in itself, but of even greater interest was the first-hand lesson in geography it afforded. From the gateway of Fort Edmonton these goods spread out fanwise to so many destinations to the north and west. He resolved that at the first opportunity his itchy feet would make their way to these destinations, for they were focal points for scores of pagan Indians.

At the moment, however, he had no need to travel to come into contact with untold other Indians of the woods or prairies. Knowing that the brigade was due to arrive, they had congregated in favourite campgrounds within a mile or two of the fort; some indeed were camped on the flats a gunshot away. All of them awaited the signal that would be given once John Rowand had despatched his pack horses and was ready to trade with them. Hitherto the young priest had met only a few Saulteaux at Pembina, and had narrowly escaped meeting hostile Sioux on his buffalo hunts. Now in the course of a few days he was to see many hundreds of natives representing five or six tribes. As he watched he was in his element, gloating over them like a man who has found creeks lined with gold and is at a loss to know which to pan first. Others might see these painted, half-naked people as redskins or savages, but to Father Lacombe they were souls to be saved. In placing him at Fort Edmonton God had rewarded his lifelong hope.

Day after day, band after band from differing tribes came in from their nearby temporary camps. They came ceremoniously and expected to be received with ceremony. Riding up, they saluted those in the fort with a friendly discharge of their muskets and waited expectantly for the salvos to spout from the old cannons in the bastions. As their echoes rolled back and forth throughout the grand river valley, the band advanced in a wild procession through the widely thrown gates and up to the trading hall, where, with Father Lacombe beside him, John Rowand greeted them — all of them as old friends and most of them by name. Finally, during the passage of days, one band after another would be given goods and ammunition on credit before setting off to hunt for furs or to make pemmican to bring in later on to pay their debts.

When the last of the hundred campfires on the nearby flats had flickered and died, when the last of the hundreds of howling dogs had been ferried across the broad Saskatchewan, Rowand retired gratefully to his counting house to watch as his staff tallied the results of the recent trade. Father Lacombe, thrilled by the multitudes he had watched so keenly, had time to wander around the fort and talk to the wives and children of the Métis employees. The men, of course, were all busy labouring in various parts of the establishment.

While trading with the Indians was the post's raison d'être, that activity had to be supported by a staff of several score labourers or artisans. With their half-breed or Indian wives and families, the resident population was about 150 souls. Since this isolated post was nearly a thousand miles from the Red River Settlement by the cart trail and 130 days' round trip by boat, it had to be self-supporting in the way of food. Furthermore, it had to lay in tons of pemmican for export for the use of other posts or for the brigades. A few fields of barley and oats kept Fort Edmonton supplied with cereal food and when the large fields of potatoes could be harvested before the Indians had plundered them, they contributed to the menu of a post which at times, in spite of them, endured periods of semi-starvation. All year long with wood to cut for the huge fireplaces and timber to be felled and brought to the fort and then sawn into planks, and cattle and horses to be tended, the staff was seldom idle. All in all, however, this self-contained establishment, this busy oasis in the endless forest, was a well-run and pleasant place in which to live.

Superintending all this activity, as well as keeping his fingers on the affairs of Fort Carlton, Fort Pitt and Rocky Mountain House, kept Rowand busy. Fortunately for the priest the trader had time to develop a liking for the younger man such as he had not felt for Father Thibault or for the Methodist, the Reverend R. T. Rundle, who had made the fort his headquarters for eight years before leaving the country in 1848. Like all Hudson's Bay Company men, Rowand could see that in various ways missionary activity was bound to help to open the country to settlement and to interfere with the company's orderly business. Nevertheless, since its policy was to help these men of the cloth, Rowand fell in line. That, however, did not prevent him from expressing his personal opinion as he did when writing to George Simpson in December 1844 when he said: "With respect to Mr. Thibault, I saw very little of him — but quite enough." Evidently a longer acquaintance did nothing to soften Rowand's distaste for that missionary because a couple of years later, when writing Simpson again, old John was in the same mood and declared: "I wish Thibault was in his mother's belly."

The passage of years had done little to change the opinion he expressed in 1843 when writing to a friend:

> "The worst thing for the trade is those ministers and priests — the natives will never work half so well now — they like praying and singing. Mr. Thingheaute [Thibault] is allowed to go back again to the Saskatchewan. We shall all be saints after a time. Rundle says that all Catholics will go to ———, for himself he is sure of going straite to heaven when he dies, but he longs to get a wife. . . ."

Although not a rigid Catholic, he was far from agreeing with Rundle's opinion of their ultimate destination. In fact, on one occasion when he was at a large dinner party at which the majority were anti-Catholic, he made his position abundantly clear by throwing his glass at one of the guests who started a ribald song deriding the pope.

Father Lacombe had been fortunate to fall into John Rowand's hands. Fortunately too, that early in his career, his friendly personality had begun to show through to the extent that he could make friends without lowering his principles in any way. At times he felt it necessary to risk an unpleasant encounter with John Rowand but even though now and then he got the trader's hackles up, the two men remained cordial friends. It took the sensitive young priest a long time to accept the apparent callousness with which pioneers had to treat human suffering in this rough and ready land where in illness a man either died or got well pretty much without human intervention. For weeks Father Lacombe had remembered his rebuff when early in the trip from Norway House he had pleaded that compassion be shown one of the sick voyageurs and Rowand had offhandedly said that any man who had not died after three days' illness was not sick at all.

One day Rowand showed him a painful felon on his finger and then a few days later when it had become worse came complaining again. He did what he could for the injury but could not resist this chance to pay Rowand in his own coin.

"You are not sick, my friend," he said. "You understand what I mean? You are not sick. Three days have passed and you are not dead. It is all imagination."

Rowand glared at him and walked away, but then, seeing the grim humour of the situation, the hard-bitten old rascal grinned and forgot the incident. In this priest he had found one of the few men who dared to stand up to him. On Lacombe's part, as on so many later occasions, his personality had held its own with the most influential man in the West — but it had done so in a manner that had enhanced rather than hindered their friendship. Though young Father Lacombe could not have realized it at the time, the blustering trader was to be only one of a long line of strong men who were to come to admire, trust and like him.

Not long after the incident of John Rowand's felon, Father Lacombe rode over to greet his confrere Father Bourassa, who was to leave the following spring and whose place at Lac Ste. Anne he was to fill.

With the help of Father Bourassa, Father Thibault had established the mission during the summer of 1844. When the pioneer missionary had first seen the lovely lake it was easy to understand why the natives had called it *Manito Sakahigan*, the Divine Lake or God's Lake. Undoubtedly with his knowledge of narrow-minded white men, he readily understood how they had twisted its name to the one in common use amongst the traders. Regarding all of the Indians' religion as pagan and therefore devilish, they had placed the Manito in the same category and called his magnificent body of water Devil's Lake. Thibault dedicated his mission to Saint Anne and thenceforth her name came to be attached to the lake.

For two reasons Father Thibault's choice of Lac Ste. Anne had been a good one. In the first place, the lake was famous for its fish and for years from its fishing station there the Hudson's Bay Company employees had sent some 40,000 whitefish annually to feed Fort Edmonton. Shortly before Father Thibault's time the few surplus Métis for whom Fort Edmonton could not find employment had gradually moved out there to live. Father Thibault's new mission was designed to serve them and to strengthen their weakening conception of the religion to which their paternal forebears had held.

In the second place, he hoped to find a location where Crees and Stonies could worship in peace. Because it lay back in the forest some fifty miles from Fort Edmonton, it was most unlikely that the warring Blackfoot would ever reach out that far to attack these woods tribes. Fort Edmonton, of course, was invariably the scene of a greater or lesser brawl whenever on their frequent trading visits the Blackfoot from the south met the Crees and Stonies from the north. From the standpoint of peaceful worship, Lac Ste. Anne was ideal.

When Father Lacombe and his guide rode out there they crossed the Sturgeon River about eight miles from Fort Edmonton and then within two or three miles came to the fire-cleared area on which the Hudson's Bay Company grazed its surplus pack horses — the company's "horseguard." There they had to leave the twenty-five-year-old portage trail heading for Fort Assiniboine and swing to the left to follow the path which was used when bringing in fish from the lake.

All this forest through which they rode was the natural habitat of the Cree and Stoney Indians with whom the Hudson's Bay Company traders found it easy to deal. Moreover, since its French Canadian voyageurs also found them more amenable, the great majority of Métis had been born of Cree mothers. When the missionaries, Catholic or Protestant, came, they too found them easy to deal with and to convert. While men of the cloth of both denominations had met a few Blackfoot, particularly at Fort Edmonton, they found it hard to make much impression on them. Consequently, because pastoral harvesters were so few and the woods Indians so many and ready to be reaped, nothing was more natural than that they should concentrate their efforts on these Crees and Stonies. The field was so vast, the labourers so few. All this, of course, Father Lacombe knew long before he had even taken the trail which led him to Father Bourassa's welcoming arms.

The sheer delight of two priests meeting when both were isolated from any of their kind by possibly five hundred miles is perhaps hard for people in our age to understand. Nevertheless, it was a delight which far transcended the genuine but sometimes studied courtesy of one priest to another. Long into the chilly September night these two talked, occasionally throwing another stick of wood into the mud and wattle fireplace.

In later life, Father Lacombe, writing of the sacrifices made by such missionaries and the wretched conditions under which they lived, also wrote that

"This wretchedness vanishes at the sight of good done to souls. We are not stopped by those trifles when consoled by the God of Evangelical Workers, when grace works miracles, finally when these poor nations come in flocks as thirsty sheep to the fountain of the sacred doctrine of the Saviour of souls. Never was heaven more lavish in its unspeakable kindness than in favour of those who evangelize the nations. The worldly soul does not understand these truths, because it serves another master, it works for an earthly reward. The missionary spends himself for another happiness."

During his short visit to Lac Ste. Anne he met many Indians and got to know most of the estimable Métis who gained much of their livelihood from the lake. He was surprised to learn that amongst his parishioners Father Bourassa counted several Iroquois whose grandparents had left their reserve at Caughnawaga, just across the river from Montreal.

As they relaxed over a pot of tea, the two priests undoubtedly rejoiced over the apparent failure of the Wesleyan missionaries in the area. Four years earlier the Reverend R. T. Rundle, who in 1840 had been the first resident missionary of any faith to reside at Fort Edmonton, had left the West and there was no ordained representative of that faith nearer than Norway House over eight hundred miles away. For a few years Father Thibault and the Reverend Mr. Rundle had had a few bitter exchanges and when occasionally they dined together at John Rowand's table their mutual coolness chilled much of the camaraderie which usually circulated around that well-laden board. On one visit to the fort in 1846, according to Father Morice, the historian, Father Thibault had "chronicled the conversion of thirty-six Indians who had previously embraced Methodism." That had done nothing at all to sweeten the relations between the contending pastors.

At times, however, the shoe was on the other foot and the Methodist, casting his net, swept in a few Catholic catechumens. But then, in spite of the devoted strivings of either missionary, it was impossible to guarantee the faithfulness of their converts. The Indians, suspiciously sampling each missionary's wares and weighing these alongside such inducements as tobacco and tea, seldom drank deeply of the cup of salvation held out to them. Now that in 1852 the Methodist missionary had been gone for four years, the field was wide open to the two Catholic fathers. They rejoiced — but redoubled their efforts.

It became obvious to Father Lacombe that if he were to travel hither and yon to Indian camps he would need a guide, dog driver and all around servant. Father Bourassa put him in touch with a Métis by the name of Alexis Cardinal who for many years served him in all those capacities and became a famous character in his own right. The priest and the man he was soon to call his "faithful Alexis" were about the same age. Alexis, the son of Rose Grise and Joseph Cardinal (one of several Cardinals who had reached the West about 1800), was born at Lac La Biche.

Taking Alexis with him, Father Lacombe left Lac Ste. Anne to return to winter at Edmonton, whence from time to time he hoped to sally forth to visit Indian camps. In all probability it was Alexis who suggested a trip to Lac La Biche that fall just as it had been his father who had heard that Father Thibault had come to Fort Edmonton, went to see him, and beseeched him to come to Lac La Biche to minister to the fifteen families in the tiny Métis colony and guided him across country on his ten-day walk to the small settlement.

Missionary affairs had progressed so far that unlike Father Thibault who had walked to that lake, Father Lacombe and Alexis were able to go on horseback. The new priest revelled in the trip which took him along the traders' pack trail which followed the north side of the Saskatchewan until somewhere in the vicinity of Saddlelake Creek they left it and headed north. On the way they passed Cache and Whitefish lakes and finally, crossing the Beaver River, hurried along to the magnificent lake itself. In all, they rode some 160 miles and all the way,

"The weather was ideal; a true Indian summer. The intense heat and the mosquitoes had disappeared. We went along happily through valleys and over hills, camping near a clear stream without fears or worries. The kettle was boiling, cooking the fat game our hunters had downed for us. Then our ravenous appetites were ready for supper. Our hunger satisfied we smoked a satisfying pipe, which was the closing act of our recreation. Night prayer fervently said, we stretched out on the soft grass to rest in peace."

At the lake they

"Camped on its shores with a goodly number of Métis and Cree Indians. All were happy to see the priest again, for, they had grown to respect and love the priest in the person of Father Thibault. I was quite at home among these people. Not able to speak Cree, I managed as best I could with the little I knew, along with the few French words the men knew. The first evening we gathered in a large hut lighted by the chimney fire. . . . I sang a hymn and recited the prayers in Cree, that was all I could do."

For the next two weeks Father Lacombe enjoyed a busy and fruitful visit. Finally when he was ready to return to Fort Edmonton, "I vested my surplice and stole, and officially founded the new mission, naming it: Our Lady of Victories. This mission was to undergo many a storm. Our Queen of Heaven would be there to defend us."

On his return to the fort, Father Lacombe settled down for the winter of 1852–53 with the firm resolution of learning the Cree language as soon as possible. Although his command of English left much to be desired and although most of the senior staff of the fort spoke English amongst themselves and were of the Protestant persuasion, his pleasant personality soon made him a welcome guest.

Operating out of the house John Rowand put at his disposal, probably the same one the Reverend Robert Rundle had used, he spent much of his time with the Métis and Catholic working men of the fort. Nearly everyone attended his masses and before spring he had a devout following amongst those Métis who previously had taken religious matters rather indifferently.

Before spring came, like so many other priests had done,

he started to compile a Cree dictionary. In his studies he was fortunate that Colin Fraser, one of the traders who at one time had been Sir George Simpson's ceremonial piper, took a fancy to him and tutored him diligently. During Fraser's long sojourn at Jasper House, he had welcomed the two Oregon-bound missionaries, Fathers Blanchet and Demers, who, in passing, had baptized three of his daughters. He was still there in 1845 to greet the Jesuit, Father De Smet. The next year when Paul Kane rode across from Fort Edmonton to Fort Assiniboine with the Oregon-bound brigade, Colin Fraser accompanied the party. Speaking of the days when he had piped Simpson into innumerable posts, he declared that on one occasion one of the Indians who had "never before beheld so extraordinary a looking man, or such a musical instrument . . . asked him to intercede with the Great Spirit for him."

Father Lacombe considered the winter well spent. With his ready ear for Indian languages he had acquired enough facility in the Cree tongue that by spring he could discourse intelligently with members of that tribe. Moreover, while more than half a dozen languages were spoken about the fort — English, French, Gaelic, Blackfoot, Assiniboine and some Beaver — he found that Cree was the common denominator and that all traders of two or three years' standing spoke it. As his command of it improved and his ability to converse in it increased, so did the number of converts he was able to make. All in all he had enjoyed a successful winter.

On one of his strolls in the early spring when the snow had pretty well melted away, he noticed the fallen cross which Fathers Demers and Blanchet had erected in 1838. It stood higher up the hill than the fort and was on the ground now occupied by the Alberta Legislative Building. Getting a shovel, and maybe some help, he replanted it, so that for some further years it should stand as a symbol of the objective towards which he and his fellow fathers directed their efforts.

That spring too, Father Lacombe cemented still further the bond between himself and his Alexis when he blessed his guide's marriage to Nancy Quintal, a Lac La Biche Métis, who in the fashion of the country had been his wife for several years. Moreover, he baptized their six-year-old girl Philomène.

Shortly after that he left Fort Edmonton to take up residence at Lac Ste. Anne to replace the departing Father Bourassa. There, despite his worries over his postponed noviciate, he carried on effectively. At last he was on his very own, free to be his own man, free to fail or succeed, but *Deo volente*, assured of his mission and his ability to follow wherever it might lead.

That summer brought him news of Bishop Provencher's death in June 1853. That news was not unexpected but was nonetheless a heartfelt shock. Some eleven months earlier he and Bishop Taché had taken their solemn last parting from this man who had laboured so long and so mightily and indeed so successfully to put Catholicism on a firm footing throughout northwestern Canada. He had come to St. Boniface in 1818 and there he had remained, striving against manifold difficulties and disappointments, and now thirty-five years later his efforts had resulted in an edifice far more imposing than any of his religious rivals could show.

For his eleven hundred parishioners at St. Boniface he had left a cathedral and a convent cared for by eleven nuns. At Saint-François-Xavier he could show a church and a convent tended by two sisters. Beyond the borders of the small area settled along the Red and Assiniboine rivers were the frontier missions at Lac Ste. Anne, Ile-à-la-Crosse and Lake Athabasca, each with some small outpost dependencies. At these missions Bishop Taché and four secular priests, Thibault, Bourassa, Laflêche and Lacombe, struggled with adversity while five Oblate fathers buckled to their tasks: Bermond, Faraud, Grollier, Tissot and Maisonneuve. Two other Oblates had recently arrived from France, Fathers Vegreville and Rémas, and were on the point of starting missions at Cold Lake and Lac La Biche. No wonder his associates revered his memory. His strenuous toil had been rewarded. Others would come and in slightly easier times would erect a magnificent superstructure but he had laid the firm foundation.

As was to be expected, while the Hudson's Bay Company had treated the Catholics reasonably well, it had shown partiality to the Church of England. Even with this help, by 1853 the Anglicans were poorly represented. Under his control David Anderson, the bishop of Rupert's Land, had fewer priests than his counterpart at St. Boniface and those he had served a much more limited area. The most westerly and also the most northerly was the Reverend James Settee, a native who had been stationed at Lac La Ronge since 1846. He had received much of his training from the Reverend James Hunter who had started serving at Le Pas in 1844.

At the time the only other missionary body in the West, the Wesleyans, had failed to follow up Reverend R. T. Rundle's brave eight-year venture which had ended when he left Edmonton in 1848. Ever since 1840 when Reverend James Evans, the inventor of the Cree syllabic, had established his mission at Norway House, however, it had been kept in operation. At the time of Bishop Provencher's death, along all the long water routes leading to Lake Athabasca or to Fort Edmonton, the Wesleyans did not have a single station beyond Norway House.

When, therefore, in the spring of 1853 Father Lacombe went to make Lac Ste. Anne his permanent residence and Father Bourassa had returned to St. Boniface, he had been left as the only missionary for a radius of three hundred miles. Several weeks later he learned that Father Rémas, one of the new Oblates from France, had been sent to start a regular mission at Lac La Biche. Rejoicing that he had an associate a mere 160 horseback miles away and delighted to have an excuse to take to the trail again, he rode over to greet him.

Father Lacombe, who had been brought up on a Quebec farm and since then had had two years' opportunity to make a somewhat gradual adjustment from a comfortable home to the starkness of Lac Ste. Anne, was appalled when he saw the wretched manner in which poor Father Rémas was existing. The newcomer had come from comfortable and crowded France almost directly to the solitude of the large lake and to the crudeness of a shack which he had built himself. When Father Lacombe arrived the local Métis and Indians were all away on a hunt and the new priest was alone. Because he had reached the lake so late, the garden he had planted was an utter failure. Consequently, suffering from cultural shock and huddling in his hut, he sustained himself by alternately nibbling on dried meat and pemmican. In his bark-roofed, earthen-floored shack, six feet high and twelve feet square, he was indeed the very picture of desolation. How glad he was to hear the hoofbeats of Father Lacombe's horse and to meet a fellow priest must be left to the imagination.

In his memoirs Father Lacombe, trying to explain some of the pioneer missionaries' feelings, wrote:

"We have to respond to and face isolation, discouragement, inclemency, poverty, antipathy and the indifference of the Indians. The missionary, with all his self-sacrifice and zeal, is a man born and raised in the midst of the benefits of civilization. Today, thrown into the midst of a rude people, lawless as to decency and morals, he is not without feeling these inconveniences bitterly."

Father Lacombe did the only sensible thing. Having Father Rémas gather up his few belongings, he led him through the fall foliage back to Lac Ste. Anne. There for several months, with the help of Alexis, the two studied the Cree language and continued the work of christianizing the local Indians.

Finally word reached Lac Ste. Anne that towards the end of February 1854 Bishop Taché would hitch up his dog team, leave his crudely constructed log episcopal palace at Ile-à-la-Crosse and make his way over to visit the two priests. They were overjoyed when he arrived. Living under much the same conditions they endured, their superior could understand their problems. They made the most of this occasion when for the first time three priests had ever been able to congregate at Lac Ste. Anne.

Meanwhile, of course, the bishop was sizing up the relative merits of the two men. He decided that now that Father Rémas had gained a few months' experience in the mission field, he should return to carry on his work at Lac La Biche. When in a few days he and Father Rémas started back to their respective posts, Father Lacombe, loathe to lose them, hitched up his dog team and accompanied them back to Fort Edmonton and even for a few more miles beyond that. Finally, after embracing all around, he started back to the loneliness of his Lac Ste. Anne mission.

Once more he had to defer his year of formal training for the Oblate order until some priest who could act as his noviciate master became available.

CHAPTER SIX

Lac Ste. Anne
1854-57

At Lac Ste. Anne during 1854, Father Lacombe's acclimatization to the West proceeded rapidly. There he was relatively comfortable, usually had a reliable supply of fish or pemmican and, best of all, behind his dogs he was only one long day's travel from that bastion of white man's civilization, Fort Edmonton. His work of lifting Métis and half-breeds to a higher level of Christian knowledge continued with enough success to please him. All the while he spent long hours improving his command of the Cree language and recording it in his notebook.

The stark loneliness experienced by the missionaries who then and later ventured into the far North fell less heavily on him. In his case that was warded off by the proximity of Edmonton where the number of Métis converts kept increasing and where he established a mission which he called St. Joachim. Moreover, the Métis colony at Lac Ste. Anne kept growing and he found that gratifying.

To the Hudson's Bay Company it was exactly the reverse. The company's existence depended upon maintaining complete control of the fur trade. For some thirty years it had enjoyed a monopoly which had been profitable to its shareholders and benign to the Indians. As long as possible, therefore, it was determined to keep free trade out of the Edmonton region.

During Father Lacombe's early lonely years at Lac Ste. Anne it had begun to rear its head. Within a very few years free traders were to squeeze in and bring with them an increasing outpouring of liquor. Before that happened, the company succeeded in maintaining much of its monopoly of the trade. In a very large measure, that monopoly was to be the factor which accounted for the difference between the more peaceful treatment of Indians in Canada and the deadly future their cousins in America suffered.

Quite rightly the priests criticized the company's use of liquor in its dealings with the Indians. So too had the company's directors in England. After it had absorbed the North West Company in 1821, the London office ordered that the use of liquor be stopped and throughout all of northern Canada that order had been carried out. If the company was to continue trading in the Red River Settlement and along the Saskatchewan River, however, it could not stop supplying some liquor to the Indians. For in the prairies and parklands lived the very mobile horse-riding Indians, the Plains Crees, the Blackfoot Confederacy and others. And they regarded liquor as essential. If the Hudson's Bay Company did not give it to them, the Americans, a mere five hundred miles away, would do so.

At Fort Edmonton, as free traders, both Métis and white, came creeping in, its use increased. While Father Lacombe set his hand against liquor, he undoubtedly realized the Hudson's Bay Company's position. He also understood the company's policy with respect to trading furs. Being a reasonable man he was always one of the foremost of the priests who recognized that in many ways, including their transportation problems, the missionaries were indebted to the company. As a result, he tried to toe the line the company had drawn — no one except its employees should trade furs.

One day during the spring of 1854 he inadvertently tripped over that line, and quite literally the fur flew. He had found a discarded, out of season otter skin and had strips of it sewn on the cuffs and collar of his jacket. The fur added a bit of warmth and a much needed touch of elegance to his otherwise unsightly coat. Though he cared little for sartorial perfection, he found the result pleasing.

But his pleasure lasted only until his next visit to Fort Edmonton, where as usual he greeted his friend John Rowand.

Instead of returning the father's cheerful salute, Rowand, seeing the fur on his coat, glared at him and exploded.

"You darned priest, you!" he bellowed. "Who gave you permission to cut up and use fur? What an example you set your Métis!"

Father Lacombe, taken by surprise, was momentarily abashed. But he was not appalled for, when provoked, he too could flash into anger. He tried to explain but Rowand was in no mood to listen. Standing toe to toe to the irate trader the priest tore off "those miserable skins from my wrists and threw them in his face." Then he flounced away.

John Rowand, however, had not acquired his reputation as a man for nothing. Nobody could daunt him; around the fort no one dared try. But here was this young priest standing up to him. When, later in the day, within the narrow confines of the fort their paths crossed again, their tempers had cooled and each was man enough to overlook the incident. Indeed, if anything, each had risen in the other's estimation.

Rowand was probably ashamed of his burst of temper. Not long before, when in his middle sixties, he had written to a friend: "I make difficulties where there are none; people after being so long in the service get useless. . . ."

At Fort Pitt a couple of months later, in a similar outburst of temper, the old man, who as usual had gone east with his brigade of furs in May, fell dead. Behind him at Fort Edmonton he had left a legacy of courage and fair dealing, and in the young priest from Lac Ste. Anne a high regard which over the next sixty years never dimmed.

The missionaries and Father Lacombe in particular had a good friend in the rugged old trader. Depending upon the personalities of the traders in charge of the posts on the one hand and those of the priests on the other, the missionaries' receptions ranged from tolerance to glad welcome. Right from the beginning, Father Lacombe was one of the missionaries who was always welcome. Some others, either Protestant or Catholic, rubbed the traders the wrong way. Idealists expecting a perfect world to unroll in front of them, some were inclined to be either snivelling or overbearing, but these soon left the West. As Father Lacombe wrote, "There were a few exceptional cases, where, we must admit, some of our missionaries, somewhat imprudent, and overly zealous, served us poorly, rather than showing themselves useful."

Only clerical men who could "roll with the punches" could succeed in the area. And Lacombe, never for a moment forsaking his high ideals, was one of these. "We had to suffer with patience and endure for the moment what we could not prevent, however unjust the affair might appear." On another occasion he wrote, "If we hadn't had the Hudson's Bay Company's help and hospitality we would have been obliged to wait for years to found the missions."

On the whole he felt that "The number of Bourgeois of the Forts of this country, equals the number of friends and benefactors that I should count among those that my memoirs must not forget."

Amongst those, of course, was William Christie who took charge of Fort Edmonton after John Rowand's death and did what he could to conduct its trade in an environment that was beginning to change. The three main changes were a slight but nevertheless noticeable decline in the size of the buffalo herds, an increase in the number of Métis hunting them and, partly as a consequence of these two factors, an increase in intertribal warfare. These changes made it ever more difficult for Fort Edmonton to obtain an adequate supply of meat.

Within what is now southern Alberta even at that time were millions of buffalo. They were not in one immense herd which made a great annual circular migration, but in many separate herds varying in size from a few hundred to a million or more. Moreover, as the fancy took them, they mingled with other herds or broke away from larger groupings, or changed their distribution as hunting pressure disturbed them. Unless they had received recent news of their whereabouts, no little group of hunters going out from Fort Edmonton could tell how many days it would have to go before falling in with the shaggy beasts.

The natives, of course, felt that it was their prerogative to hunt the buffalo themselves and to sell the meat, either fresh, dried or as pemmican, to the fort. Since, however, their deliveries were most unreliable, Fort Edmonton had to send out paid hunters to supplement the supply. These were generally Métis who, because their numbers in the area were still relatively small, did not organize annual hunts on a grand scale such as their cousins in the Red River area did. Naturally the Indians made it hot for these hunting Métis interlopers.

In spite of that, small venturous hunting parties of Métis or Cree kept coming in to Fort Edmonton with news of affairs on the plains. And, much like their successors a hundred years later hung on radio broadcasts, Edmontonians of 1854 hung on the news from the plains. A few typical bits of information gleaned from the Fort Edmonton journals starting the fall of that year indicate how important was the question of meat supply.

Late in October the plains hunters arrived with ten carts and seventeen loaded horses. They said that they had been five days coming home with the meat. Early in December some Hudson's Bay Company men came in from Rocky Mountain House and reported that since a war party of Crees had set fire to the plains, there were no buffalo near there. From time to time all winter Father Lacombe went back and forth between the fort and his mission and usually accompanied small bands of Métis hunters coming or going. About the middle of January a messenger came in from one of these bands to report that they had made a good kill and to ask the fort people to go out to help bring in the meat. When these men returned a week or so later they brought thirty-six dog trains of frozen meat which had evidently been taken in a pound. About the middle of February, Maskepatoon, the famous Cree chief, sent in word that he had killed many buffalo and wanted someone to visit his camp and bring goods to trade for the meat.

Besides carrying on his priestly duties whenever he came in to his St. Joachim chapel in the fort, Father Lacombe and his faithful Alexis set off in the spring of 1855 on a long trip out into the prairies to visit some Cree camps. Wherever he encountered these people, some of whom he had met at Fort Edmonton, they received him kindly and with a modicum of interest. Here and there he baptized some children, but perhaps the main result of his trip was to familiarize himself with some of the geography of the parklands as far south as the Battle River.

Visiting the Plains Crees merely whetted his appetite for travelling, so in May 1855 with Alexis to guide him, he set out from Lac Ste. Anne to make his way to the Peace River country. Taking the portage trail to Fort Assiniboine and paddling down the Athabasca River to the mouth of the Lesser Slave Lake River, he eventually reached the lake: "After meeting up with every form of difficulty and unexpected obstacles, on Pentecost Sunday, accompanied by my faithful Métis, I roused the Indian and Métis population camped on the shores of Small Slave Lake which is a splendid sheet of water. In an instant my canoe was surrounded by the crowd which was delighted to see a priest again."

His friend Colin Fraser, who was in charge of the Lesser Slave Lake post, was undoubtedly there to welcome him and probably provided horses for the continuation of his trip to Fort Dunvegan. At both these places, "My fatigue, privations and difficulties were well rewarded by the religious enthusiasm shown. So, I set to work. Night and day I was kept busy, teaching catechism, prayers and hymns."

Remembering the generosity Colin Fraser and other Hudson's Bay men had shown him, he returned to Lac Ste. Anne in September. In his memoirs written in later life he was kind to the Hudson's Bay Company's employees and after mentioning some of the company's many courtesies, he continued:

"And, after all these testimonies what can I add? Let it suffice for me to recall my intimate relationship with Mr. William Christie, who, during his five years' residence in Edmonton, did me much good and was most amiable. It is in such cases that we cannot understand the designs of God in leaving such persons in the error of protestantism, they who have been so kind to the Apostles of truth."

He was not at Fort Edmonton on September 20, 1855, when the brigade arrived from Norway House with some goods for his mission along with the annual trading supplies for the post. Whoever carried the news of the brigade's arrival also hastened to impart the unwelcome news that a Wesleyan rival, the Reverend Thomas Woolsey, had come with it and was taking up residence in the fort. But that was not all; the courier was able to tell the father that another missionary, the Reverend Henry

B. Steinhauer, a full blooded Ojibway Indian, was even then making his way through the woods to Lac La Biche. With Woolsey around, Father Lacombe's chances of straightening out William Christie's error of protestantism began to appear dim. Nevertheless, after a flying trip to the fort to get his supplies and mail and to size up this Wesleyan rival, he hurried back to Lac Ste. Anne to increase his already strenuous efforts with his Indians.

In sending Woolsey to Fort Edmonton and Steinhauer to Lac La Biche, the Wesleyans, of course, were reactivating their role in the far West. They were not to do so without opposition because Bishop Taché at St. Boniface was also obtaining men to step up his church's activity in the same area. For instance, a new and seemingly inconspicuous Oblate from France had arrived at his palace in August 1854. His name was Vital J. Grandin and he was soon despatched to Lac La Biche and before long went on to serve the missions in the far North. Part of Bishop Taché's stepping-up process led to the wise decision to upgrade the Lac La Biche mission so that it could become the supply depot for the priests down the Athabasca and Mackenzie rivers. In the fall of 1855 this decision led him to replace Father Rémas at Lac La Biche with two stronger men, Fathers Tissot and Maisonneuve, and to move him to Lac Ste. Anne where Father Lacombe was to be his superior.

Bishop Taché instructed Fathers Tissot and Maisonneuve to abandon Father Rémas's old mission site which was within present-day Lac La Biche town and start construction of a far more imposing establishment on the lake shore several miles west. From there, with the purpose of testing a transportation route down the Athabasca, he took a canoe and successfully negotiated the fearful Grand Rapids of that river. About the same time, he assigned Father Maisonneuve the task of cutting out a road whereby the Lac La Biche mission could bring in its supplies from Fort Pitt. To do that he had to find and clear a route south from the mission to the vicinity of modern St. Paul to intersect the pack trail from Fort Pitt to Fort Edmonton.

Father Rémas's removal from Lac La Biche rankled. Evidently in spite of his courage and sacrifice, he had failed. As a devoted Oblate his duty bound him to obey his superiors and being a pious and a good man he tried not to let Bishop Taché see how hurt he was and made his way to Lac Ste. Anne about the time Father Lacombe returned from his trip to the Peace River country.

At that mission he found himself in an anomalous position. On the one hand he was to obey his immediate superior Father Lacombe. On the other, he was to become Lacombe's novice master for the period during which he entered upon his year of seclusion and prayer leading to his elevation to the high calling of an Oblate. For both priests, the scholarly man from France and the devout man from Quebec, minor difficulties lay ahead.

Father Lacombe, of course, was delighted that the late Bishop Provencher's promise was finally to be fulfilled. Three years had gone by since that promise had been made; three years during which he had carried on faithfully but had always felt that he needed the support which an introduction to the devotion and discipline of the Oblate order would give him. Originally he had dreamed that he would receive one year's instruction in a cloistered atmosphere similar to that in Bishop Bourget's Montreal palace, where by prayer and meditation he could come to discern the mystic heights of his objective. Under the circumstances at Lac Ste. Anne that was not possible; instead, Rome made valid, by special permission, a "flying noviciate." During it he was to take instruction from Father Rémas, O.M.I., but was occasionally to divert his attention by visits to serve the Indians. Had he been a solitary type of man needing seclusion, he would have felt deprived by the lack of formality in his training. As it was, both he and Father Rémas, a devout scholar and a devoted savant, prayed and studied together. If Father Lacombe ever regretted his skimpy noviciate, he never let on, but there were times when Father Rémas wondered how much his neophyte had absorbed.

From time to time Father Lacombe interrupted his training sessions by trips of varying duration to Indian camps. One of the longest of these took place in the fall of 1856 when he made his way to visit the Iroquois who called the Jasper valley their home. At that time Jasper House had reached a low ebb. The brigades bound from Edmonton to Oregon, which for so many decades had crossed the mountains by way of Jasper, had ceased doing so. The Hudson's Bay Company, reducing Jasper House to a minor outpost, had left one man in charge and his main task was to keep an eye on some 350 half wild horses which the company owned and to transfer some of these to Fort Edmonton. Indeed, in October 1855 three men from Jasper reached the fort, driving fifty horses before them along what some day soon would become a pack trail from the mountains to Lac Ste. Anne.

When, therefore, about a year later Father Lacombe decided to go to see the Iroquois and Chippewas (Nipissings) he followed this very primitive route. For some reason Alexis did not go along so that the priest had engaged Michel Nipissing as guide and packer. Riding their two ponies and hazing along two pack horses carrying their supplies and Father Lacombe's portable chapel they made slow progress through the fallen timber and muskegs west of Lac Ste. Anne. As they neared the Pembina River a fierce forest fire swept towards them. Michel, the experienced frontiersman, felt that they were doomed but Father Lacombe's energetic action, far outweighing his experience, saved them by hurrying the party off to the right down the slope to the river.

Even there the fire pursued them, but by keeping the horses immersed in the water and wading in beside them while the flames and smoke rushed past, they escaped with little more damage than a few singed hairs. They were delayed there two days before they dared proceed through the miles of burning stumps and glowing embers west of the river. A few days after they left that stream Father Lacombe stopped by another.

"Overcome by fatigue and fever brought on by the heat and mosquito bites I fell sick while camping on the banks of a river. I was sure I could go no further. My companion, worried about my condition, said: 'Father, I am afraid that you will die here. Then what will become of me? Everyone will say that I mistreated you, perhaps even murdered you. Give me a paper so that I can prove that I was good to you.'"

But the weary father was a Lacombe from St. Sulpice and as he was to find on several subsequent occasions, it took a lot to kill a Lacombe. Perhaps it was only natural under the isolated and sometimes almost hopeless conditions in which he was often to find himself that many a time he concluded that he could never recover from his current malady. The fact of death he often faced, but the fear of it never. He always felt a twinge of disappointment that he was not to be left to carry on his work, but as a dutiful servant, he gladly left the outcome in higher hands.

At the end of the eighth day he camped at Jasper House, which he said was at the foot of Mount Millet. As he and Michel set out on their way back to Lac Ste. Anne, the natives of the magnificent valley, sorry to see him go, rode out a long distance and finally by firing off their guns gave him a parting salute.

In the little chapel at Lac Ste. Anne on September 28, 1856, shortly after his return from Jasper, Father Lacombe pronounced his vows of poverty, chastity and obedience into the hands of the superior general, represented by Father Rémas. At last he was a member of the Congregation of the Oblates of Mary Immaculate. His dream was fulfilled. As a much older man thinking back to those days spent with Father Rémas, he was to write: "Père Rémas, a man who was truly a man of God . . . a wise and prudent man. . . . During those twelve months there were occasional clashes which were inevitable due to Father Rémas's position and mine."

While Father Lacombe's noviciate was under way, buffalo continued to blacken the hillsides in the parklands south of Fort Edmonton and Indians continued to hunt them and to skirmish with one another. Frequently the Plains Crees, led by men like Maskepatoon, Laputange (Lapotac) and Sweet Grass came in to trade at the fort. Rarely, but always with aloofness and hauteur, some Blackfoot came in. Slowly, and mainly at Lac Ste. Anne, the number of Métis in the area kept increasing and from time to time they set out to the plains to hunt buffalo. Priests and preachers, Fathers Rémas and Lacombe, and the Reverend Mr. Woolsey and his associate, the Reverend Mr. Steinhauer, kept coming in to the fort and then going away again to meet with various bands of Indians.

More and more the Hudson's Bay Company factors worried about free traders. As early as April 1856 a man by the name of Hamlin was reported trading in opposition to the company at Lac La Biche. Then in the same month the fort journal recorded a startling development. "We beheld with vexation five of the Lake St. Anns Freemen with 21 horses crossing the river below the Fort on their way to Red River carrying away with them 500 martens together with other valuable furs to be sold there."

This move by the Métis was the thin edge of the wedge which before long would make life as difficult for the company at Fort Edmonton as it had already become at the Red River Settlement. Though the company could not forestall it, this was in some measure the result of its policy of assisting missionaries who were endeavouring to gather colonies of Métis around them.

Towards the end of October the Lac Ste. Anne Métis were reported as coming home from the Red River Settlement with carts laden with supplies. They had been six months on the return trip.

On January 7, 1857, the journal contained the information that "Old Lacombe dies — He was upward of eighty years of age." Was this man some relation of Father Lacombe? The author can find nothing amongst Father Lacombe's papers which indicate any concern for this particular old voyageur. Other entries in the fort journal going back several years mention a Lacombe who seems to have been this same reliable freeman. Whether or not he was closely related to the St. Sulpice Lacombes, at least one of that line had made his way to the West. Writing in 1890, Father Lacombe said:

> "Like several of his contemporaries he had married a Cree Indian squaw, in the manner of the country. They had a few children. Upon my arrival in this country, one of his sons, I never heard of others, an old man, had just died in the midst of the Indians of the prairies. He left a numerous family of boys and girls of whom only one remains today, a man of fifty some years, named Corps-Rouge, Omikkoiyawe, (Red Skin) who lives among the Blood Indians. So, you will no longer be surprised that I love the Indians and am interested in their lot."

During the February following Lacombe's death several small bands of Blackfoot, risking their lives by passing through predominately Cree country, came to the fort. Undoubtedly they brought meat to trade and by the middle of the month the journal indicates that 760 buffalo tongues had been salted down. Towards the end of the month Father Lacombe started for the plains with his men "to trade provisions." Evidently a missionary was permitted to barter for meat if not for furs. His trade goods, of course, he would have purchased from the company.

In the middle of March a messenger came in from the Blackfoot to announce that a large party was on its way to the fort. He came partly to find out if many Crees were about and partly to tip off the traders that the Blackfoot expected to be received with proper ceremony. Three days later a large band arrived with their furs and meat. Some seven hundred strong, they crossed the river and camped on the hill behind the fort. For a few days their great smoke-stained tepees glowed in the sun. While the men were trading and carousing, the busy life of the camp went on. Horses were picketed all about or grazed freely farther back, dogs and children ran barking and shouting hither and yon, while the women folk, gathered into groups about the campfires, sewed and cooked.

Then one morning the lodges were pulled down and, led by the warriors, the band filed down the steep path to the river. Lusty, strong-featured, bronzed men and women with lithe bodies and faces streaked with vermilion, they formed a picturesque procession. The leaders wore eagle feathers in their hair, the men were for the most part naked but for a buffalo robe caught around them, while the women wore decorated tunics of antelope skin or blue cloth and richly beaded gaiters. Men and women alike sat their sure-footed broncos with the ease of plainsmen while they dragged their primitive chattels on travois behind their ponies.

Some weeks later another messenger came announcing the imminent arrival of a large band of Crees, which included Maskepatoon, Laputange and Sweet Grass, all very important chiefs. The main band reached the fort on May 1, and since these chiefs were so outstanding, they were received with a salute from two cannons. As a preliminary to serious trading, they were given some rum and, having had their thirst whetted, they traded five horses for more rum and were reported as camped on the flats below the fort drinking all night. A day or so later, when the throbbing in their heads had eased somewhat, the trading began.

Unfortunately, while the Hudson's Bay Company journals mention various chiefs in a general way, they do not provide much information about them. What little we have comes from the writing of the missionaries who could not help extolling the virtues of those Indian leaders who, nominally at least, adopted their particular faith. Some chiefs scoffed at their teachings and were recorded as being inspired by the devil; others listened to them and were baptized and were listed in the records as on the side of the angels. The Indians, neither angels nor devils but men worried by a changing environment, were superstitious like any other human beings and were ready to nibble at any new sorcery that came their way.

Amongst these chiefs, Maskepatoon, the Plains Cree, gave a lot of thought to the new philosophy espoused by the missionaries. When Father Lacombe went to Lac Ste. Anne this leader was a man of about forty years of age whose ability had raised him to the status of a chief. As such he was a thinking man, ready to weigh the missionaries' arguments. Unfortunately their inter-faith bickering discouraged him. As he explained to Paul Kane in 1848,

> "Mr. Rundell [Rundle] has told him that what he preached was the only true road to heaven, and Mr. Hunter [Anglican] told him the same thing, and so did Mr. Thebo, [Thibault], and as they all three said that the other two were wrong, and as he did not know which was right, he thought they ought to call a council among themselves, and then he would go with them all three; but that until they agreed he would wait."

As a thoughtful leader and in spite of occasional drinking bouts at Fort Edmonton and Fort Pitt, he made several attempts to conclude a lasting peace between Cree and Blackfoot. About 1850, under dramatic circumstances, he succeeded in bringing about a temporary peace which ever since has been commemorated in the name of the Peace Hills near modern Wetaskiwin.

In May 1857, while Maskepatoon's party lingered at Fort

Edmonton, Father Lacombe came in from Lac Ste. Anne to make final plans for a long anticipated trip back to St. Boniface. While as far as Fort Carlton he was to travel down the Saskatchewan River with the annual brigade taking the furs to Norway House, he also superintended the despatch of a number of Métis who with their carts set out on his behalf for the Red River Settlement. On May 13 as he boarded one of the company's thirteen boats he was aware that a further eleven also loaded with the year's returns were to leave two days later.

This trip down the river during the high water of the middle of May was a striking contrast to his voyage upstream during September five years earlier when the water had been low and the trackers had struggled wearily to lug their boats along. Then, as an uninformed newcomer feeling his uncertain way into the West, everything had been new and strange. Now, as an experienced missionary of five years' standing, he had gained the respect of natives, bourgeois and crew. Now he understood the ways of the West, the methods of trade as well as the economics of the area and of the company's well-organized transport system.

To Father Lacombe, a young man of thirty looking forward keenly to his welcome at faraway St. Boniface, the trip as far as Fort Carlton was sheer pleasure. Rowing all day, the crews sped the craft along between the high sloping forested banks and when night came they tied several boats together and, except for a man or two left on the watch, all stretched out to sleep away many more miles. The long hours of each day glided away as the landmarks were ticked off — the Redwater River, the mouth of Saddlelake Creek and the Snipe and Snake hills. On they went noting the Moose Hill to the north, the mouth of the Vermilion River coming in from the south, and then, as they entered the parklands, watching the more open hillsides which indicated that they were close to Fort Pitt.

When the priest had left Fort Edmonton the leaves had not appeared. Each day's progress brought a little more greenery to the wide valley walls until at Fort Carlton far out in the prairies, the scent of opening buds, the sight of dangling red balm catkins and the sheer delight of shining new poplar leaves set his heart tingling.

After a delay of a day or so at Fort Pitt, the brigade, augmented by another two boats, swept on. Here and there they saw small herds of buffalo crossing the river and, scattered along the banks, lay a few carcasses of these animals which having been weakened by the hard winter had drowned on their way across the wide stream. At nearly every one of these, one or more wolves which had been feasting drew back if the boats passed too near them. Occasionally a large or small party of Blackfoot hailed them and the boats stopped within gunshot while the bourgeois went ashore to smoke with them. One day a violent wind made it unsafe to continue and the men, relieved of the toil of rowing, relaxed. What with minor delays of this sort, the brigade was over a week in reaching Fort Carlton.

There Father Lacombe left the brigade. With a few mounted companions he set out along the Winnipeg trail for the five-hundred-mile trip over the hills and valleys of the prairies which, through sunshine and bird song or days of continual rain, took nearly a month to complete. On his arrival, Bishop Taché and his confreres were overjoyed to see him. At St. Boniface, on what in effect was a well-earned holiday, he had little to do but sit and talk or stroll around the growing settlement. There, for over a month, he learned of the progress made by his fellow Oblates at their even more lonely missions and also had an opportunity to talk to the Sisters of Charity and to hint that they should extend their endeavours to include his Lac Ste. Anne mission. Some weeks after his arrival the Métis he had despatched from Edmonton arrived with their carts.

CHAPTER SEVEN

Steady Progress
1857–60

Father Lacombe had to schedule his horseback departure for Fort Carlton so that he would arrive there about the first of September in time to catch the westbound boat brigade. His cart-bound Métis had to leave much sooner than he. While he purchased supplies for his mission, they relaxed in the settlement for about a week before setting out again. Then about the first of August, climbing into the saddle, the priest began his return trip. Undoubtedly on his way west he would have met an occasional traveller but one whom he did not meet, Captain John Palliser, was to note one indication of the father's passage over the prairies.

For two or three weeks after Father Lacombe had passed through Fort Carlton, various Indian bands coming in had reported a great fire as having licked up the ripe prairie grasses and swept south and east over the country along the trail through the Touchwood Hills. A week or so later Captain Palliser set out along the trail to Fort Garry and when he reached the vicinity of the Quill Lakes came upon a campsite of the guilty party and noted how the fire had spread from it. As Palliser wrote, "It was kindled from the camp-fire of Mons. La Combe, the Roman Catholic missionary to the Crees, on his way to Edmonton; this is learned from a notice planted there, in the shape of a post, on which was carved his initials and the date of the encampment in September."

At Fort Carlton Father Lacombe embarked with the company's brigade, which after its usual upstream struggle reached

Fort Edmonton on October 4, 1857. On his round trip to get groceries — some salt, sugar and a box of tea — he had been 145 days. His Métis and their carts took even longer. Knowing that their beasts would be wearied by such a long trip, Father Lacombe hurried out to Lac Ste. Anne, returned with fresh horses and set off east along the trail to meet his tripmen.

Once he returned to Fort Edmonton again he had time to absorb all the news from the prairies and parklands. The Indians had been in a bad mood. On June 26, 1857, according to the Fort Edmonton journal, "A Cercie [Sarcee] arrived and tells us that the pease [sic] is broken, that several Cercies have been killed by the Crees." All summer, various reports of minor skirmishes came in and about the middle of September six Blackfoot arrived at the fort saying that down the river near Fort Pitt their tribe had killed thirty Crees. Skirmishes of one sort or another were the order of the day and not even the happy-go-lucky Métis of Lac Ste. Anne dared penetrate the prairies except in large, well-armed bands. Some of the leading men amongst these Métis were Abraham Salois, Louis Paul, Alexis Nault, George Ward, one of the Hamlins, a Loyer, Joe Gray and Gabriel Dumont, the elder. Like their relatives in the Red River Settlement, most of them scratched at little cultivated patches which due to neglect produced very little.

The mission garden was quite a different matter. In it the priests worked hard and tended very productive plots. When about the time of Father Lacombe's arrival cows were added to the little mission farm, the priests lived in relative comfort compared to some of the missionaries in the Athabasca-Mackenzie watershed.

Even at that, the garden and the cows could only supplement their main fare, which was fish from the lake; freshly caught in summer or dried or frozen in the winter. For weeks on end the missionaries might breakfast, dine and sup exclusively on fish washed down by tea, which they could sweeten during the months that their sugar lasted. Bread in Father Lacombe's early days was something to dream about and he and all missionaries jocularly remarked that they were beyond the longitude of flour. At times, for wearisome weeks, they might switch from fish to rabbits and, once the waterfowl returned in the spring, might vary these by a period of gulping down eggs in all stages of in-

cubation or of switching to moulting ducks. Whenever Lacombe's Métis killed a moose or two, he shared in their good
fortune, while all looked forward to the day when the hunters
would come back from their foray south of Fort Edmonton with
buffalo tongues, marrow bones and back fats. Then, indeed, all
would feast as ribs roasted by the fire. Yet even then as Father
Lacombe went from fire to fire accepting the hospitality of his
flock, he could not repress visions of his mother's kitchen in St.
Sulpice with its bread and butter, its potatoes and even pud-
dings.

Nevertheless, in Father Lacombe's own words, "it was not so
much the privation, fatigue and work that were difficult in these
missions, but above all, the isolation to which the missionary is
abandoned, especially in their first years of apostolate." Some
men could stand the isolation and the many hardships of a frontier mission and fortunately Father Lacombe and most of his
associates were men of that calibre. Father Frain, however, a
relative newcomer, soon broke down under the strain. It was
because of his illness that Father Lacombe had his first meeting
with Dr. James Hector of the Palliser expedition.

The doctor, who by dog team had taken a mere thirteen days'
travelling to cover the 393 miles from Fort Carlton, entered Fort
Edmonton on December 30, 1857. When in the course of two or
three days the news of his arrival and of the fact that he was a
physician reached Father Lacombe, he decided to take Father
Frain "who was ill, from Lac Sainte Anne to Edmonton, that he
might see that Doctor. In those days I was strong, vigourous [sic]
and a good runner. I ran this distance of fifty miles in 12 hours
with our patient well covered in our sleigh drawn by our dogs.
Because of his poor health Father was soon obliged to leave us
and return to the old country."

In this remote land where educated men were such a rarity
Dr. Hector and Father Lacombe rejoiced in each other's company. But each was a busy man and in a day or so the priest returned to Lac Ste. Anne, while the physician and geologist prepared to set out for Rocky Mountain House.

About three weeks later Father Lacombe passed through Fort
Edmonton again as, hoping to fall in with some Blackfoot, he
accompanied some of the Métis on their trip south in search of
buffalo. On February 8, as he hurried to return to his mission

from his seventeen-day trip, he found that Hector had also come back from his journey. The doctor remained at the fort long enough to note the return of some of the Lac Ste. Anne Métis.

"The fort assumed a lively appearance this afternoon from the arrival of the hunters from the plain with 40 horse sleighs loaded with buffalo meat. There were 18 men, and the horses were all half-broken animals that had been brought from the mountains at Jaspar [sic] House the previous summer."

On February 12, to ask Father Lacombe's advice about recruiting Métis for his summer's trip, Dr. Hector set out for Lac Ste. Anne in a horse-drawn sleigh. After sleeping once in the open during the "coldest night I have ever camped out, the thermometer at Edmonton falling to −47°'" he was glad of Father Lacombe's warm hospitality. He wrote:

"There are two villages, each with 30 to 40 houses, but there is very little ground under cultivation. Barley, potatoes, and turnips are the crops that succeed best, and wheat has never been raised. . . . We attended the little chapel attached to the mission, which is neatly built of wood, with a spire and bell. The attendance was small, and, the thermometer being at −20°, it was bitterly cold work, so that the priests had to officiate in their great coats and mittens."

When Captain Palliser spent Christmas 1858 at Fort Edmonton he also came to know Father Lacombe and spoke highly of him.

"While we were at Edmonton we were frequently visited by the French priests of the Catholic mission at Lake St. Ann's. Mons. La Combe, the head of the order, was a most excellent benevolent gentleman, possessing many estimable qualities most valuable in a missionary. He spoke Cree well, and had obtained a good deal of influence, not so much, however, among the Indians as among the half-breeds. . . . Mr. Rundle, who must have been a very able and influential man, is spoken of among them with reverence and enthusiasm to this day. Mr. Woolsey also, the present missionary, is a most excellent benevolent person. . . . At Christmas . . . the catholic missionaries from Lake St. Ann's performed mass, and Mr. Woolsey conducted the Church of England service in the principal room of the fort."

In May 1859, in a letter Palliser wrote Governor Simpson, he was not so certain that the missionaries, no matter of what denomination, were really doing the Métis any good.

"Poor Christie is terribly annoyed with these Lake St. Annes rascals, they really are a rotten set. I fear the Popish Priests you are nursing so carefully in this country will be a thorn in your side by and bye. The Stoneys are wretchedly off, the priests are playing the deuce with them they seem to do nothing but pray, sing hymns and starve! The 'Cardinal' came down on them the other day, and divorced about 50 of their wives. All the priests of all denominations dine with us. It is great fun to see the black looks of the hostile divines, I understand that sometimes hostilities have proceeded further than mere looks. . . ."

Aside from the pleasure he derived from meeting such of its members as Palliser, Hector and Monsieur Bourgeau, the botanist, Father Lacombe was glad to see that the expedition had been sent out. At last someone had been delegated to study the prairies with an eye to seeing what resources, other than fur, lay in them. Amongst other things, Palliser and his associates had come to peer into the possibility that the prairies might be fit to farm.

Father Lacombe had no doubt that when their final report was released it would confirm what he and various Protestant missionaries already knew. On his wanderings over a period of ten years and embracing the vast region from St. Boniface west to Jasper, he had wondered how long it would be before this immense arable area of some half a million square miles would become settled. Whether his many real friends amongst the Hudson's Bay Company's traders liked the idea or not, he knew as few other men did that some day it would become the home of millions of immigrants.

Indeed, he and his fellow Oblates had come out as the forerunners of that wave of immigration. But while the profit-minded Hudson's Bay Company men came — and indeed, the

grasping immigrants, who were bound to follow the missionaries, would come — with mercenary motives, he and his associates were pioneering in the land without any motive of personal
or collective gain. They had come to serve their God and their
church, to increase its converts amongst the Indians and Métis
and thus save the natives' souls.

And yet active missionaries such as Father Lacombe often
turned another problem over in their minds. Through their
ministrations the souls of the flock could be saved, but what of
their material well-being? His and his associates' duty lay in
fighting the unequal and often discouraging battle which led to
hundreds of nominal converts — a desirable end in itself — but
left his catechumens still faced with an uncertain temporal future. To prepare them for that future, each missionary did his
utmost, but there was so little time to do that, so little time —
maybe thirty years — in which to change their centuries-old life
style. Invariably the missionaries ran aground upon the rock of
the natives' unwillingness or inability to face the future and
prepare for it.

If the missionaries should fall short of accomplishing that
goal, however, Father Lacombe and his fellows had the satisfaction of knowing that in the northwest, by their hardship and
toil, they were laying a firm and lasting foundation for their
church. When settlers came flocking in they would find firmly
rooted Catholic missions ready to serve them. And it was to be
hoped that many of those who came would be Catholic, and
French to boot. Meanwhile, he watched the members of the
Palliser expedition travel back and forth across the prairies until
they gradually came to see the resources of the West in much
the same light as he did.

When their report came out it proved to be a mine of information and is still particularly useful to the modern student who
tries to piece together the picture of conditions on the prairies
in those days. Several of the journals referred to the constant
friction between the Crees and the Blackfoot. In June 1858, for
instance, John Sullivan, one of the senior members of the expedition who appears to have fallen under the influence of a Blackfoot public relations man, made the following comment:

"The [Cree] Indian informed us that the peace between the

Blackfoot and his own nation had been violated, and that a very large war-party of the former was on the road to the Cree country. The cause of rupture as usual, was horse-stealing. The Crees are invariably the first offenders, and, comparatively speaking, the Blackfeet exercise great forbearance towards them in return."

This sort of warfare, of course, made it dangerous for the Métis of Fort Edmonton and Lac Ste. Anne to bring in a reliable supply of meat and there were times when the fort staff was on the verge of starvation.

Up till that time the reason for the hunger was not lack of buffalo. Nevertheless, it was already evident that their numbers were decreasing and some of the more responsible Indian chiefs were becoming worried about their future. As Lieutenant Blakiston, another of the expedition members, wrote:

"They are aware that the buffalo are rapidly decreasing, and foresee that their descendants will have to take to some other way of living than the lazy yet not luxurious mode followed at present . . . year by year they see the animals decrease, and although they consider that they will last their time, and that by them they will be able to keep themselves in tobacco, ammunition, and other requisites, and have an occasional drinking bout, yet they know too well, as one man expressed himself to me, 'If this continues our children cannot live.' "

On several occasions Palliser spoke highly of some of the Indians, but he had reservations about the Métis. In February 1859, for instance, he wrote:

"There are several kinds of employees of the Hudson's Bay Company, now diminishing very much throughout these portions of their district, viz., — the old Canadian voyageur, a hardy, jovial, respectful, and well-conducted man; also the old hands which used to be engaged from the Orkney Islands and other parts of Scotland; their places are now fast supplied by lazy French half-breeds from Lake St. Ann's, who, if they are desired to work or ordered to do anything they dislike, may go away as soon as they have received their advances, and join the Indians out on the prairies."

Nevertheless, he was struck by one of their attributes, which endeared them to Father Lacombe, their piety, and speaking of Sunday observance on the plains, he wrote:

"All my Red River men belonged to the Church of England, consequently I read prayers for them; but, also, the St. Ann's men, half-breeds, who, although of Catholic persuasion, asked and obtained leave from me to attend Divine worship, and I conducted the lessons and half the prayers in Cree through the medium of an interpreter. I mention this circumstance to show the respectful tendency and absence of bigotry of these men, in their appreciation of Divine service."

Their piety was a marked contrast to that of another class of men, the American gold miners, who began dribbling across Canadian prairies at this time. Because they hated all Indians, they angered the natives and made it even more difficult for the staff at Fort Edmonton to deal with them. Though many of the miners were Irish and of Father Lacombe's faith, he too wished that they had not entered the area. That is, all but one of them, who reached the fort on April 8, 1859. Strangely enough this man, C. A. Loveland, a Scandinavian and presumably a Protestant, did the father a good turn. When he arrived he was short of supplies, although he had plenty of American currency to pay for them. Chief Factor Christie, another Protestant, refused to honour his money and put him to work at wages of a shilling a day to earn the goods he needed by building a church within the palisades for Father Lacombe.

How long Loveland stayed working at the fort is not recorded but all during 1859 the journal reports the progress being made on the church. Finally on December 24 the journalist exclaims triumphantly that the chapel was completed that afternoon ready for mass that evening.

Its completion by competent carpenters marked an important milestone in the progress Father Lacombe had been making. His new chapel, St. Joachim, the first church edifice ever built solely for that purpose in Edmonton was a tribute to his endeavours and to the value the Hudson's Bay Company placed on them. It was also a tribute to his congenial personality and his diplomacy. His rival, the Reverend Mr. Woolsey, a Protestant working out of the company's fort where nearly all of the senior staff were Protestants, still had to be content with holding his services in a room in what everyone still called Rowand's Big House.

For Father Lacombe, however, his new St. Joachim church was but the high point of a year marked by various successes. His adherents amongst the freemen and Crees kept increasing in numbers and in dedication. His unceasing efforts to bring some of the Crees into his fold were showing results as whenever they were in the vicinity more and more of them took every opportunity to attend his services and to be baptized. He had even aroused a mild curiosity amongst the Blackfoot who came in to trade at the fort.

On the more secular side, his endeavours had turned the small clearing around the log shacks of the Lac Ste. Anne mission into a comfortable haven; a little garden patch on the shore of a beautiful lake, one spot of domesticity in the otherwise endless wilderness. Using his farm boy's experience and harnessing the energies of his associates Fathers Rémas and Frain, he had developed an establishment which surprised and delighted the few white men who passed that way. Lord Southesk, a travelling Briton who spent a night at the mission in August 1859, was highly complimentary.

When much to the priests' regret he left to continue his journey, they loaded him with "provisions — fish, potatoes, dried meat, etc. God bless them and prosper their mission." In his diary he referred to "Pères Lacombe and Le Frain" as "agreeable men and perfect gentlemen," and added that in his opinion Rome has an advantage in the class of men she assigns to her mission, as she always sends out "polished, highly-educated gentlemen."

Pleasing as Southesk's sojourn may have been to him, it was infinitely more so to the isolated fathers who for a few hours could discuss affairs of the outside world with a man of culture comparable to their own. Comfortable they may have seemed in their log shack surrounded by a garden and flowers and remote from the rumours of warfare that constantly buzzed about Fort Edmonton, but their comfort was but a temporary respite between journeys back and forth from Indian camp to Indian camp.

Nevertheless, Father Lacombe had already taken another

step to improve his establishment in this wilderness in which he had chosen to cast his lot. It involved bringing into play one arm of the Catholic church's unique organization which, by sending lay brothers and nuns to assist the priests, multiplied their effectiveness many times. In the existence of these orders of workers lay much of the credit for the fact that the success of the Catholic missions was much more spectacular than that of their rivals. Lay brothers provided the labour and skills to construct more elaborate missions and to provide for the people who lived in them, while the nuns came to teach, run infirmaries and orphanages. By assigning such tasks to brothers and nuns, the priests were left free to celebrate mass and catechize in the various Indian camps.

Father Lacombe's mission, therefore, took a long stride forward when on September 21, 1859, Father Rémas reached Fort Edmonton after his fifty-one-day one-way trip from St. Boniface. That day his small train of carts drew up to the fort — twelve horses, six carts, and a wild dog. And stiff and bruised from their long trek from St. Boniface, three Grey Nuns climbed down from a cart. Three days later these Sisters of Charity, Sister Emery, the superior, Sister Lamy and Sister Marie-Alphonse, reached Lac Ste. Anne and immediately started tidying up what had hitherto been an all-male establishment. Fortunately Sister Lamy, in writing to her parents, left us a description of the mission as she first saw it.

"After a hearty meal, Father Lacombe invited us to visit his house. It is rather small, at the most only twenty feet long and fifteen feet wide. It is sealed with mud and covered with bark. The house is divided into two bedrooms and a living room. The furniture consists of a chair, two stools, a table, a sofa that is used as a bed at night, a stove and a desk.

"The chapel is also very poor. There are two altars. One is dedicated to the Blessed Virgin, the sanctuary lamp being made of wood by the missionary. A wooden chandelier is trimmed with pieces of tin and coloured birds' eggs. Three prayer stools and the vestry complete the chapel. . . .

"We visited the good Indians and the Christian Métis as soon as possible. These poor people could not demonstrate enough their happiness. The richer families brought us some pounded meat, while a woman of the Cree nation offered us a dish that she said we had never before tasted. How right she was. It consisted of raspberries that the woman chewed into a paste and then dried in the sun. So as not to offend her, we accepted some. We found that it tasted something like a mixture of spices. . . ."

Adding to Father Lacombe's pleasure at seeing the Grey Nuns was the fact that Michel Normand and his wife, née Rose Plante, returned to Lac Ste. Anne at the same time. Their association with that mission began when as a childless couple which had grown up and been baptized at the Red River Settlement they had accompanied Father Thibault west. When Father Bourassa finally left Lac Ste. Anne, they had returned to their native parish. Then at Father Rémas's request they came back to the lake. As Lacombe wrote:

"How happy I was to see Michel and Rose with us again! Since that time they have not left us. Like real missionaries they became attached to and interested in all our work. Their fidelity, their honesty, their piety are recognized throughout the countryside, especially so among the missionaries, who esteem and venerate them."

With the arrival of all this help the mission progressed rapidly. Noting its increasing stability, Chief Factor William Christie decided to upgrade the company's outpost there by replacing a shack he had rented from John Cunningham, an enterprising half-breed, by a new log building twenty-five feet by thirty feet. Unfortunately this new structure was destroyed by fire a day or so after it had been completed, so that the company had to build another. Nevertheless, this new post at the lake was a sign that lay civilization was sending out tentacles to embrace it.

In another guise these tentacles of the contact between white men and Indians required some changes at Fort Edmonton. The Indians camped on the flats near the fort played havoc with the large potato patch as soon as the tubers developed. While it was almost impossible to take measures to prevent the loss of potatoes, when it came to losing rum, steps to stop that loss were soon taken. The men were directed to make shutters for the rum shed "as parchment windows wont do now-a days the Indians are becoming too great rogues & thieves."

Out at Lac Ste. Anne Father Lacombé, who was trying to break the Métis into a semblance of sedentary agricultural people had begun to wonder if perhaps he could start another mission in a location having better soil on which his Métis might find their efforts more rewarding. Such a location, of course, should be at or near the Saskatchewan River and thus be more accessible to the Blackfoot with whom his contacts so far had been only sporadic. Lac Ste. Anne had been located as a mission mainly for Crees and so as to be out of reach of the Blackfoot. Now it appeared desirable to start another establishment aimed more directly at them.

Moreover, his itchy foot had begun reasserting itself. Mainly through his efforts over the last eight years, Lac Ste. Anne had been put on its feet. From here on all it needed was intermittent attention to see that it followed in the path already blazed for it. Although devoted to it, the mission was a fait accompli and he began looking for a new venture against which he could pit his exuberant energies. This new goal glimmering in his mind must have been what caused the writer of the Fort Edmonton journal to record: "August 20, 1860 — Mr. Lacombe and his man started down the river, to see a place and get some hay cut if convenient to commence another station to settle."

Four days later he was back, stating that he had found such a spot and had cut some hay "at a place he intends to make a farm." Since he was away such a short time it must have been somewhere downstream, possibly near the future Fort Saskatchewan. There is no further record of any development there, so his enthusiasm for this site must have evaporated quickly.

News of renewed Indian warfare may have occupied his attention to the detriment of his new location. Near at hand, towards the end of September, some Sarcees came in to trade and on the way one of them was killed by Fort Pitt Crees "across the river." Three weeks later news from Fort Pitt indicated that in a recent battle much like one which had taken place three years earlier, the Blackfoot had killed twenty Crees and, of course, had lost some of their own men.

That episode in which the aroused Blackfoot had again put on a show of strength succeeded in cooling some of their enemies' ardour. Less than a week later the Crees were reported as fleeing to Lac La Biche where Fathers Tissot and Maisonneuve could console them and to Whitefish Lake where the Reverend Steinhauer, the Methodist who in 1857 had abandoned his mission on Lac La Biche, had recently started another.

In the midst of his worries about this renewed warfare, Father Lacombe received word that his revered Bishop Taché intended to come across from Lac La Biche and would probably reach Lac Ste. Anne at Christmas time. On December 18, 1860, all anticipation and with a train of dogs and a horse cariole in which he proposed to take the bishop to Lac Ste. Anne, he arrived at Fort Edmonton. Next day his eagerness to see his friend prompted him to head out east along the trail to meet him. That night the bishop stayed in the fort, examined the new church and had a pleasant visit with Lacombe's friends the traders.

The following morning he left for Lac Ste. Anne where some days of the utmost exhilaration passed in a flurry of Gallic excitement. For not only was this brilliant man cordial and friendly but he understood the hearts of all present. The days he spent there were taken up not only with the usual inspection of a bishop but were filled with the glow of a helpful superior greatly pleased with the progress made by this handful of devoted men and women. All present, bishop, priests, nuns and lay workers, were knit together by their common dedication and their common language, but above all by their being a small band united in establishing a bridgehead of civilization in the midst of almost unlimited barbarism.

Much of Bishop Taché's discussions with Fathers Rémas and Lacombe centred around the need and the methods to be taken to expand the church's service to the Indians, particularly to the Blackfoot. In these discussions Father Lacombe played a leading part and quickly demonstrated that his plans even outdistanced his superior's. And with an executive's gratitude to a thinking junior who has ideas and can carry them out, he was more than willing to fall in line with those of the eager young priest. He was more than willing, also, to acknowledge that in Father Lacombe he had a valuable subordinate — one who looked ahead, one who could plan and one who could pull the proper strings to bring his plans to fruition.

In Father Lacombe he had not only a devout and nearly indefatigable priest but a tactful politician of no mean order who knew which side his bread was buttered on. All of the handful of priests in his diocese were dedicated men, but like other mortals, varied greatly in their makeup. Some worked stolidly, some complained, some in an unbending rigidity fought with the Hudson's Bay Company men, but in Lacombe he had a man of diplomacy who, without yielding on any essential point, nevertheless could turn almost any situation to the church's advantage. At Fort Edmonton, for instance, where the Hudson's Bay Company's senior staff were nearly all Protestant and were one and all disturbed by the presence of missionaries of any faith, Lacombe, a Catholic priest, was perhaps the only man of the cloth invariably received with smiles. There, in an anti-Catholic and anti-missionary milieu, stood the only nicely built church in the land — a Roman Catholic one. Such a diplomat as the thirty-three-year-old Father Lacombe was indeed a man to value and to encourage.

It was obvious that part of that encouragement should lie in allowing him to carry out his idea of starting a new mission near Fort Edmonton. For he was not only enthusiastic about this new venture but he had the ability to bend others to the task of bringing it into being. So on his way back from Lac Ste. Anne to Fort Edmonton in January 1861 Bishop Taché allowed Father Lacombe to guide his hand in selecting a site for it. As Father Lacombe wrote almost forty years later:

"In my travels from Edmonton to Saint Ann, then I'd stop on a hillside to have my dogs rest, I'd gaze towards a certain hill with a lake in the distance, and just opposite a forest. As I'd gaze, I'd murmur to myself: 'What a lovely place for a mission.' So, it was to this site that I led Mgr. Taché. As we stood admiring the view from all sides, all enjoying a bit of pemmican, His Excellency said: 'Father Lacombe, you were right, this is a magnificent site! I choose it for our new mission, and desire that it be named Saint Albert, in honour of your beloved patron.' I submitted to such an agreeable order, with gratitude. His Excellency stood his walking stick in the snow and said: 'The chapel will be here.' There where he stood his pastoral stick in the snow . . . today stands the altar of Saint Albert Cathedral. . . ."

CHAPTER EIGHT

St. Albert Mission
1861-65

The decision to build a new mission was based on varying motives. One of them perhaps barely perceptible at the time lay in Father Lacombe's makeup. He had to be up and doing. Largely due to his efforts the Lac Ste. Anne mission had settled down to an orderly, almost humdrum existence. Its challenge had been overcome and its purpose was being accomplished. Now he needed another challenge.

Awaiting the return of spring, Father Lacombe turned his attention to the Blackfoot. Father Caer had come to replace Father Frain and during the early winter he was assigned to take care of St. Joachim at Fort Edmonton. Father Rémas, reliable as ever, carried on the work at Lac Ste. Anne. Then on January 22, 1861, Father Lacombe set out for Rocky Mountain House to establish more formal relations with the Blackfoot.

Sometime previously, apparently while Bishop Taché was still at Lac Ste. Anne, one of the Blackfoot chiefs arrived to ask that a priest be sent to visit his people. It is hard to believe that his appearance at the mission just when the bishop was there was altogether a coincidence. Moreover, Father Lacombe's diplomatic hand in bringing about this well-timed request appears to be evident in the suggestion that the priest come carrying a white flag with a red cross on it. He promised that during his visit his people would see that its bearer was protected and that they would refrain from warring on the Crees.

To fulfil his promise Father Lacombe set out for Rocky Mountain House where he hoped to hold services for some or

all of the wandering Blackfoot oriented tribes, the Bloods, Piegans and Blackfoot and their allies the Sarcees. His mission
seems to have met with encouragement, and after an absence of
about three weeks he and Alexis, his combined dog driver, guide,
interpreter and confidant, returned to Fort Edmonton by way of
Buck Lake and Lac Ste. Anne. Unfortunately since the recent
deaths of three of the leading Blackfoot chiefs, relations between the traders and that tribe had been deteriorating. The
Hudson's Bay Company was beginning to notice the effect of
the new leaders and Chief Factor Christie at Fort Edmonton
reported that the Blackfoot were becoming increasingly dangerous, destroying the small crops around the post, trying to
pick quarrels, thirsting to rid themselves of all white men and
eager to burn the fort.

The Crees, although most hostile to the Blackfoot, were much
less difficult to live with. Some of them indeed were highly regarded. Such a chief was Laputange or Lapotac whose sudden
death by bleeding at the mouth the Fort Edmonton journal
lamented by referring to the "melancholy news of the death of
our greatest and best chief . . . [who] never tasted a drop of
liquor, his loss to Edmonton House is irre-parable. . . ." By his
death his family was left to the charity of the Hudson's Bay
Company and of them the journalist opined that they "deserve
to be taken care of."

A couple of weeks after his death and shortly after Father
Lacombe returned from Rocky Mountain House, five bands of
Crees, mainly from the Fort Pitt area, 150 men besides their
women and children, came riding up to the fort. Although each
chief was given a keg of rum, the group camped on the flats
below and outside the fences of the fields conducted themselves
well. Only one incident marred the occasion when, because a
woman refused to give her brother-in-law a rope which he
wanted to trade for rum, he shot and killed himself.

About the same time another band of Crees, this time from
Beaverhill Lake, came in with nine horses pulling sleds loaded
with 4,370 pounds of fresh meat and news that there was lots
more where that came from. The company immediately sent
ten men with ten trains of dogs to bring in the rest.

Later in March, Blackfoot belligerence became noticeable
again when according to the journalist they came in armed and

would only trade for liquor. "The Blackfeet have been unbearable for the last 3 years or more. . . ." The present outburst was "all . . . owing to the Blackfoot [Sarcee] Chief that was killed here last fall by the Crees. . . ."In a reflective mood the journalist wrote that "this liquor business is a terrible thing and must be stopped for there is no dealing with the Indians when drunk, it is only give, give, give, for nothing. . . ."

While all this was going on, Father Lacombe and his associates, Fathers Rémas and Caer, had been kept busy with services at Lac Ste. Anne and St. Joachim "not counting our numberless visits to other groups, living on fish near the lakes, or on the hunt in the forests."

But at last spring came, the spring to which for so many years the father, as a missionary wandering here and there over Alberta's magnificent countryside, always looked forward.

> "The snow, eternal snow, which enveloped us during long months, gave sign of leaving us. Once more we were going to see good old mother earth as the Indians say. We made preparations for a new expedition to Jasper. Father Rémas was to enjoy this. Father Caer was to go to the prairies as chaplain to the buffalo hunters. For four long months he was to follow the caravan. During this time he would pitch his chapel-tent anew each night in the vast desert, on the shores of some small lake, or on the banks of a small stream, where brackish waters flow. I was to remain in charge of Lac Sainte Anne all in starting the foundation of Saint Albert."

So, during the first week of April 1861, "accompanied by Michel Normand, his wife, Rose Plante, and a young orphan named Nancy, I went to the large lake I was to name Saint Albert. We camped at night and then reached the hill. We had with us four oxen, some horses, a plow and the tools we needed. A beautiful large shelter made of hides served us as a residence."

On Monday, leaving Rose Normand busily cooking in her tent on the site of the church, Father Lacombe led her husband Michel and two Métis across the river to the south slope of the valley. There,

> "Once in the midst of these deep-rooted spruce giants, I spoke to my companions: 'My children, we are about to fell these

beautiful trees which will serve as lumber to build the Fathers' residence and the House of God. Let us kneel and say a prayer and ask the Master to help us, and bless us.' Leaning on our axes, we made the sign of the cross, and recited the Our Father and the Hail Mary. 'Yes, that God's holy will be done. . . .' In no time, three beautiful trees fell to the ground with a crash. During ten days my men continued preparing the necessary wood for our buildings. Our beasts of burden hauled this material to the chosen site."

It is interesting to note that though the father also had an axe, only three trees fell during the first round. A pit was soon rigged up at which the men whipsawed the boards needed for the structure. Before many days this building, twenty-five feet by thirty feet, stood over the spot where the bishop had stuck his cane into the snowdrift. The mission of St. Albert had been started.

But gardens and fields were as important as cabins and churches, so the priest, seeing some Métis whose curiosity had impelled them to watch the unusual activity on the hilltop, set them to work ploughing. By using two oxen to pull the plough during a day shift and two more to continue the work during the evening, it "was possible for us to seed a large field in a few days. At the same time the women who were as courageous as we, were busy preparing their garden plots in which they sowed cabbage, carrots, turnip, onions, etc."

Some twenty Métis families mainly from Lac Ste. Anne soon settled along the Sturgeon River and by the shores of Big Lake. To each Father Lacombe assigned the usual Quebec type of river lot about two miles long but having a narrow frontage on the stream. He watched as at his urging they built neat shacks with wooden floors and parchment windows. For the happy priest had a finger in every activity, working now in the saw-pit, now on the church and then in the gardens, urging everyone on by precept or performance. His gregariousness and the combination of the respect his Métis held for him, with his own deep love of them made this period one of his happiest.

Then, when the crop was springing from the soil an inch a day and all work was progressing well, he took a few days off. Towards the end of June his itchy feet and his sheer Gallic sociability sent him off to Lac La Biche. There he could visit his brethren, Fathers Tissot and Maisonneuve, who like himself were striving mightily to build up their mission to be ready for the demands that would soon be made of it. Perhaps too he went to consult them on some building problems.

At the same time, of course, the trail would take him past Whitefish Lake where he could assess the progress Steinhauer, his Methodist rival, had made since in 1857 he had left Lac La Biche and started afresh. Moreover, he stood a fair chance of picking up some information about how the Reverend Mr. Woolsey was getting along. For Woolsey, with a mission to serve the Assiniboines or Stonies at Pigeon Lake, halfway to Rocky Mountain House, was also a fly in Lacombe's ointment. He had heard that about ten days after he had felled his first tree at St. Albert, Woolsey had set out for Smoky Lake with the intention of starting another establishment somewhere along its north-east shore. He considered Woolsey a bumbling old man who found it hard to adjust to the crudeness of the frontier, but a man with a "zeal worthy of a better cause."

On many a Sunday at Fort Edmonton Woolsey had held his services in the dining-room of the Big House, while Fathers Lacombe or Caer preached to a much larger crowd in their new chapel. Whenever a priest and a minister were at the fort at the same time, they had sat across from each other in that dining-room to enjoy the company's hospitality.

It was in that same room that an open break in relations between Woolsey and one of Lacombe's associates (undoubtedly Father Caer) had been avoided narrowly. Woolsey, knowing not a word of French and but a smattering of Cree, and Caer, if it were he, having a mere nodding acquaintance with either English or the Cree *lingua franca*, were thus mutually spared the embarrassment of having to talk to each other as they sat together to break pemmican. On these occasions it was the factor's custom to ask one of them to say grace at one meal and to ask the other at the next sitting.

Invariably, with a lack of courtesy and an excessive zeal having its immediate roots in Caer's inflexibility, but more remotely in the bitter animosity existing between the two religions, Caer would jump in with a Latin grace, leaving the phlegmatic Woolsey sitting with his mouth open. Finally one day, after half a dozen such performances, Woolsey motioned the priest to stay behind while the other diners left the room. Then straightening his shoulders and towering over the man of lesser stature and jabbing his finger in his direction, he mustered all his broken Cree to ask the other to change his ways. The combination of the straightened shoulders, the jabbing finger and the broken Cree seems to have conveyed the message for, from then on, the Methodist had his turn at grace.

On June 21, bringing Father Tissot with him from Lac La Biche, Father Lacombe stopped overnight at the fort. There Father Tissot applied his builder's knowledge to one of the fort's problems and thereby started a new industry. On June 24 the journal states: "Rev. Mr. Tissot to the River Bank in the evening and found several stones which he called lime stone, tried two in the forge, he proved correct." The factor seems to have seized on this new knowledge, because about two weeks later the journal states that two men were sent to look for lime stones. An entry a week later indicates the rapid progress being made in producing lime. "The lime kill dug is eight feet wide and 11 feet deep it will take a great quantity of stones."

In the relations between the Hudson's Bay Company and the missionaries the flow of help was preponderantly from the company to the men of the cloth. This business of making lime, however, was but another instance of some of the favours the priests rendered the traders. Undoubtedly some of the produce of this kiln eventually found its way to Father Lacombe's St. Albert mission. An instance of help going the other way occurred after the mission had reaped its first surprisingly successful harvest that fall. Once all the vegetables had been stored in root houses and the wheat threshed out and the Métis got their first glimpse of how richly the soil would produce, Father Lacombe sent some wheat to the company's wind-driven grist mill to be ground into flour. At last the mission staff and some of the Métis were able to supplement their pemmican and fish with bannock.

About the same time the fort experienced its usual influx of Indians coming in to trade for the goods brought in by the fall brigade. On September 9, 1861, about five hundred Bloods, Blackfoot, Piegans and Sarcees (generally spoken of collectively as the Blackfoot) arrived and camped on the south side of the river. Then for a couple of days two men worked from dawn to dusk to row them across to the fort. For the next two or three days the journal mentions how the natives were drinking and trading and how, to complicate matters, a number of Stonies and a band of Crees under Maskepatoon's leadership arrived until there were eight hundred Indians all together.

They were an explosive mixture and every man about the fort stood armed and ready to try to ward off an eruption. During this time a Piegan was wounded by a "rascally Cree or Stoney" and one Sarcee was killed by Maskepatoon's Crees. Then, even as the company's men were rowing the last of the Blackfoot back across the river, some twenty Crees attacked them but were frightened off. The next day a relaxed and thankful journalist could report that the spate of trading had added 40,000 pounds of dried meat to the company's stores. Everyone breathed a sigh of relief.

Tension, however, was not confined to Fort Edmonton. In a different guise unrelated to Indian animosity, it had broken out in Father Lacombe's bailiwick. Perhaps his success at St. Albert had made him a bit overweening, but Father Rémas's distaste of him had begun to strain relations between them. Father Rémas had been hurt by his removal from Lac La Biche eight years earlier, he had been disquieted by some aspects of Father Lacombe's noviciate and now finally had given reluctant voice to some of his sentiments. This had started a correspondence with Bishop Taché who had evidently chided him. Now it appeared that St. Albert was to supersede and downgrade Lac Ste. Anne. Already Father Lacombe had obtained approval to move the Sisters of Charity to St. Albert as soon as he could build a proper home for them. He had become the golden-haired boy. Everyone, the bishop, the Hudson's Bay Company officials, the Métis and even the nuns made a fuss over him and in conscientious Father Rémas's breast it rankled. By December 1861 he found himself writing to Bishop Taché about Father Lacombe's "touchiness and his predilection to want everyone to like him."

Father Lacombe suffered too. In the midst of his outstanding achievement at St. Albert this coolness between himself and his highly respected fellow priest was the only cloud on his otherwise bright horizon. It worried him.

Nevertheless, trying all the while to mollify good Father

Rémas, he had to carry on his work. High on his list of priorities, of course, was the need to visit the Blackfoot and at least twice during the winter of 1861–62 he set off "for the plains" on trips of about three weeks' duration. For most of 1862, however, affairs at St. Albert kept him fully occupied. As he was to write, "I began this year axe in hand."

First of all he applied his axe to timbers which he had a gang of men erect into a convent for the nuns. Then he applied it to cutting and shaping piles and stringers for a bridge he proposed to build over the Sturgeon River immediately below the mission. Following mass on a Sunday when he deemed the river was in such a state that his Métis could work in it, he announced what he had in mind. "My friends, I am through crossing the river, walking in the mud on the bank, and pushing the scow. I'll build me a bridge. All those who help me will cross over it free. The others will not. I will have a man there to watch."

The next morning every able-bodied male turned out and, with axes, saws, ropes and horses, within a few days the new marvel, two hundred feet long and fifteen feet wide, was finished. "While they worked I fed them with pemmican and tea."

However important it may have been, the bridge was only one of Father Lacombe's accomplishments that year. More significant in terms of developing the West was his move that spring to start the church's own freighting system. As his two missions grew, they needed more and more supplies which had to be brought in from the East. Up to this point the Hudson's Bay Company had been reasonably generous to the missionaries in bringing in their goods and in its charges for this service, but as their establishments both grew and multiplied, carrying their freight had become a burden and the company began making suggestions about the priests hauling in their own supplies. Father Lacombe was quite willing to fall in line with this suggestion because he felt that the church would save money by so doing.

At St. Albert, a new factor in missionary life and one which made more supplies necessary, had begun to raise its head. The Métis, who during the earlier years had been glad to pitch in and help the priest voluntarily now began reconsidering their stance and demanding pay. That pay had to be in goods.

Father Lacombe, having organized his brigade, started it

along the trail which ran south of the Saskatchewan River. Although there was a pack horse trail on the north side, up to this time no one had taken carts along that portion of it which ran from Fort Edmonton to the site of the modern town of St. Paul. The portion from that point east to Fort Pitt had recently received attention from axes wielded by the fathers from Lac La Biche and had been improved until it could accommodate carts. At the same time, the priests cut a new trail from St. Paul north to their mission. In any event, in 1862, Father Lacombe's Métis became the first clear-cut brigade of freighting carts to be sent from Edmonton to Winnipeg. While he may have started down the river with the Hudson's Bay Company's boats that May, the father undoubtedly travelled overland either from Fort Pitt or Fort Carlton to St. Boniface. On May 5, 1862, the Fort Edmonton journal records: "Mr. Christie started in the morning in company with Mr. Lacombe. . . ."

An entry for the following Sunday expresses an interesting sense of relief on the journalist's part. Apparently Mr. Woolsey was absent and, of course, Father Lacombe was on his way east. The sole entry for that day states: "Men all at rest, no parson or priest today."

Meanwhile the carts were creaking their way east over the plains and rolling hills and about a month later reached Fort Garry and St. Boniface. During their stay there Fort Garry was filled with excitement as the famous Overlanders of '62 descended upon it and began preparing to follow the trail to Fort Edmonton and then to go on to the Cariboo mines. This party, some 175 strong, left Fort Garry on June 5 with oxen, pack horses and cows, and came straggling in to Fort Edmonton about July 22. When Father Lacombe's loaded carts started on the homeward leg of their trip they had a much more well-defined trail to follow to Edmonton and also had the benefit of the bridges the Overlanders built over such water courses as Beaverhills Creek and Deep Creek.

Father Lacombe spent two or three congenial weeks at St. Boniface while he purchased his supplies, discussed matters with his friend Bishop Taché and relaxed in the company of several fellow priests. Referring to them, he was to write: "During my pleasant stay with Mgr. Taché, I had the pleasure of meeting the newly arrived Father Mestre and Father Ritchot, my former pupil at L'Assomption College. I didn't get to see our valiant Father André who had left for the prairie with the hunters. Oh! to be able to relate how promising this brave among the brave was!" We can be sure that he and Father Ritchot spent many hours living over again their days at L'Assomption.

Whether or not his bishop alluded directly to the complaint he had recently received from Father Rémas is not revealed, but undoubtedly he used Father Lacombe's stay in St. Boniface to guide and uplift his ambitious priest and probably to chasten him.

When Father Lacombe set out west again it was to travel as far as Fort Pitt in company with Father Maisonneuve's brigade of carts which was taking three sisters who were to add to the personnel at the Lac La Biche mission. In the matter of additional help, he too was taking a new man west, Constantin Scollen, an Irish lay brother about twenty-one years old.

When the brigade of some thirty carts returned on August 26, 1862, the settlers at St. Albert buzzed with excitement. Everyone turned to watch as bags and bales and barrels of provisions were carried into the storehouse where they would take their place beside other freight which a few of the Hudson's Bay Company carts had brought from the East. But of all the loads, those which contained gears, levers and a set of millstones excited them most. For Father Lacombe had brought along another symbol of civilization, the parts for a horse-driven flour mill.

Unfortunately he was too busy to assemble it that fall. As well as his priestly duties in the settlement and what few visits he could make to outlying Indian camps, he had to double as an unofficial mayor of St. Albert. Handing out homesteads, working in the forest or the fields or the saw-pit, directing, encouraging and helping everyone, as well as dispersing farm tools, kitchen equipment and all the lares and penates of the colony, he was busy from daybreak to dusk. His enthusiasm kept him ever on the move. And he enjoyed every moment of it.

Four days after his return he received an official visit from his friend, Chief Factor William Christie, who was showing the sights to his superior, Governor Dallas. The governor was on his way back after having visited Oregon where the company had recently been driven to the wall by a rapid influx of settlers. The presence of the new St. Albert colony irked him, for he knew that it, a little cloud in the company's sky at the moment, was but a foretaste of the settlement which would some day take place in the Saskatchewan River valley. It is said that because Father Lacombe's bridge was another symbol of future settlement, he vented his spleen against it and ordered William Christie to have it torn down — an order which, of course, the chief factor would never dream of carrying out. If indeed Dallas did and allowed his momentary temper tantrum to overcome his judgment, he must surely have regretted it moments later when at Father Lacombe's table he enjoyed the mission's bread, thick cream and fresh vegetables. When he turned his judgment to the splendid progress Father Lacombe and his associates had made in such a short time, his discernment was faultless, for he is reported as saying:

"See the thrifty way in which these missioners make the most of everything, in spite of their poverty. See how with all our resources and our hundreds of servants, our Forts are falling to ruin, while these priests who come into the country with nothing but a little book under their arm are performing wonders."

A day or so after Governor Dallas called at the mission, Father Lacombe wrote Bishop Taché telling of the visit and how well it had gone and how the next day he hoped to see the governor again to discuss the question of a school at Fort Edmonton. His letter does not mention any hard words over the bridge and yet when writing he had it in mind, because in another context he stated that the bridge, presumably having withstood the spring flood, was as sturdy as ever and had not moved an inch.

It was well that the Catholic church had provided Brother Scollen as another assistant to Father Lacombe, because less than a week after Governor Dallas's visit another thorn bush had sprung up. On September 4 the Reverend Woolsey brought the Reverend George McDougall and his son John to the fort. The father was merely on a tour of inspection but it was known that the son was to remain in the country and to set up a new mission.

Brother Scollen, who was rapidly acquiring a knowledge of the French language, had come west so that he could teach an English school at Fort Edmonton. As soon as Father Lacombe had time to turn his hand to the matter, he installed Scollen there and in December the teacher began instructing his charges. Without doubt it was the very first formal school within what is now the City of Edmonton. Whether or not it was the first such institution in what is now Alberta is another matter. Wherever missionaries of any faith set up an establishment, one of the first things they did was to provide some schooling, usually religious, to the native children. This type of work was also done by the Methodists and by the Sisters of Charity at their various missions. Scollen's school, located in an empty building in Fort Edmonton, was perhaps a more formal one particularly since it was devoted to teaching in the English language. But so was the Reverend Steinhauer's school at Whitefish Lake, which by the summer of 1862 was being carried on in a separate building.

In any event, while he was at Fort Edmonton, Brother Scollen soon found himself becoming familiar with prairie Indian ways. He was undoubtedly present when on November 27 Father Lacombe, worrying about the Blackfoot, set out from St. Albert with a party of Métis on his way to make another contact with some bands of that tribe. He was probably at the fort also when a couple of days later one of the mysterious white men who lived with the Blackfoot visited Fort Edmonton. This was Jean L'Heureux, one of the early West's erratic characters.

L'Heureux had started out to be a priest, but when for some reason he was cast out of the seminary, he had headed west in search of gold or adventure. He ended up with adventure, and about 1860 came to live with the Blackfoot and to wander as they did. A devout Catholic in spite of his rejection for the priesthood, he found himself teaching and exhorting his native friends. Perhaps to strengthen his influence among them, or maybe due to his streak of eccentricity, he made a cassock of brownish material much like that worn by the Franciscans. Dishevelled, untidy and unkempt, he lacked the orderly deportment of a regular priest. Nevertheless, he learned the Blackfoot language and his hosts came to esteem him highly.

On the occasion of his visit to Fort Edmonton in November 1862, L'Heureux brought in a white man whom the Blackfoot had wounded. Evidently about dusk one evening, on the lookout for their Stoney enemies, they had seen the tent which two

American miners had set up and, thinking it housed Stonies, fired upon it and killed one of the partners. Once they discovered that its occupants were white men, they had fled, leaving the wounded wanderer in the tent. Sometime later Jean L'Heureux had happened along.

In December, in the intervals between classes, Brother Scollen must have been interested in an action which for four days unfolded within earshot of his school. The fort journal reports its opening move as follows: "50 Crees, headed by 'Broken Arm' [Maskepatoon], 'Sweet Grass' etc. arrive. Sue for peace with Blackfeet."

Some Crees from the Fort Pitt-Fort Carlton area were there at the time and they expressed a desire to be included in the proceedings. To ascertain how the Blackfoot felt the factor sent a messenger bearing tobacco to their camp, which could not have been far away because he returned that day. The next morning J. E. Brazeau, one of the fort traders, visited the Blackfoot camp to tell them that when they came in, and for the duration of the conference, both parties were to deliver up all their guns, knives and other weapons. The following day after all had been disarmed, the leaders were introduced to each other and amid a lot of promises both parties agreed and went so far as to have the factor write out papers of agreement which they carried away with them.

Though the peace seems to have lasted for nearly a year, its terms did not include the Stonies. In February 1863 the Blackfoot killed two of that tribe, and in April a Blackfoot came hurrying across the river with his wife and child and explained that over on the south side the Stonies had ill-treated him, taken his horse, gun and some of his furs and killed all of his dogs. The factor sent Abraham Salois after the culprits and he managed to talk them into giving up the horse and the furs, but they kept his gun.

Much of the credit for the endurance of that peace is probably due to the Cree Chief Maskepatoon who devoted a great part of his time to bringing about a lasting peace between his tribe and the Blackfoot. Most of our information about him comes from the Methodist missionaries whose writings smack of the fondness lavished on a neophyte, but he appears to have been a great man.

While for the time being the peace kept the Indians more or less away from each other's scalps, Father Lacombe was scratching his over a tremor of unrest amongst his priests at Lac Ste. Anne and St. Albert, in which his associates were pointing their fingers at him. The trouble had first erupted towards the close of 1861 when Father Rémas had written Bishop Taché. It was followed by another letter from the same sincere author while Father Lacombe was away at St. Boniface and explains what had touched off the unrest.

"The trouble with Father Lacombe is that he wants to do everything himself, he does not know how to delegate work to his brothers; he has too much confidence in himself, and very little or none in others. His second fault is to have the knack to persuade his superior to let him do what he wishes. His third fault is his very excessive sensitiveness in that he cannot tolerate being told anything, even something ever so small offends him. It ends up that when he has succeeded in making himself liked, everything is fine; everything is fine although everything is wrong; the consequences of these small troubles will be felt everywhere, even at confession."

For a while letters flowed back and forth between St. Albert and St. Boniface. Reading them, one comes to the conclusion that Father Rémas had been influenced by Father Caer, who seems to have lacked some of the desirable qualities so necessary for the priesthood. As Caer's animosity towards Father Lacombe reached its peak in May 1863, one of his letters says: "As soon as I arrived here I noticed that Father Lacombe was seeing people of the opposite sex much too frequently and for no good reason; especially the Nuns and the girls in the kitchen," and much more in a similar vein. At this point Brother Scollen seems to have become aware of the unrest and in a rather effective way put a stop to it by intimating to the bishop that it was not Father Lacombe but the devious-minded Father Caer who was playing the role of which he had accused his colleague. Perhaps the best judgment on the matter is that Father Caer's charitable qualities were not fully developed.

For many a day Father Lacombe must have chewed the cud of reflection over that period of unpleasantness. For many a year he must have profited by the insight into human psychology it had brought him. His drive and enthusiasm, the very qualities that endeared him to Bishop Taché, could backfire. Diplomacy towards the rest of the world was not enough; one had to be especially careful not to ride roughshod over one's staff members.

Undoubtedly Bishop Taché laid the whole problem before Father Lacombe and cautioned him. Furthermore, he must have preached the virtues of delegating work. This tempest in a teapot appears not to have lessened the love and respect between the bishop and his ardent follower. Nevertheless, in his mental notebook Bishop Taché probably tucked away some doubts as to his protégé's qualifications for ever assuming a bishop's mitre. Some day soon the St. Albert district would need a bishop.

As St. Albert entered the spring of 1863, signs of progress abounded. In March the nuns had moved over from Lac Ste. Anne, and as soon as the men could work with bare hands Father Lacombe put some of them to erecting his horse-driven mill. About the middle of May when priests and nuns were planting their gardens and small grain crops, Dr. W. B. Cheadle, an English traveller, paid Father Lacombe a visit and thought the priest to be an exceedingly intelligent and agreeable man. He noted that he spoke English fluently and that the Métis acknowledged that the father's command of the Cree language was superior to their own. Cheadle enjoyed dining with him in his small one-roomed house with its sleeping loft above. After walking around the settlement of some twenty houses, Cheadle concluded that "altogether this little settlement was the most flourishing community we had seen since leaving Red River, and it must be confessed that the Romish Priests far excel their Protestant brethren in missionary enterprise and influence."

Coming from a well-educated Protestant this generous and well-merited praise for Father Lacombe's establishment is all the more noteworthy. Cheadle's respect for missionaries in general and what good they were doing the Indians was not invariably so lavish and is perhaps best indicated by some comments he made about their effectiveness as he had seen it at Fort Edmonton. "Priest catches a convert and baptizes him. Wolsey [sic] hears of it and baptizes him over again, and so on ad infinitum, it being with great difficulty that convert knows whether he was made Papist or Protestant last." Having confided that to his diary, he reported the story that trader Richard Hardisty told him about the affair over saying grace at meals.

It may not be amiss here to quote the feelings of the writer of the Fort Edmonton journal in an entry he made on the day Dr. Cheadle arrived and which, since the Reverend George McDougall had also been holding services at the fort, probably took in all missionaries. "They are fast taking possession of the Fort and if no change is made with regard to their proceedings, I expect the Company will sooner or later feel the consequences. As it is the Priests can come and stop the men from their work whenever they please."

Dr. Cheadle had passed on west towards the mountains long before Father Lacombe, with the help of an American miner, got his mill assembled. When it did operate it "was a very imperfect set up."

> "Much time was needed to break our ponies in to this new type of exercise: to turn a large wheel which interlocked with a smaller one, setting into motion a belt which in turn set the grindstones in movement. Having neither blacksmith, iron nor tools, this invention of ours was often out of order, etc. However, we did manage to make some flour, to the great admiration of our people. . . . It should be mentioned that the Hudson [sic] Bay Company had, prior to this, built a flour wind-mill, but it functioned very poorly and was finally abandoned."

As it turned out, his mill never worked too well either and at times the mission's grain had to be taken to the wind-powered mill at Fort Edmonton. To try to remedy this situation, Father Lacombe set crews to work to build a dam just below Big Lake so as to use water-power for this work. Although at times it became a source of worry to the missionaries, when it did work it did so "famously."

Like so many other matters which he had set in train, his mill added to the ease of life at his new mission. Even at that the itchy-footed farm boy from St. Sulpice, having set his establishment on a firm base, was beginning to tire of it. The old call of the big skies over the parklands and the open prairies kept reasserting itself. So did his need to get out amongst the Indians and to help them. As early as January 1863 he had written his bishop asking, "Won't you let me leave St. Albert? Send me to the land of the Crees and Blackfeet. You know how much I would like to go." Moreover, the recent unpleasantness at the mission had made him more eager than ever to get away.

Up to this point he had made as many brief visits to the Cree camps and occasionally to those of the Blackfoot as he could. So too had Fathers Rémas and Caer and yet though all of them had tried to change the natives' outlook and to curtail the warfare between Cree and Blackfoot, they had had little effect. Father Lacombe, however, had another string to his bow; if visiting and preaching did little, perhaps formal education would do more, and Brother Scollen with his school in the fort seems to have made good progress. In December 1863 the fort journal shows that the chief factor had inspected the school and was pleased at the results he observed and at how many of the students could already read and speak English.

But if by means of preaching and schooling Father Lacombe hoped to save them from their own indifference, it was equally imperative that they be saved from the errors of the Methodists who had recently stepped up their crusade.

As with all missionaries, the Hudson's Bay Company was also helping them, and during the summer of 1862 had assisted the Reverend George McDougall and his son John to come in to begin their campaign. The pair were quite active and within months John McDougall had started a mission which he called Victoria, some eighty miles down the river from Fort Edmonton. Although it was said that the Reverend Mr. Woolsey was about to leave the field, these two newcomers, from all reports, appeared to be a much greater threat to Catholicism.

As it soon turned out, they were indeed a greater threat. The elder McDougall, a Methodist of the old rigorous school, was not only a deeply devout man but one who had come of pioneer Ontario stock. He was exactly the adaptable type needed to overcome the hardships and the inconveniences of the West. His son John, not yet ordained, but a muscular, athletic lad, seemed likely to follow in his father's footsteps.

During the early months of 1864 Father Caer, who had been moved over to take charge of Lac Ste. Anne, spent many weeks out in the parklands visiting the natives and began hearing echoes of the new blows the McDougalls were striking. Then in December young John McDougall passed through Fort Edmonton on his way to reestablish the mission at Pigeon Lake, which the Reverend Mr. Rundle had started nearly fifteen years earlier.

Moreover, the McDougalls' Victoria mission had developed rapidly and had attracted several curious Crees. During 1864 the Hudson's Bay Company, watching the growing pains of the new mission much the same as it had done at Lac Ste. Anne a few years earlier, decided to set up a trading outpost there.

All this activity Father Lacombe reported to his beloved Bishop Taché who had been expecting increased opposition along the Saskatchewan River and was doing his very best to augment his own forces. He, like the Hudson's Bay Company, keeping abreast of the times, had been watching the gradual and as yet minor changes that were taking place in the West — some of them at the time mere straws in the wind of the future.

One of these straws, inspired by the Hudson's Bay Company in 1864, however, did catch him unawares, but his surprise was no greater than his pleasure at the news. For that year the company's famous explorer, Dr. James Rae, came walking into Edmonton on July 28, with the explanation that he was picking out a route for a proposed telegraph line which was to cross Canada to the Pacific Ocean. Writing to his mother exactly a month earlier, the bishop, rejoicing at the very thought of what a near miracle that would be, said: "Voila! Won't it be wonderful when we will be able to ask you in three minutes how you are."

That fall when the valleys of the Saskatchewan and the Sturgeon rivers were a blaze of yellow foliage, Father Lacombe welcomed another most unexpected visitor when, having come across the prairies with a cart brigade, his much younger and only brother, Gaspard, walked in on him. In physique, appearance, open-hearted friendliness and in his predilection towards travelling, he bore a striking resemblance to the founder of St. Albert. On the other hand, he was much less emotional and much less disciplined, and completely lacking in the determination by which Father Lacombe had driven himself through college and which had steeled him to endure the rigours of his earlier missionary days. For big-hearted Gaspard was a wanderer who had left home two or three years before in search of adventure. Hearing that there was gold to be panned on the Saskatchewan River, he had harkened to its call.

Not knowing what to do with him, Father Lacombe took him along when he went to evangelize a band of Crees, which for the time being was camped in the vicinity of present-day Elk Island Park while they drove buffalo into a pound. Gaspard could endure the Cree camp for three days only and when a couple of Métis decided to return to St. Albert he came back with them. "Ugh!" he exclaimed. "The dirt, the cold and the lice!"

On that trip he also learned more of his brother's characteristics — his utter unselfishness and his generosity. These qualities which throughout his long life were ever to mark his passage through the land had already been noted by Father Lacombe's fellow workers and they had warned Gaspard of his brother's proclivities. Laughing, though vexed, about his experiences in the Cree camp, Gaspard explained, "He gives everything away. The first day he gave away my shirt — the only one I had in my duffle bag — my red flannel shirt. And all because he had nothing left of his own to give away!"

While Gaspard was watching an Indian pull on his red shirt, Bishop Taché at St. Boniface was looking forward to making another trip across the prairies. Later in the fall he was to escort the European, Father Vandenberghe, a delegate from the superior general of the Oblates, who was touring the country. As it turned out, the pair reached St. Albert on December 3 on a visit which was to be of great moment to Father Lacombe. Writing of that visit, Bishop Taché said:

"Sunrise permitted us to contemplate with pardonable pride and complacency the beautiful Mission of St. Albert, so advanced and yet so new. What a great work had already been done. Handsome and vast constructions had been erected as if by enchantment; broad meadows had been cleared and put under cultivation, and were already yielding abundant harvests. All this, we could not leave without admiration."

All this, as he knew, had come into being under Father Lacombe's inspiration, perspiration and stewardship. By that time the settlement could boast of some forty Métis families and a population of about three hundred souls. As such, as Father Lacombe himself expressed it, "St. Albert was becoming too civilized for me."

He had completed his task here. Let others take over the mundane matter of operating it. He was ready to fight on other fronts; ready and anxious to confine his efforts to carrying the gospel to Cree and Blackfoot camps. This he considered a missionary's main objective, not planting potatoes. If in the course of that work other missions should arise under his hand, all well and good. But his duty lay with the far-flung camps.

To his joy, Bishop Taché and Father Vandenberghe agreed with him. Starting January 1, 1865, he was freed from St. Albert and given "the mission of roaming the prairies in an attempt to evangelize among the ever-wandering Crees and Blackfoot."

Such roaming, such complete merging of his life with theirs, he felt to be the way leading to the Indians' salvation. It was to turn out to be the way leading to his own greatness.

CHAPTER NINE

St. Paul des Cris

In every man's life there is a period which establishes his reputation. It is usually a period when, because of his total absorption in his work, the days, months and seasons slip by imperceptibly to form the happiest years of his life. In Father Lacombe's case that period started in 1865 and continued for seven years. During it while coursing the parklands in an unending round of visits to Indian camps he baptized thousands of natives. During it he endured starvation, illness, great hardship and a gunshot wound but, nevertheless, enjoyed many satisfactions.

He had arrived on the scene while the natives were still in full possession of their magnificent open countryside and before the bloom of their unique civilization started its rapid decline. Emotionally, perhaps more so than some, he needed friends who were ever glad to see him and as the Indian leaders of both the mutually hostile Crees and Blackfoot came to understand him, they reciprocated his deep love for people. Then, too, his wanderings satisfied his longing for the open trail and his desire to see over the next hill and to look down upon the next valley and then over all the West's vast region of rolling parkland and prairie.

Enjoying these rewards for seven years, he became an authority on conditions in the West and on the problems of the Indians. He came to know every chief of every Cree, Stoney, Sarcee, Piegan, Blood or Blackfoot band and each of them knew him. For years he had mingled with them, sharing their sorrows, hardship and happiness, urging them to adopt his concept of the will of the Supreme Being, begging them to keep peace amongst themselves, and advising them to prepare for the day when the country must inevitably be invaded by a horde of white men. Though they paid little heed to his entreaties, they nevertheless regarded him as one of but half a dozen men, all missionaries, whose truthfulness they could trust. At times they played him off against his most prominent rivals, the Methodist McDougalls, George and John, but that did not lessen their trust in him.

As they sat smoking around their campfires they discussed what they could understand of the differences between these two competing sects who seemed to worship the same God, and wondered why they could not agree among themselves. In spite of that disagreement, many Indians felt that it would be well to sample this new religion and to add some of its rituals to their own repertoire. Consequently, many of them became nominal converts to Catholicism or Methodism and some indeed became devout and believing converts. As a result, both Father Lacombe and young John McDougall became welcome visitors to their camps.

It would be an incautious judge who would state that during those years one achieved more good than the other. If, however, the number of converts were to be used as a criterion, Father Lacombe's church would undoubtedly have to come out well ahead of the McDougalls'. But regardless of that, each of these long-suffering, faithful missionaries came to have great influence in Indian camps and thus on the history of the West.

While up to 1865 the Catholic church had obtained gratifying results with the Métis and the Crees and while the Methodists had scored heavily with the Crees and also with the Stonies, neither had really come into more than sporadic contact with the Blackfoot. About that time, both groups began the very difficult job of impressing that tribe.

During his time at his missions of St. Joachim at Fort Edmonton, Lac Ste. Anne and St. Albert, Father Lacombe had perfected his command of the Cree language. Now in Alberta's plains he was to turn his mind to mastering the Blackfoot language. Freed at last from the petty politics of a mission, he turned

to the larger politics of keeping peace between the battling Indian tribes and outreaching his Methodist competitors.

On January 1 he had been released from St. Albert — as he
said, "My die was cast." On January 7 he set off for six weeks
with the Crees.

"With my ever faithful Alexis' help, I prepared for my travels: four dogs, a sled, our blankets, my rackets [snowshoes],
our axe, a pail for the meat, another in which to boil tea,
provisions for ourselves and our dogs, pemmican and dry
meat, the whole tied and bound to our sleigh. And, off we
went. . . . We climbed the hills on the southern bank of the
river [at Edmonton], only to discover that three Blackfeet
had been massacred by their enemies, the Cree. The scalps
had been taken and the hands and feet were hanging in the
trees. The surrounding snow was covered with blood. I sent
Alexis back to the fort to notify so that someone would come
for these bodies and bury them. Under the impression of this
savage hate and murder we continued on our way. We had
a three day trek to make before reaching the first Cree camp.
The cold was intense. We suffered greatly when camping
beneath the open sky."

For three or four days he and Alexis pressed on, camping at
night in the open and one morning:

"The snow falls, the wind whistles, the fire crackles, and the
kettle is boiling. We must hurry to eat for today we must
reach the Cree encampment on the Labiche [Red Deer]
River. 'Move on, Butterfly, and you, my dogs, run.' We put
on our snow shoes, the dogs follow us as we advance across
this immense white sea facing a gentle 40 below zero zephyr!
  " 'Are you cold, Alexis?'
  " 'Not yet. . . . And you, Father?'
  " 'Carry on. I'm alright.'
"Thus that evening we reached the Cree encampment. One
must have witnessed such an arrival to have any idea of it.
The darkness, the deafening howling of the dogs, the shouts
of all, the cumbersome piles of cut up carcasses, and the bit-

ing cold, are enough to discourage one. But, we have arrived. A good christian Chief, Abraham Kiyiwin [Kehewin], has recognized me. He seizes me and brings me into his cabin. At last I can rest, remove my outer clothing and take much needed food. A large helping of buffalo meat will comfort me. The men begin to pay their visit. But it is night. Let me sleep, tomorrow we'll see each other. A smoke, a bit of prayer, and abed! What a sleep! The dogs, those thieves, visited the hut in the night. You can well imagine how pleasant it is to have these beasts roaming around, even stepping on you, or fighting over you. Well! we sleep anyway."

In some tepee for three or four days before moving on to the next Cree camp perhaps twenty miles away, Father Lacombe set up his small altar and said mass. During the forenoon he taught catechism or prayers and hymns to the women. "Each woman has her little one in her arms. Imagine fifty mothers with fifty crying babies, each trying to outdo the other." At noon he assembled the children for catechism. Then in the evening with the father's little bell in hand Alexis invited the men into the tepee.

"This is more serious and done with more dignity. The pipe of peace is brought along. I take on a majestic and more reserved attitude. When each is in place according to his rank, I intone a fitting hymn, in my best singing voice. Next comes my harangue. It must be pious, but must not hurt. . . . Then on our knees or seated on our heels, we pray, sing and finally smoke the pipe of peace whose smoke seems like an incense crowning our religious ceremony. I visit the sick and care for them with my remedies. I make effort to approach the infidels and bring them to the faith. My remedies and care of the suffering are powerful means to help convert the pagans."

When the time came to set out for another camp he and Alexis urged their dogs across flats and along creek beds where, as dark shadows, the soft folds of snow cornices lining the banks punctuated the brilliance of the morning sun. Here and there, showing up as black spots in the all embracing white expanse, individuals or groups of grazing buffalo diverted their attention.

In one of these camps "a man of high rank and a great charlatan" called Father Lacombe into his medicine tent, saying:

"Prayer Chief, listen to me. I am not one of yours. I have my own method of serving the great Master. Today I invited you to my tent to ask you a favour. God listens to you when you ask Him for something. You see my son. He has seen seven winters. He is my only child and I love him greatly. If, by your prayer, you can cure him, with my wife I promise we will adopt the religion you preach. Have pity on me."

The kindly father, believing the boy to be on the point of death, baptized him. When some two or three months later he met this sorcerer who was to become one of his most fervent Christians, the boy was in excellent health.

In another camp the priest met an old friend, Chief Sweet Grass, "still an infidel but a great friend of the missionary. To our entreaties he was content to reply: 'Leave me be, when my time comes, I'll tell you.' "

Nevertheless, in the camps, probably near present-day Ponoka, the sturdy, friendly priest strengthened his bond with these wandering Plains Crees. On many another occasion he was to meet them away out in the sun-kissed parklands. For they ranged over the land from Fort Edmonton to Fort Carlton, a distance of four hundred miles and at any time might be met anywhere from Lac La Biche to the Neutral and the Hand hills. On their war expeditions, of course, they travelled much farther south.

Before ending his mission to the Crees, Father Lacombe sounded them out about the possibility of establishing a rendezvous for other meetings. He hoped that he could start teaching them the rudiments of farming as he had done the Métis at St. Albert. In this way he could prepare them a little for the inevitable day when the buffalo, which in their thousands now covered the prairie's rich farming lands, would have been swept away and replaced by white farmers in their thousands. At such a rendezvous perhaps he could begin to anchor the Crees to an agricultural way of life. In his planning he had already chosen the spot where he hoped it would be — more or less in the midst of the area where the Methodists from Whitefish Lake and Victoria were gaining some influence. His Crees applauded his suggestion and with the same tact which he had led Bishop Taché to put St. Albert where he wanted it to go, he led them to suggest that the meeting place be at the spot where the "prairie gives on to the river" — at modern Brosseau.

Then about the end of February, sorry to leave a field so largely untilled, the persistent priest, nearly worn out by his exertions, made his way back to St. Albert. The mission there had never looked so good to him. With a feeling of satiety and surfeit he had left it. Now, grateful for its rest, comfort and food, he was glad to climb the hill to it and to head towards its spotless kitchen, which was so unlike what his memoirs describe of its Indian camp equivalent:

> "Their kitchen comprises of a pot destined to every use. In it they cram the fish as it is taken from the water, for them this is the ne plus ultra of culinary art. The meal is served on a piece of bark, a piece of wood, or on the ground. One must let show no weakness if one doesn't want to stir up irritability, and if one holds to keeping the esteem and confidence of these Indians. Overcome with hunger one soon learns to devour this food without dislike; for under the control of this cruel tyrant (hunger) everyone becomes somewhat savage."

And yet despite this he was to return again and again to serve his God "in the midst of Indians whose boorish habits, repulsive morals, and disgusting uncleanliness inspire but disgust."

While Father Lacombe had been with the Crees, Maskepatoon had been absent with the Methodist McDougalls making overtures of peace to the Blackfoot. Travelling as they were through hostile territory Maskepatoon's group was more or less surrounded with scouts, some of whom kept ahead and sent back information of possible enemies. As an indication of how hostile the country was and how carefully a party had to proceed, it may be well to quote some of John McDougall's description of that trip. On its third day, they camped within a few miles of what their scouts told them was the site of the Blackfoot camp in the valley of the Battle River.

"Our scouts that morning were like telegraph bulletins. We knew how the camp was arranged, and changed our course to suit this arrangement. We were told of the windings of the coulee, or valley, down which the Blackfeet lodges were standing. We were told of hunting parties that had gone out that morning; of the bands of horses, and how closely these were guarded; of the long strings of women and ponies, and dogs and travois, which were coming and going in various directions, packing wood to camp; all of which was literally true, for our scouts had been there and seen it all."

Later that day as the party came in sight of the camp, "a swarm of men and boys, all armed and anxious" came out to meet them.

It may have been this same camp of Blackfoot which a few weeks after Maskepatoon's visit came down with scarlet fever and sent to St. Albert for Father Lacombe. Though they were still "infidels" who had made only cursory contact with the missionaries, they turned to them in the distress of an epidemic of scarlet fever. Father Lacombe responded immediately.

His approach to the stricken Blackfoot was much less spectacular than McDougall's and the state of the camp much different. Since Maskepatoon's visit the buffalo had moved and all the priest knew was that the camps were said to be near Buffalo Lake. So with that information and with Alexis driving his dogs, he made his way out along what had already become a well-marked cart trail that ran as far as the lake. At dusk, near Bittern Lake, he stopped for the night at a Cree camp.

"When they learned of my destination and my determination to reach it, they did all in their power to dissuade me, giving as prime reason that these wicked Indians [the Blackfoot], enraged by an illness they believed had been given them by the white men, would not receive me but would no doubt kill me.

"After two days, in spite of a snow storm during which we had lost our way, we came in view of their camp. We signalled, and I unfurled my white pennant which bore a red cross. In a short time I was surrounded by a crowd. What a scene! I beheld a crowd of half-naked men, women and children, with bodies reddened by fever, and that, in a biting cold. For a few minutes I was at a loss as to what to do. Everyone wanted me. Some held my hands, others the edge of my cassock. They tried to lift me heavenwards, saying to God: 'Master of life, have pity on us, because of this man whom you love.' I finally managed to escape their grasp and enter a hut, one of the sixty.

"In this tent I found three dead, a father on the point of despair, holding in his arms his daughter, dead since two days, and from whom he would not be separated. Everywhere there was the sound of lamentation. It was heartbreaking. With my companion's aid, I set to baptizing the children and the adults who were in danger of death."

For about three weeks he spread his attention over ten camps, each about five miles apart. In one of these he encountered Jean L'Heureux by whom he sent a message back to Fort Edmonton, telling of the mortality he was witnessing. Of it on March 24 the journalist at the fort wrote: "more than 1,100 persons, men, women and children have died among the Blackfoot."

At each camp, according to Father Lacombe, "we heaped the dead by tens or fifteens, in a closed tent which was held down and covered with stones and snow. Then we would move on further from this scene of desolation, leaving forty or fifty corpses in one place. Soon the wolves would contend with this."

Then in his turn the worn-out priest "was stricken with the disease. Without medicine or care, exposed to the cold, and a burning fever, I thought the end had come for me. But God had pity on me. . . ."

By the time he had recovered enough to travel, the epidemic had subsided. Then, the spring having swept away the snow, priest and guide and dogs had a difficult trip back to St. Albert. At last, however, Father Lacombe had made a telling contact with the Blackfoot. In their distress they had called for his magic and he had answered. Never again would they scoff at his religion. Thenceforth, his white pennant with the red cross was welcome in Blackfoot camps. For this he was thankful, but he was especially gratified that out of four hundred whom he had baptized, "all the little children who had died after their baptism were already in heaven praying for their parents' conversion."

But there was to be little rest for the kindly black-robed medicine man. No sooner had he eaten a good meal at St. Albert and stretched out his tired frame to relax for a day or so than word came that more Blackfoot bands at Rocky Mountain House in the clutches of the dread disease were calling for him and that his friend, the red-haired Hudson's Bay Company man there, Richard Hardisty, begged him to come to their aid.

By the time he returned to St. Albert shortly after the middle of April the snow had gone and a barely perceptible green had tinged the poplar and balm trees as once more their reactivated buds announced the new season. Spring had come and its cleansing winds had swept away a winter marked with disease and death. Another of the parkland's magnificent growing seasons had begun.

So had another season begun for Father Lacombe. Now he was free to embark upon a summer-long mission of ministering to his bands of Crees and Blackfoot and camping with them as for months they ambled back and forth over Alberta's glorious flower-strewn parklands.

First of all, of course, he had to establish a base from which he could exercise some influence over them. He had already made up his mind and indicated to the Crees that this mission was to be on the Saskatchewan River at the point now named Brosseau and that it would be called St. Paul des Cris. On April 29, 1865, the Fort Edmonton journal records lending him a boat with which he could start for his new field of endeavour. A few days earlier he had sent his brother Gaspard and Noel Courtepatte with a team and cart to take some farming tools to his new site. Along a clearly marked trail towards St. Boniface which kept well south of the Saskatchewan River and made its way past Whitford Lake and on to the beginning of the chain of lakes, they travelled as far as modern Two Hills. There they headed some ten miles north and east until they struck and crossed the North Saskatchewan River. Father Lacombe wrote:

"As for myself, with Alexis, a half Cree half Blackfoot widow and her young son who both spoke both languages . . . we placed fifty barrels of potatoes, seed grain, a plow, some food, etc., and then pushed off from the shore. After two and a half days, carried along by a swift current, we were opposite a large Cree encampment. They were faithfully awaiting me at the place we had agreed upon the preceding winter.

"Immediately the raft was taken by storm, and all that was on it carried to the top of the hill. Noel had already arrived with the oxen. We hitched them to the plow. All, men, women, and children watched me and impatiently awaited my movements. It was solemn. To me even the oxen seemed impatient! The word was given and the plow dug into the virgin earth. I guided it. I called Saint Isidore to my aid. A multitude of women followed me and reduced the furrows to dust. In a few days a piece of land was prepared. The potatoes were put into the earth. Our carrot and turnip seeds were sewn, and the first seeding of the establishment was completed."

It should be noted that it was the women who did the cultivating. The men watched. For that kind of labour was beneath a man's dignity. Father Lacombe may have come imbued with ideas of putting hoes into their hands, pushing Christianity into their hearts and pouring peace into their heads, but they were Crees, not Métis. If the good father wanted to plant potatoes, they would applaud, if the women were willing to dig and hoe, they would acquiesce, but with buffalo to be found over the next hilltop this was no job for a man.

The women, however, did learn some of the rudiments of agriculture. At the same time Father Lacombe learned too. With the Métis at St. Albert he had been fairly successful, but in these free people of the plains there was no white blood and no heredity harking back to husbandry; there was but half-hearted assistance and tolerance.

Nevertheless, though not without twinges of disappointment, Father Lacombe encouraged these people in their work. Busy from morn till night, sandwiching in his holy offices whenever he could, he kept everyone else busy till the gardens were planted "in the first furrows in which these poor savages confided their seeds for the first time to mother earth." It should be noted that no reproachful connotation was implied when Father Lacombe used the word savages or *sauvages*. To him it signified wild in the same sense that he or we might speak of *sauvage* or wild fruit or flowers.

But his labour and the unsanitary conditions in the Indian

lodges had taken their toll. By the time the grass at the edges of his garden plots was springing up lustily, he was attacked by the same dysentery which had "brought to the tomb all those stricken by it. For the last two days I feel that I have it, but, I have not yet stopped and can continue my ministry. If this contagion is to carry me off my sacrifice is made."

Fortunately he was able to remain on his feet and dragged himself around administering the last sacrament to many of his converts. Though frequently ill with one trouble or other, he was always too busy to dwell upon his illnesses. On this occasion the best tonic of all, the magic of the new mantle of spring's leaves, swept away his distress.

Far up and down the three-mile reach of river visible from the mission the gnarled old balm trees along the banks had come alive with the aroma and the newly washed greenery that signalled the start of the new season. Farther away, as the land liberally sprinkled with crocuses rose gradually for three or four miles to the south, the park-like poplar clumps beckoned, and off to the right even the darker pines exuding their soapy smell announced that once more spring with its plenty had burst over one of the fairest landscapes on earth.

The call of this new magic sweeping down from the hills was too much for the Crees to resist. After all, out of deference to the "blackrobe," they had slept in one place for nearly a month. Now, nothing could hold them back from the joys of a summer spent wandering at will over the magnificent parklands. This great assembly of some two hundred tepees, hundreds of horses and veritable hordes of dogs had been camped on the north side of the river; some on the flats extending east from to-day's bridge at Brosseau and some on the bench of land higher up. Now it was time to break camp and move off. Now it was time to cross the river.

In a letter Father Lacombe wrote to his superior general, he described their departure saying: "You will have difficulty forming any idea of the spectacle presented by all these savages to the number of at least a thousand when they crossed the large and rapid Saskatchewan." By means of his description we can visualize this great camp of horsemen as they pulled down their tepees, bundled up their possessions and then, spread out over a distance of several hundred yards along the river bank, waded in to cross the swiftly flowing stream. Some built rafts, others converted the buffalo hide coverings of their tepees into crude coracles. Then, loading the family and its possessions on them, a good swimmer, holding a raw-hide rope in his teeth, pulled the wobbly craft across the twelve-hundred-foot stream. But, as Father Lacombe wrote, "to fully comprehend this spectacle one must hear the cries of the crowd and the tumult which they made during the two days it took to transfer the camp to the south side."

Next morning on the south shore the real preparations for the journey began: saddling and packing the horses, catching the dogs and loading up both the dog travois that were to carry some baggage and the horse travois on which the sick, the aged and some of the children rode. The rest of the children sat up with the mother on the horse. Then in a remarkably short time family after family moved off to form themselves into small bands riding with the morning sun on their left as they ascended the gentle slope. Soon, a mile or so away, as Father Lacombe stood looking longingly after them, the last of the great cavalcade disappeared over the ridge.

Although they had appeared to have straggled off, he knew that on their march south they were making for some definite area four, six or eight days away and fanning out as they went. Some would bear to the left on a course that would take them past Sick Man Hill and on to Birch Lake and on till they encountered sizeable herds of buffalo. Some would bear to the right, swinging around by the Hairy Hill, ascending the Vermilion River and scouring the plains out Beaverhill Lake way and finally perhaps striking the Battle River near Dried Meat Hill. And though they travelled as separate bands, they kept in constant communication along the face of their advance. For this was not a war party slipping stealthily into enemy territory but a summer hunting expedition, watching for game, working hard but enjoying every minute of their trek.

And yet carefree and romantic as their wandering appeared to be, it was well organized into several parallel lines of march. The farther they advanced towards the Battle River valley, the more care they exercised in keeping guards well out ahead and behind, as well as on their flanks. At night the guards were posted at intervals around the camps and all the horses were either tethered or hobbled close within the circle of tepees. For, any moment the belligerent Blackfoot might come swinging out of some coulee or sweeping over a nearby ridge. Indeed, all day long the Crees noted and talked of some creek or lake they passed where in recent memory they had fought with their foes, or where their camp had been when the young men had returned bringing in so many scalps or horses. Almost every hill, copse or lake brought forth some reminiscence.

Having watched his Crees depart, Father Lacombe returned to St. Albert for a brief rest. There he spent two or three weeks enjoying his discussions with Father Tissot, the new superior of the mission. All the while, of course, he was making plans to follow his Crees out into the prairies. These plans included having the Fort Edmonton staff make a scow on which he and Gaspard returned to St. Paul des Cris about July 10. There with his brother's help he was able to make improvements to the "skeleton of a house" which had been thrown up in the spring. As soon as these were accomplished, Gaspard returned to St. Albert and at last Father Lacombe was free to head south to join his Cree neophytes.

CHAPTER TEN

Coursing the Prairies
1865

"And now, off to the prairies! With Alexis, my excellent Blackfoot cook, my horses, my cart, and, my portable altar, my catechisms, some objects of piety, these made up my church and my rectory. Truth to tell, I was as happy as a Prince of the Church! My people, half of which are now Christians, in the stature of great hunters before the Lord, respected and loved me. I was as a new Moses in the midst of this new Israelite camp. We were not to be fed with the desert manna, but, of the tasty prairie meat sent to us by God."

After travelling south for three or four days from St. Paul des Cris he arrived at the first of the Cree camps. Like all others, it was a most impressive sight which, as he looked down upon it from the last ridge, was made up of a number of white buffalo hide tepees arranged in more or less concentric rings. Some were smaller than others but all were of the same conical shape, although each was distinguishable by the paintings which depicted some of its owner's exploits or by other symbols indicated the supernatural sources of his secret powers.

Perhaps next in prominence in the scene were the horses, often hundreds of them, some tethered here and there near their owners' tepees and others grazing within about a mile of their camp. Those that fed freely were carefully guarded and on almost every knoll nearby a small knot of guards could be seen. Their job was to see that the horses did not stray too far and, more importantly, to scan the horizon for any possible enemies bent on stealing them.

Intermingled amongst the few horses which were tied up beside the tepees was an assortment of poles and meat-drying racks. On these in different stages of curing were spread the produce of recent hunts. And amidst them were women scraping hides, dressing skins, slicing up fresh meat and hanging it on the racks or pounding dry meat, rendering tallow or making pemmican. Some were cooking and some sewing with an awl and needle. For women, there were few idle moments.

Then to make the scene even more lively, scores of children, very often naked, played about, some shouting, some eating and some crying, but all of them in motion. Hundreds of dogs fighting, stealing, barking or just lying in the sun, added their share to the prevailing din.

As Father Lacombe entered the camp he was greeted as an old friend and taken to some head man's lodge. There he was quickly filled in on the camp's adventures since the party had left St. Paul des Cris. As he could see from the drying racks, buffalo had been numerous and luck had been with them. Moreover, because of the way the buffalo were moving that year their prospects seemed bright.

As it turned out, the moving camp encountered another large herd within three or four days of his arrival, and once more, as he had done some fifteen years earlier, he witnessed another successful buffalo run. In his memoirs he recalled the outcome of the present hunt, writing: "Hundreds of buffalo lay dead on the prairie. They are cut up and the meat is brought to camp to the great joy of all, and to the supreme satisfaction of stomachs which will be filled with fat marrow, tongue, etc."

After the success of the hunt and the feasting which followed, Father Lacombe got in his work.

"And what do I do when appetites have been satisfied? I send an urchin to ring my little bell to call the children to catechism. Night has come and the sun is about to disappear behind the hills. Once more, the tinkle of my bell is heard. This time it is to invite all to night prayer. All are seated on the grass having the star studded sky for a roof to our House of Adoration. Silence reigns. The crows and other birds are

147

asleep in their nests. The wolves and foxes are sleeping in their lairs, but reasonable creatures are awake. Listen to the songs of gratitude and good night to the Great Spirit. Oh! but it is great and sublime to hear these hymns and prayers, these entreaties of the desert children, repeatedly echoed and re-echoed by the valleys and mountains, in the calm of night when all nature is at rest. And there in the midst of this happy crowd behold the 'blackrobe' presiding over this assembly of his neophytes. He seems eloquent in this tongue which he has learned from proud prairie warriors. 'Go, and sleep in peace, my children. May the Great Spirit bless you. Adieu till tomorrow.' "

Father Lacombe's estimate of his success with the camp of Crees could not help but be coloured by his enthusiasm. At last his hard work and sacrifice seemed to be making headway against paganism and, if deceived by appearances he overestimated the degree to which Christianity was taking hold of his wandering flock, who can blame him? But as many a man, including his rival John McDougall, had noted, the Indians were instinctively courteous. Because of that courteousness the natives had a propensity for saying what they thought their guests would like to hear. The average Indian, of course, was no less intelligent than the average white man, had no less imagination and was no less shrewd.

The result of this combination of qualities was that very often their seeming eagerness to fall in line with this new religion sprang from convictions only shallowly rooted. Many a time they were merely momentary enthusiasms stirred up by the missionaries' sincerity and salesmanship; frequently their acclaim of the white man's religion was also salesmanship on their part which was aimed at obtaining goods, trinkets or attention from the missionaries. Despite an understanding of native nature which led these men of the cloth to discount some of the Indians' protestations, the priests and preachers were often victimized. As we shall see later on, Father Lacombe could see how gullible were the McDougalls in letting the Indians impose on them, but was not so clear-sighted when his own leg was being pulled. Nevertheless, in the long view of the overall good the missionaries did, perhaps it was well that Father Lacombe and his associates and rivals chose to appear to be deceived by the Indians' blandishments.

Not all Indians, however, stooped to blandishments. Neither the medicine men nor those band leaders of a more perceptive turn of mind were easy to sway to the side of Christianity and these failed to fawn on the missionaries. The medicine men, often maligned by the missionaries and often misinterpreted in the white man's world as being mere frauds, were important members of any Indian tribe. Undoubtedly they had considerable knowledge of medicine in its physical sense and, by combining this with a more than average insight into psychology, were valuable and sometimes leading men in their tribes. Many of them were of a pronounced philosophical bent. Realizing that the new religion would undermine the practice of their profession, it was natural that they should be unfriendly to the preachers.

The natives were consistently religious. To them religion was not merely something to attend to at certain hours or on certain days but was part of their everyday life. It was woven into every one of their acts and thoughts. All creation — the sun, moon and stars, the weather and the seasons, rain and snow, daylight and dark, birds, animals and even trees — was inextricably interwoven with it. But above all these minor spirits, an Indian paid homage to a Great Spirit who ruled everything and possessed incomparable powers. Perhaps because of that outlook the Indians had a breadth of view in religious matters and were not so hidebound that they could not adopt elements of others' beliefs, including those of the white man.

It was this broad outlook that made them curious about Christianity, of which the Métis had been the first to tell them and in part had predisposed them towards Roman Catholicism. Too, the sublime and intricate forms of Catholic worship, including the sacrament of the mass, gave the priests some advantage over the more prosaic Protestants. Moreover, the business of baptism was a new wrinkle.

With all this in mind then, it was no wonder that the Crees listened attentively to Father Lacombe. For they found him a sensible man who in his turn listened patiently to their long-winded speeches and the often fanciful narration in which they clothed their tales of great deeds on the hunt or in war. If he ever became bored with these recitals he never let his disrespect show. When they were disposed to listen to him as a missionary, he talked; when they were not, he turned his talents to trying to help their sick people. And in all his intercourse with them they found him a man who inspired their liking and confidence. His sunburned, open, kindly face and his manner which reflected honesty and unqualified goodness, drew them to him. Indeed, by this time they were calling him *Ka-miyo-atchakwe* — the Man of the Beautiful Soul.

And well he had earned such acclaim. His ability to mix, his sincere love of ordinary people, white, red or Métis, as well as his natural longing for the open trail, fitted him well to earn this acclaim and for the task he had undertaken. With the panorama changing from day to day, views of slopes and valleys, humpy hills, meadows and trickling streams, how close he must have felt to his flock. How close too must have been his spiritual union with them and indeed their mutual union with the Great Spirit which had allowed him and them to enjoy this unblemished paradise.

Amidst this magnificent backdrop their life had to go on.

"And soon dawn and the rising sun appeared. We rise early. The horses are brought in. The women prepare breakfast. I say mass in my tent, and those who are not occupied come to it. According to orders received from the chiefs or captains of the camp, we will move camp in view of a new hunt if other herds of buffalo have been seen close by; or, we will remain where we are to give the women time to complete their work on the meat or hides."

Then one afternoon,

"The men were smoking their pipes in the shade of their tents. The youngsters were running about in the ravines or on the hillsides. The women were drying the meat or tanning the hides. I had assembled the children on a grassy hillock, and was teaching them catechism when the alarm was given. At the cry of 'The Blackfeet! — The Blackfeet' . . . the camp became terror-stricken. 'Make haste to prepare! The enemy! The enemy! We have seen them! . . . They are hiding behind the hills preparing to attack us under the cover of night!' This is repeated by all with certainty.

"I who had learned to know the tactics of the savages did not want to give in to these fears which I believed unfounded. But, when I saw the commotion I let my Indians prepare for the attack. They began by surrounding, or rather, covering the camp, by spreading out our hide tents to shut us off from the sight of our assailants. Within, each family, with the aid of its little axe and knives, dug a hole for the women and children. Our best horses were also sheltered. The men had their guns in position, ready to fire. I mounted my horse and rode around the camp speaking to my people and encouraging them to defend themselves well. Then, I cried out: 'On your knees! Act of Contrition!' . . . I gave general absolution."

In the midst of this alarm they waited through the long summer evening expecting an attack any moment. Finally,

"At midnight I went forth a certain distance from the camp to a hilltop, and there, shouted at the top of my voice in the Blackfoot tongue summoning them. . . . I named myself. . . . No answer. Day dawned. Cautiously we searched the surrounding thickets and discovered that some two hundred enemies had hidden there in view of attacking us before dawn. At the sound of my voice in the middle of the night they had fled. A few days later, when, accompanied by some Métis, I visited the Blackfeet, I was able to affirm our supposition. This circumstance, where, my presence and my words prevented a massacre, helped in no small way to increase the priest's influence among these barbarians."

But even that influence was not enough to persuade every Cree in the camp to accept the good father's religion.

"One fine Sunday morning in July, while I was preparing for mass, and putting order in my tent in view of this, I noticed a savage busy saddling his horse and preparing for the hunt. I went to him, though he was an infidel, and tried to dissuade him from his plans in telling him that this was the Lord's day, and, having a plentiful supply of meat, there was no need for hunting. He replied rudely enough that this was his affair; that for him this day was like any other ordinary day. And, he rode away. The day passed, and no one noticed his absence. As he had not returned at nightfall, his family became anxious and sent someone to look for him. It was useless. The darkness prevented them from making any discovery. The next day his horse was found with the saddle hanging under it. Immediately we supposed that misfortune had befallen him. In spite of all searches made, no clue was found as to his whereabouts."

So, amidst alarms, excitements and buffalo hunts, Father Lacombe passed some six weeks in the parklands and began to make ready to return to see how St. Paul des Cris was getting along, when they discovered the answer to the missing man's disappearance.

"One day in September, when the hunters came upon a large herd of buffalo, they noticed one strange looking animal among them. They felled it in a shot. Imagine their horror when they noticed a human spine entwined in this buffalo's horns, and dry human flesh stuck to the animal's hair. The explanation was easy. The unfortunate one, in pursuing this buffalo would have fallen from his horse in the midst of this herd of furious beasts, and, was run through by this animal's horns, taken up and carried off. Unable to rid itself of this burden by shaking its head, for a part of the summer the animal carried about a portion of the human remains, which gradually decomposed, leaving but bones caught in the horns. It was a terrible punishment, the narration of which I repeated many times when speaking on the observance of the Lord's day."

Not long after that, Father Lacombe went to visit his friends at Lac La Biche and then, returning by way of St. Paul des Cris, he went on to St. Albert by following the pack trail along the north side of the Saskatchewan River. At that time of year riding along that trail was sheer, unalloyed joy. For long stretches it followed the edges of large river flats a stone's throw from the water and then for reaches of a few miles took to the level table-land above. Invariably these yielded rewarding long vistas of the silvery stream making its way through the broad valley. For some miles it threaded its way through open jackpine groves where prairie chickens burst from the sandy path and, flapping and sailing, disappeared into the depths of the open woods. For a few miles here and there the horses padded their way through dense poplar forest to the accompaniment of retreating bush partridges pattering away on the thick carpet of September's yellow leaves. For its whole length of over a hundred miles from St. Paul des Cris to Fort Edmonton it was a continuous blaze of golden magnificence. After the clatter and clutter and stench of Cree camps, Father Lacombe savoured its soothing silence and solitude.

But even such a golden paradise could not be entirely flawless. And at the close of his first day's ride the devout father encountered its most serious flaw — the McDougalls' Victoria mission. As he wrote to his superior general, this was the third time he had seen this mission where the Wesleyans' "fanaticism had made very great expenditures to make their establishment important" and where by means of presents and promises they were seeking to subvert the Indians. Moreover, very recently the Hudson's Bay Company had built a post there and it was doing its part to draw the Crees closer to the clutches of *"le ministre et ses catéchistes."* That year, also, some thirty families of "English" half-breeds, that is, Protestant half-breeds, had left the Red River Settlement and in a body moved to Victoria where along the adjacent river flats they were building homes.

It had been partly to counteract the effect of the Victoria mission that Father Lacombe had started his St. Paul des Cris. Thereafter, while many Cree bands continued to congregate and camp on the flats near Victoria, many others came to the priest's mission. Thenceforth for some years, the duplication of missionary effort continued. During the summer of 1865 there was a remarkable, though entirely natural, parallel between John McDougall's exertions and Father Lacombe's. In the spring both had gone out to help the victims of scarlet fever and later both had spent nearly a couple of months out in the Cree camps. While there each must have known that his rival was with a nearby band, but if the two ever met in the field neither deigned to report the fact. Although John McDougall's writings are sometimes hard to follow, what he recorded of the Cree activities that summer gives us a clearer picture than the information left us by Father Lacombe.

About the time that Father Lacombe left St. Paul des Cris

to follow after his share of the Crees, John McDougall left Victoria to overtake Maskepatoon's camp. Somewhere along the river he caught up with that famous Methodist chief and accompanied his band out through the Birch Hills and south into the watershed of the Battle River. On the way Maskepatoon explained that they were heading for a rendezvous in the hills overlooking the big bend of Iron Creek, north of modern Sedgewick, where the Crees proposed to hold one of their customary thirst dances. This, the most solemn event of any year, was to be the usual occasion for the fulfilment of vows, for the more devout to make sacrifices and generally for all the Crees to meet the requirements of the faith of their fathers. Apparently neither priest nor preacher remained for the actual ceremonies during which the Indians sought to understand and follow the wishes of the Great Spirit.

Father Lacombe, however, returned to St. Albert about the beginning of October. He had enjoyed a zestful summer amongst his Crees, had baptized a gratifying number and had made a favourable impression on the remainder. Now it was time to try to duplicate that success with the Blackfoot. He was fully aware that dealing with these aloof warriors of the plains amidst snowdrifts would be a much more difficult task than influencing the more amenable Crees as they cantered over sun-drenched meadows aglow with roses and tiger lilies. Moreover, while his command of the Cree language had become exceptionally good, his knowledge of Blackfoot was rudimentary. The fact that he had left his trusty Alexis at St. Paul des Cris was another liability hard to overcome. To partially offset that he would carry his passport to the warriors' camps, his well-known identifying flag with its red cross on a white background. So, on October 23, 1865, putting his flag into his baggage, taking along his dogs and his snowshoes, he joined a party of Hudson's Bay Company men which was going to Rocky Mountain House.

There Richard Hardisty welcomed him much more ardently than he did a handful of Blackfoot who had come in to sell some pemmican. During the last few years all of the Blackfoot Confederacy had been troublesome to the traders. During the summer of 1865, while Father Lacombe had been wandering with the Crees, a band of the Blackfoot tribe had actually breached the defences of Fort Pitt. Apparently, more to show off their strength than to commence active hostilities, they had scaled the walls of that outpost, stolen whatever was not locked up and destroyed thirteen carts. Consequently, Hardisty at Rocky Mountain House treated them with scant civility. They were pleased to see Father Lacombe because some of them had met him when seven months earlier scarlet fever had laid hands on their camps. When they left Rocky Mountain House to rejoin their bands many miles east along the Red Deer River, they gladly took the priest with them.

Winter was tightening its grip on the land when he and his friends picked their way over an inch of snow on their six-day leisurely trip to the vicinity of the modern city of Red Deer. Ice was running in the Medicine and Blindman rivers when they crossed them and they were glad to reach the nearest camp, which Father Lacombe found to contain Piegans. They, like all the Blackfoot Confederacy, had spent the summer far out on the prairies but at the approach of winter followed their usual practice and retreated to the wooded areas along the upper Red Deer River and the Battle River. As was also customary, the Blackfoot tribe wintered the farthest north of any of the confederacy and this year, as in many a previous one, were scattered in small bands in the good buffalo hunting area of the valley of the Battle River.

After spending a couple of days with one band and two or three days with another, he completed his rounds of the Blood and Piegan camps. His unfamiliarity with the language was a definite drawback but he soon found a man who could speak Cree fluently and therefore could interpret for him. With his help he wrote out some prayers and hymns in Blackfoot. At the same time, he said, "I spent day and night studying the language."

Even in such good buffalo country as that east of Red Deer the camps now and then found themselves on short rations and during Father Lacombe's week or so of wanderings with the Bloods and Piegans he frequently went to sleep hungry. One night after he had left them to make his way north to the Blackfoot camp and had tramped all day in the snow and in the cold *"le plus piquant,"* he went to bed supperless. As he toiled onward the next day he fasted but at dusk came to a Blackfoot camp near the Battle River. There on December 3, 1865, he was welcomed and fed by his friend Natous or The Sun, who was sometimes called Three Suns.

According to his letter to his superior general, the Blackfoot tribe had three camps strung out along the northerly bend of that river from the vicinity of the present Samson Indian Reserve down towards Camrose; one of forty-five lodges, another of fifty and a third of sixty. Natous's camp, where the missionary looked forward to "relax a little after my long trip, to study the language and carry on my evangelistic mission," was the smallest of the three. His account of these camps is different from that given in Dempsey's *Crowfoot,* and since it is possible that he may not have been there long enough to be aware of all aspects of the situation, it may be as well to compare it with Dempsey's.

According to it, there were four camps; two large ones farther down the Battle River, as well as those of Natous (twenty-seven lodges) and Crowfoot (twenty-one lodges). Ever since his father's recent death, Natous's ascendancy to the chieftanship had caused friction in what up till then had been one band. At the time of Father Lacombe's visit, to avoid further trouble, the faction favouring Crowfoot's claim to the leadership had moved off and camped a few miles downstream from Three Ponds where Natous entertained the priest.

The fact that the band had split worried the priest because such small camps in such a frontier area were very vulnerable to attack and he advised them to reunite in case of attack from the Crees. They, of course, were thought to be over two hundred miles away in the area northeast of Beaverhill Lake, but that distance was an insignificant one for a well-fed war party to cover. More concerned with their internal strife than with this interloping magician's presumptuous advice, they ignored it and went about their business.

Next day after relieving his hunger with a good meal and his fatigue with a sound sleep, Father Lacombe busied himself with his usual religious duties. Natous's camp, of course, had been well-sited near wood and water and not far from a large stand of bush. Many of the men were away on a two- or three-day hunting trip but, after they had posted guards for the day and sent out the young men to keep an eye on the horses, those left in camp had little to do but lie around and talk. The women, however, were busy all day long cooking and scraping hides, hustling out to the pond to crack the ice to get their water or bustling back and forth to the clump of trees to snap off dry branches for fuel.

After the dusk of the short winter's day drew in, the father sat around the fire in Natous's lodge practicing his Blackfoot and discussing the affairs of the day. Eventually the visitors left and one by one all of Natous's family stretched out.

The fire had burned low and the cold, intensified by the breeze sifting across the snow, seeped into the tepee to which no light penetrated to relieve the gloom of the dark, stormy night in which neither moon nor stars showed. Though warmly clad, the priest found the cold keeping him awake. While he tossed and turned, listening to the regular breathing of the slumberers and remembering the comfort of his cosy cot on the farm at St. Sulpice, his mind kept returning to the nagging worry of how defenceless this camp was, separated from other camps and with half its men away hunting. It was a long time before he finally dropped off to sleep.

His awakening was to be much more abrupt.

"All of a sudden Natous jumped up, and as he seized his gun, he yelled mournfully: 'Assinaw! Assinaw! The Crees! The Crees!' He hadn't finished these cries when a terrible explosion was heard, and shots from every direction pierced our lodge."

With the terrifying cries of the attacking Crees and the slash of bullets ripping into their lodges, pandemonium swept the camp. Warriors, women and children rushed about. "My chief had thrown himself and his family out of his lodge and was yelling at the men to give up their lives courageously. The first shooting cracked off two of our lodge poles and flaming gun-wads fell at my feet. With the first attack our lodge was completely destroyed.

"I got up, without being too frightened, because for the last few days, I had expected what I saw. I snatched up my surplice and my cape and quickly put them on, I tied my shoes, then I kissed my cross, and gladly made a promise to God to sacrifice my life. I then hung at my side the bag containing the holy oil. During all this time the bullets whistled around my ears. Then I went out, turned towards the enemies, and tried to make myself heard and be recognized; but it was impossible, the tumult was at its height. One can't imagine the confusion at this time.

"Imagine a dark night, lit only by the sinister flash of burning gunpowder from the rapid volleys of Cree and Blackfoot guns; add to that the war cries, the chief's ordering and cheering on the young men, the desperate cries of the dying and the injured, the laments of the women and the crying of the children who did not know where to flee, the neighing of the horses and the muffled and continuous barking of the dogs."

In the pitch dark with the snow sifting through the camp, all this terror, confusion and death made up a black hell which even Father Lacombe found hard to describe. Death rattles, war cries and yells of unbridled passion swept the camp as the living fell over the dead and the wounded pleaded for help.

"When I saw that it was impossible to make myself heard by the Crees and to stop this nocturnal combat, I exhorted the chiefs to give up their lives courageously. Myself, I ran towards the dying and the injured. Those poor savages took my habit, clasped my hands, which they didn't want to let go, and said to me: 'Kimmo kinnan, djimo hikkat': 'take pity on us, pray for us.'

"The first victim which I found was a young woman who had been hit in the forehead by a bullet, as she came out of her lodge. As I was entering it, I trod on her blood-soaked body. I bent down immediately and asked if she wanted to die a Christian. With her nod, I seized a pot of water which fortunately was near by, and which I saw from the flash of light from the firing guns. I poured some water on her head and baptized her. A few minutes later the Crees swept into this woman's lodge and scalped her. They also killed a baby who was being nursed, which I hadn't seen even though he was in this same lodge. . . . Everything I possessed was taken and I don't know where they took them. Only my breviary was left. I was told an Assiniboine had already taken it, when a bullet knocked him down and he died near the bed in which I was resting just a few moments before. A Blackfoot who had noticed him, had jumped on him, scalped him and taken my breviary which he later returned to me."

The hell of this confusion, as fighting men swayed back and forth, lasted from about one o'clock till six in the morning. In the falling snow the Blackfoot, starting their defence with only sixty guns, fought convulsively against an overwhelming force of Crees, Assiniboines and Saulteaux. Three times during the long night the Crees surged into the camp. Three times they were repulsed, but with each onslaught more bodies crumpled on the snow. A couple of miles away Crowfoot, hearing the shooting, rushed his warriors to the rescue, but even with this addition to their forces the Blackfoot were badly outnumbered. By dawn half their camp had been destroyed.

When that dawn gave him some hope of being seen, Father Lacombe, holding his crucifix high and waving his red cross flag, made his way to the top of a rise whence he could look down towards the enemy lines. As they watched the black-robed medicine man mount the slope and yell to the Crees, his friends held their fire.

"Hear! You Crees. It is Ka-miyo-atchakwe who calls."

But the Crees did not hear this voice in their own tongue competing against the din and as yet the morning was too dark to see his flag. Bullets whizzed by him or smacked into the drifts near his feet. One, glancing off a stone, struck his shoulder and grazed his head. He staggered and fell full length in the snow. Two Blackfoot rushed up to carry him down to the dubious safety of their tepee.

But encouraged by his bravery and reinforced by Crowfoot's band, they made a last desperate sally and caved in the enemy's front. The Crees, momentarily disorganized, slackened their fire and, fearing a rout, backed up long enough to hear one of the Blackfoot shout, "Stop, you dogs. Have you not done enough? You have shot your blackrobe!"

Immediately, abashed at the thought of killing their Man of the Beautiful Soul, they fell back. The battle was over.

Back at the Blackfoot camp, Father Lacombe, rubbing his throbbing head, was already on his feet. His wound had turned out to be merely a bleeding scratch from a spent bullet. Amidst the desolation he was able to help bind up his friends' wounds. Natous's leg had been severely wounded but eventually he was to recover. Twelve Blackfoot men, women or children were past recovery. Many more suffered severe disablement. Two children had been carried away and some two hundred horses, including Father Lacombe's team, had been driven off. All of the camp's pemmican had been taken and half the lodges — about twenty-five — had been ripped to shreds.

The enemy had not escaped unscathed. When the Blackfoot had restored more order to their ravaged camp they found eight Cree corpses and word eventually reached them that, to save them from mutilation, twelve other enemy bodies had been borne from the field.

The Blackfoot estimated the number of their assailants as about a thousand but that is a combatant's calculation. Father Lacombe stated that the force was made up of Assiniboines, Saulteaux and Crees and that some had come from as far afield as the Lac La Biche country.

After the battle, Father Lacombe spent a few days consoling his friends, who gave him a horse with which he made his way to Rocky Mountain House. He rested there for a while and then, travelling in Richard Hardisty's cariole, reached Edmonton within a day or so of Christmas — a welcome present to his friends at the fort to whom the Crees had reported that he had been killed.

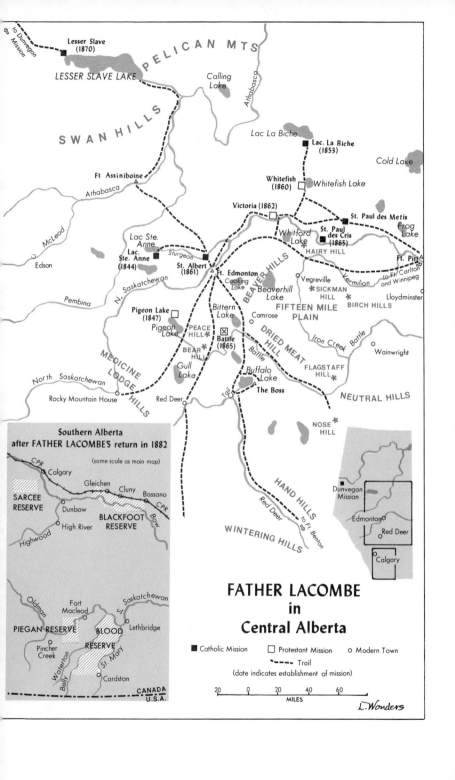

Lesser Slave (1870)

PELICAN MTS

LESSER SLAVE LAKE

Calling Lake

SWAN HILLS

Lac La Biche

Lac. La Biche (1853)

Cold Lake

Ft Assiniboine

Whitefish (1860)

Whitefish Lake

Athabasca

McLeod

Victoria (1862)

St. Paul des Metis

Frog Lake

Edson

Lac Ste. Anne

Lac. Ste. Anne (1844)

Sturgeon

St. Albert (1861)

Ft. Edmonton

Whitford Lake

St. Paul des Cris (1865)

HAIRY HILL

Ft. Pitt

to Ft. Carlton and Winnipeg

N. Saskatchewan

Cooking Lake

BEAVER HILLS

Vegreville

SICKMAN HILL

Vermilion

Lloydminster

Pembina

Pigeon Lake (1847)

Beaverhill Lake

FIFTEEN MILE PLAIN

BIRCH HILLS

Bittern Lake

Pigeon Lake

PEACE HILL

Battle (1865)

Camrose

DRIED MEAT HILL

Iron Creek

Battle

Wainwright

BEAR HILL

MEDICINE LODGE HILLS

Gull Lake

Battle

Buffalo Lake

FLAGSTAFF HILL

North Saskatchewan

Rocky Mountain House

Red Deer

Trail

The Boss

NEUTRAL HILLS

NOSE HILL

HAND HILLS

Red Deer

to Ft. Benton

WINTERING HILLS

Dunvegan Mission

Edmonton

Red Deer

Calgary

Southern Alberta
after FATHER LACOMBE'S return in 1882

(same scale as main map)

CPR

Calgary

Gleichen

Cluny

Bassano

SARCEE RESERVE

Dunbow

BLACKFOOT RESERVE

CPR

Bow

High River

Highwood

Oldman

Fort Macleod

S. Saskatchewan

PIEGAN RESERVE

BLOOD RESERVE

Lethbridge

Pincher Creek

St. Mary

Waterton

Belly

Cardston

CANADA
U.S.A.

FATHER LACOMBE
in
Central Alberta

■ Catholic Mission   ☐ Protestant Mission   ○ Modern Town

- - - - Trail

(date indicates establishment of mission)

20   0   20   40   60
MILES

L. Wonders

The house in St. Sulpice parish in which Albert Lacombe was born in 1827

The church of St. Sulpice, Quebec

Father Lacombe's mother

Father Lacombe as a young man

John Rowand

Father Lacombe's first church at St. Albert, erected in 1861

Father Constantin Scollen

Bishop Taché

...ishop Grandin

Father Leduc

Father Doucet

Father Rémas

Father Valentin Vegreville

Chief Factor William J. Christie

The Roman Catholic mission at Calgary, 1883, possibly Father Lacombe at left.

St. Boniface Cathedral and the "Turrets Twain"

St. Mary's Church and rectory, Calgary, 1886. From the left:
an unidentified Indian, Father Leduc, Father Foisey and Brother Little.

Father Lacombe's sister Christine Harnois, her husband and three sons raised after the family's diphtheria losses.

Father Lacombe and Jean L'Heureux in Ottawa with the chiefs..
Crowfoot centre, Red Crow on the right.

ather Lacombe and Lord Strathcona at Edmonton, September 1909

he Lacombe Home at Midnapore

Father Lacombe on his diamond jubilee as a priest

CHAPTER ELEVEN

"In Prairie Journeyings Often"
1866–69

The battle at Three Ponds spread Father Lacombe's reputation far and wide throughout the Blackfoot country and after that battle, no matter where he went, he was welcomed as *Arsous-kitsi-rarpi*, the Man of the Good Heart. Already, to the Crees, with whom he had spent much of the summer of 1865, he was *Ka-miyo-atchakwe*, the Man of the Beautiful Soul. Amongst all the plains tribes of Alberta and Saskatchewan he had become one of three or four white men whom all regarded as utterly unselfish.

For the next four years, "in journeyings oft," he continued to endear himself to all these tribes. Acclaimed in Cree camp, esteemed in Blackfoot lodges, applauded in the missions of Lac Ste. Anne, St. Albert and Lac La Biche and welcomed at Forts Edmonton, Pitt, Carlton and Rocky Mountain House, where Richard Hardisty had recently married the daughter of George McDougall, his tranquil, open countenance and his friendliness opened every door. These years when he was never tied down to any one spot, these years of perfect freedom to wander the wilderness purposely were undoubtedly the happiest of his eventful life. Without going into his thousands of miles of travelling by snowshoe or pack horse, we can select some highlights of this period.

In the middle of February 1866, he and Alexis set out to visit a number of small Cree camps spread through the thick forest well to the north. The pair's progress was slow and, of course,

177

involved camping in the open. Alongside their fire each night, covering themselves with buffalo robes, and, alternately napping, shivering and watching in awe the frosty sparkle of the myriads of stars that made up their roof, they endured till daylight.

On the second night as they lay hoping that sleep would soon come, Alexis heard what he took to be someone crying. When Father Lacombe concentrated, he too could hear eerie sobbing sounds most unusual in the silent forest. Leaving the fearful Alexis to cower in his robe, he went out to find the source of the moaning. Hurrying forward and stopping at a dead campfire, he found a young Cree woman cradling her baby in her arms and huddling in her blanket to spend what she believed would be her last night on earth.

Her husband had brought a second wife to his lodge and, unable to endure his harshness and her own humiliation, she had run away. For two days she had wandered and hungered and for two nights in her open camp with her freezing feet, she had whimpered to the unpitying stars. Calling Alexis and helping her over to his fire, the priest soon restored her will to live. When next evening he reached her people's camp with her and sought out the errant husband, not even his priestly scorn could induce him to take her back. A few days later Father Lacombe had Alexis take the mother and child to St. Albert where the sisters welcomed her to their home.

While he waited for Alexis to return, he heard that the Blackfoot were camped about fifteen miles away and that they were on their way north towards the Cree camp to avenge the humiliation of the December battle at Three Ponds. Hurrying out to meet them, he succeeded in persuading them to call off their expedition. Their respect for him had been so great and his arguments so convincing that they headed back towards the valley of the Battle River. Even then on his return to St. Paul des Cris on March 14 he wrote, "I do not know, and God only can know how long this peace will last."

By Palm Sunday he had traversed the miles that lay between his mission and Fort Pitt. As well as holding services there, he took the opportunity of having a start made on a log building dedicated to St. François Régis so that it would stand as witness to the fact that his church considered the area as under its aegis.

Within about a week he was back at St. Paul des Cris "celebrating the Resurrection of our Divine Saviour in the greatest poverty one could imagine. Chapel ornaments and everything poor, very poor. . . ."

During that spring, to take his last look at the poverty of his brother's mission, Gaspard Lacombe stopped for a day on his way back to the East. He had spent the previous panning season with a couple of gold miners not far from the Victoria mission. While he had been in the West he had helped his brother whenever he could, but having none of Albert's fervour he had no inclination towards missionary work. To him the very thought of sitting in a lousy skin garment gnawing frozen fish or dried meat or even pemmican helped to speed his return to the East, where for a few years he wandered happily if fruitlessly.

All summer long Father Lacombe travelled back and forth waving his red cross flag, tinkling his little bell and carrying the word to camp after camp. That fall a large aggregation of Bloods, Piegans and Blackfoot sent to Fort Edmonton to ask that a trading party be sent out to meet them. When the company responded by sending out thirty Red River carts under John Cunningham, the Indians were in such a haughty mood that they pillaged the party. It was only Crowfoot's intervention that permitted Cunningham and his men to escape with their lives and to take their empty carts with them.

Under such disheartening conditions and with an increasing outpouring of free traders' liquor leading to growing Blackfoot belligerency, Father Lacombe kept plugging away. While he continued to add more converts to his already long list and while he continued to enjoy his constant travelling, nevertheless, in a secular sense the results of his ministry had been discouraging.

It was with some relief, therefore, that during the fall of 1866 he received instructions to meet Bishop Grandin, coadjutor bishop of St. Boniface, at Fort Carlton the next spring and to proceed to St. Boniface with him. After a laborious trip the two clerical men received heroes' welcomes at the palace there. There too they learned the latest rumours about the progress being made in the discussions that some of the maritime colonies were having with Upper and Lower Canada. It was hoped that these discussions would lead to a confederation of all these colonies to which indeed the prairies of Rupert's Land might be annexed. With more and more Protestants from Ontario coming out to the settlement and a few of them actually coming out to farm, Bishop Taché was gravely concerned about the fate of the Métis and the future of the Catholic church in the West.

Most of these rumours originated across the river in the hamlet of Winnipeg, which was beginning to spring up around Fort Garry. As yet, without counting the Hudson's Bay Company employees, the village had a population of a mere two hundred people housed in a few stores and shacks. But it was a busy place with adventurous men filling its streets and saloons — men who could perceive opportunities which the Métis and the long established white settlers had failed to see. Already these opportunities had produced a newspaper and for the last eight years steamboats had been descending the Red River and docking near the mouth of the Assiniboine. Across the international boundary an American railway had been thrusting out towards the northwest and now ran as far as St. Cloud, less than four hundred miles away. From its terminus while Father Lacombe was at St. Boniface it was estimated that some two thousand Red River carts were kept busy hauling goods to the Red River Settlement. These carts and the newly-arrived American and Ontario businessmen they freighted for had all contributed in their own way to undermining the Hudson's Bay Company's authority and its long established system of law and order had practically broken down. The relatively stable fur-trade order was on its last legs.

While Father Lacombe was observing what was happening along the Red River in 1867 and wondering how long it would be before the civilization of saloons and brothels would flow westward across his prairies to Fort Edmonton, the balmy days of spring slipped by. When in June the leaves were fully out and a yellow blanket of buffalo beans overspread the prairies, he set out west once more. This time his caravan was led by Father Hippolyte Leduc, who was shepherding a bevy of five Grey Nuns along the first part of a long route which was to take them to Lac La Biche and on north into the Mackenzie River watershed. Parting from them at Fort Pitt, Father Lacombe hurried to St. Paul des Cris where he arrived in August.

There, still thinking about the rapid and disturbing changes that were taking place in the Red River Settlement, he determined to redouble his efforts amongst Cree and Blackfoot. The handwriting on the wall was becoming increasingly visible — the benefits of "civilization" were ready to burst over the prairies and he had so little time to prepare them for it. Even the Métis he met were concerned. During his absence and undoubtedly with the knowledge of his brother priests, the Métis of St. Albert had sent a delegation to see Chief Factor Christie at Edmonton and had expressed the wish that steps be taken to institute laws "among them for the good Government of the Colony etc. etc." He had told them to embody their thoughts in a petition to be presented to the governor of the company. The writer of the post's journal commented that they seemed well disposed towards the company but ended that day's entry by writing: "but there are no leading head men among them capable of laying hold of carrying out their plans."

As just one indication of the changes that were on their way, Father Lacombe, no stranger to Red River carts or freighting brigades, was surprised when a few days after his arrival the company's 1867 brigade of no less than eighty carts creaked along the trail. Year by year since in 1856 the Lac Ste. Anne Métis had returned from Fort Garry with carts and since in 1862 Father Lacombe had brought in the mission's first brigade, the volume of goods demanded by Fort Edmonton and the missions had increased considerably.

But it was camps that called Father Lacombe, not carts, and as soon as he could he set off south to find his Cree converts and to continue his catechizing. Once more he headed out through the parkland and for many a day made his way over miles of magnificent, unspoiled buffalo pasture. Day by day as he headed south past Birch Lake and around the Viking moraine, he saw recent signs of his Crees' passing and in the great southerly bend of the Battle River caught up with them. As the terrain rose and fell his course finally brought him right out into the bigness and the wideness and the strangeness of this vast land of waving grass.

It was not entirely new to him, for along many stretches of the Winnipeg trail he had crossed similar prairies. But then he had been in a Métis brigade hurrying along. Here, after he attached himself to the Cree lodges and lived and moved with these camps, crawling along through this land of ripening grass fringed with goldenrod and blue asters, he absorbed the full significance of this endlessly free land.

Slowly, living on the bounty of relatively small buffalo bands, they bore southeast, keeping an eye on Flagstaff Hill rising on their right. Finally crossing the Battle River they ascended the slope which would bring them to the Neutral Hills, a dim blue outline far ahead but with their western outlyer, the Nose Hill, standing out clearly. In this area they were treading on debated ground and as they moved the guards kept farther out and relays of messengers galloped back and forth to the main camp. For the Blackfoot also claimed this territory in much the same way that Flagstaff Hill, disappearing in the distance, was a favourite resort of the Sarcees.

One September evening as the camp Father Lacombe stayed with was sited by a pond which supplied moisture to a small surrounding copse of trees, he sat smoking a contented pipe with a score of older men. The leaves were turning yellow and as the sun was setting over a ridge, the priest and these old sages talked freely of their differing philosophies. Suddenly a small knot of horsemen topped a distant rise and in due course, after dropping into a draw, galloped up the long slope to the camp.

As they dashed into its midst, women, children and dogs gathered to receive them and Father Lacombe soon found out that this knot of galloping youths had been on a foray — a successful one against a small camp of Sarcees off to the west. As he and the elders walked over to hear of their adventure, the young men, still aflame with the excitement of victory, waved two matted scalps and unshackled a captive young woman still staring in horror at her husband's scalp and crying bitterly. Suddenly she saw the blackrobe — the Man of the Good Heart — and dashing to him, fell at his feet.

With all his humanity aroused, he instantly sought to help her and after hearing a fresh recital of the killings and the capture, extended his hand to this Sarcee woman who had sought his protection. There was only one way to help her — to take her under his own wing. As his mind raced to cope with the situation, his long-headedness mingled with his merciful instincts. Here was a young woman of the Sarcee, to all intents and purposes a member of the Blackfoot. What gratitude would fill Blackfoot breasts if he could return her unharmed to her tribe. What an impression he could make — what an entry to their hearts — if only he could carry out his good intentions. With these young men flushed with victory and particularly the one who was now her legal owner gloating in anticipation of how he would enjoy her, Father Lacombe knew he faced a dangerous prospect. But he knew that he must take the risk.

"Who owns this woman?" he asked.

"I do," replied the triumphant captor, "I killed her husband. I do."

"Well then I want you to give her to me."

"Give her to you? She's mine. I won her, I caught her, I want her."

And then laughing scornfully he continued, "Ah! you priest you! You say you never want women."

"Then," said Father Lacombe in later life as he recalled the incident, "I lost my temper. I was determined to have her and I berated her captor. For if you let an Indian be rude or too familiar with you he keeps on and you lose control of him.

"Bah! You say such a thing so stupid to me? Ha! You are a big brave man, you are so strong you catch this young woman. Bah! You know why I want her — to take her back to her people."

Nevertheless, the young man, on the defensive now, persisted. "I want her myself. Look at her. Is she not fine? I have no wife and nothing to buy one with and I want her."

Then, as Father Lacombe recalled, he turned on the crowd which, sensing an impending fight, was no longer laughing. "You Crees," he said, "do you not know me? Do you not come to me in your sickness and your sorrow? When the Blackfoot take your daughters and wives as prisoners do you not come to me for comfort? Now, I try to save one of their wives and you laugh and sneer. Alright! Alright! I warn you, when you are in trouble do not come to me. For I will tell you and I will tell God that the Crees have deserved all the bad they get. So do not come to me and cry for I say God has no pity on those who do wrong."

Diplomacy was all very well, but as he expected, his needed touch of anger and authority worked wonders.

Turning to the warrior he said, "You want goods to buy a wife — I will see that you get them. I will give you a horse and blankets and food."

The young man hesitated and the priest raised his offer. Finally, looking hungrily at the girl, the young man gave in.

"I was sorry for him, really," Father Lacombe reflected, "but I had to get her to take back to her people."

As a result, the following expenditure was later entered in the St. Paul des Cris journal.

"A Sarcee woman, captive of the Crees, bought for:

  1 horse, valued at 30 skins.
  1 Hudson's Bay wool blanket — 6 skins.
  1 Hat — 4 skins.
  1 Fringed sash, a large knife, a scarf and some sugar, tea and tobacco."

Once he had acquired her he left her in charge of a good Christian Cree family until shortly afterwards he left the natives and made his way back to St. Paul des Cris.

Soon after that he took her to St. Albert where the Sisters of Charity welcomed her. Thus far his plan, started with such risk, had gone well. The first acts of his little drama had been well played. Time, he was sure, would carry it to a happy ending.

On his way back through Fort Edmonton he spent a pleasant day or so with William Christie and arranged to have the blacksmith make some fittings for a new contraption he had in mind. His request for this service was gladly granted as were several favours which the fort could do for the missions. The miller there was expecting some loads of wheat to be brought over from St. Albert to be ground in the company's mill and he had acceded to the request of the good fathers of Lac La Biche that if they also sent over their wheat he would mill it.

Having placed his order for fittings, Father Lacombe hurried back to a bleak sojourn at St. Paul des Cris. There he kept himself busy obtaining many tanned buffalo hides and cutting twenty lodge poles in the grove of pines to the west. With the skins, the poles and the fittings, he was ready to assemble his portable house-tent which, when dragged along to an Indian camp by a team of horses, he could erect into a structure fifteen feet by twenty-five feet. He had also purchased a small iron heater so that when the curious Indians came into his tent — dare we call it a trailer? — he could preach and celebrate mass in relative comfort.

Finally on December 12, 1867, accompanied, of course, by Alexis and by an aged Blackfoot woman who went along to cook for the party and to help him improve his command of her language, he set out for a winter's mission in the parklands. When they made their way across the ridge to the Chain of Lakes near modern Two Hills they knew their food supply was precarious. Tending his sick Indians for two or three weeks at St. Paul des Cris had nearly exhausted the stock he had been saving.

For the time of year the snow was deep so that at the end of their second day the party had to camp somewhere in the vicinity of modern Vegreville. When they stopped Alexis saw a thin wisp of smoke coming from a clump of poplars not far ahead. Making their way over to it they found a couple of Cree families, eighteen persons in all, huddling, starving and miserable in two tepees. "Only skin and bones, almost starved — poor people. . . . So thin, and the children too weak to play or cry."

Their story was soon told; they had come down from far beyond the Saskatchewan River. Their hunting had been nearly fruitless, they had eaten their dogs and horses, had headed south to try to find their relatives or buffalo and now had come to the end of their tether. Camping beside them, Father Lacombe went through the motions of asking permission of Alexis and the Blackfoot woman — a permission readily granted — to feed the remaining five or six frozen fish and the bit of pemmican left in their own larder to these suffering people.

That help enabled the famished ones to plod along in the trail the father broke the next day while Alexis, ever alert for game, brought in one rabbit and one partridge. This food they cooked and divided amongst the children. Next morning more snow fell and through it for several more days the weary priest and his weakening party dragged their way across the hostile white expanse towards the faraway Battle River, where Father Lacombe expected to keep a rendezvous with a camp of his Cree people.

But while a few tepee poles standing starkly against the leaden sky showed where the camp had been, his friends were gone. The recent snow had covered their tracks and Father Lacombe and his bitterly disappointed, starving folk were ready to take the last desperate measure of killing one of his horses. To do so, however, would have frustrated all his winter's plans and he resolved to let it live one day longer.

Bright and early the next morning he sent his good Alexis out to hunt again. The father also put on his snowshoes,

> "and set out trusting in God. I am the only one with the strength to go ahead. But, I am weak, and at moments my mind goes blank, and my vision is blurred. Today, we ate, or rather, drank a broth made from old hide sacks and straps from old parchment skins. Alexis rejoins us at camp, but has only a few pieces of buffalo meat from a scabby, sick and dying buffalo which he killed. The sight and odor are repulsive. And, in spite of the fact, my savages quarrel to have of this distasteful bit that they have hardly cooked. I try to swallow a bit, but vomit it as quickly, for I can't stomach it. I was reluctantly planning on killing my horses; I would need them so for my winter's travels. But, that is over, and we can wait no longer. It is now ten days that we are suffering from hunger, and with that, the cold and deep snow, and no other shelter but our poor covers, and exhaustion from constant walking. Tomorrow, Sunday, we will kill one horse if we do not come upon the camp."

Long years later, thinking back to this experience, the aging father wrote:

> "My dear friends, and all you who are seated at a table covered with appetizing food when you need it, let me tell you how sad and torturing it is to be hungry in circumstances such as I have just described. Till then, in my sermons and instructions to lazy Indians I had oft' times repeatedly proclaimed that he who does not want to work should not eat. But now, after such an experience I have changed my mind, and, am resolved that from now on I will share my bit with my hungry brother. It is only after having felt the pangs of hunger that one really understands the Father's words, 'I was hungry and you gave me to eat.'
>
> "Then the Lord's day dawned. This clear sunny day per-

mits of our seeing into the distance. We are not mistaken! It is the camp! Our spirits rise. A few hours later I am with my Christians who have plenty of buffalo meat. They eagerly come to our rescue, but we must be prudent, for, after such a long fast it would be dangerous to load our stomachs with solid food. After two days of dieting on broth, we can eat as the others, and devour quantities of tongue, hump, and fat side dishes!"

Father Lacombe and Alexis had no sooner recovered from their ordeal than Christmas was upon them. With his roomy tent pitched in the afternoon shadow of Nose Hill, he was able to celebrate this great religious feast on the prairies for the first time.

"Hail, lovely Christmas night! For the first time our cold prairie and our people will witness this anniversary. . . . Firstly, confessions for those who have already made their first communion. At midnight, the first mass, only for the men. . . . Having vested, I announce that the feast has begun. . . . I am so happy and moved that my heart seems ready to burst. A few more minutes and the Infant Jesus is in our midst. *Tasay Manito Awasis:* 'He is Born, the King Divine.' In truth my uncouth shepherds sing like angels. . . . Ah! Your beautiful churches, your cloth of gold vestments, your organs, and orchestras, do not promote more heart-felt devotion than do our Indian hymns and prayers. *Gloria in excelsis!* Now my beloved shepherds go, and smoke your Christmas pipe full and rest.

"It is three o'clock. Time for the mass of dawn for the women and the not to be forgotten babies! 'Sing, my good women. The white people call you squaws, but, you are the wives of our noble warriors and hunters of the prairie desert, and consequently, you are the queens of the prairies. . . .'

"At ten o'clock it is time for the third mass which is attended by our youths of both sexes. In the evening the tent-chapel is filled to capacity. The chief, Wikaskokiseyin [Sweet Grass], though not yet a catechumen, is there in the midst of his people."

Throughout the celebration, illustrating the courtesy and tolerance of the Indians, the prominent Chief Sweet Grass, though still an unbeliever and one who also listened to John McDougall, was there to rejoice with the black-robed father.

For several weeks in the heart of the winter in Sweet Grass's camp and in others, Father Lacombe continued his ministry. Occasionally his entourage returned to St. Albert or St. Paul des Cris and during March 1868 spent about three weeks at Rocky Mountain House. Starting in the spring Father A. André went to reside at St. Paul des Cris to enable Father Lacombe to continue his incessant coursing over the prairies and to free his hand to set the stage for the coup de grâce he had been planning ever since he had taken the Sarcee girl under his wing. It would have been relatively simple to have sent word of the girl's rescue to her people, or indeed, to despatch Alexis to take her back to them, but if he had done that the Sarcees would have been grateful and would have remembered the event for a few weeks. By adding a touch of drama to her delivery they would talk about it for years.

So when he was ready he called on the Sisters of Charity at St. Albert and picked her up. They had found her an exceptionally fine woman, had bestowed on her the name of Marguerite, and had become so fond of her that they tried to dissuade the black-robed venturer from taking her away.

But with his innate feel for a dramatic situation, he persisted in his plan and, along with Alexis and the Blackfoot woman, started off south. For many days they travelled, meeting a few Crees and Blackfoot here and there, until finally, looking across a broad, shallow valley, Marguerite was able to make out a distant camp which she thought might be that of her own Sarcee people. Approaching it slowly the priest's procession stopped, set up a tent and raised the well-known red cross flag. Assured by seeing it flickering in the breeze about half the members of the small Indian band, warriors, women and half-grown boys, started out to greet the Man of the Good Heart.

When they were near enough Marguerite was able to identify them as Sarcees — her people. Ordering her to hide in the tent, Father Lacombe watched them with a mixture of excitement and chagrin.

"They come," thought he, "not because they want or believe in my religion. They come out of curiosity, for something to do. Fortunately, however, they come because they do like me and maybe in the end their kindness to me may be turned to good account."

Once this small mob had dismounted and were crowding around him, he noticed by the black paint on some of their faces and by the cut of their hair that a few of the band were in mourning. Restraining his eagerness, he asked why they mourned.

"Last fall," they said, "over near Flagstaff Hill a band of Crees caught a handful of our people, killed two young men and ran off with one of their wives. We mourn for these."

"Didn't you pursue the Crees and try to take your woman back?"

"We sent out men — I am her brother — I went out, but the Crees were too clever for us and we never found her. Maybe she is dead. See, there is her mother who mourns daily. But we will never see her again."

"Never again? Are you sure?"

Then rising to the drama of the moment, he shouted, "Marguerite, come here!"

As the tent flap opened and Marguerite, healthy, strong and active, ran towards them, they fell back in disbelief. But in a moment she caught up her crying mother in her arms and they came to realize that it was true — in effect, Marguerite had been brought back from the dead. Surrounding Father Lacombe they bore him in triumph to their main camp. It was, as he said, "an ineffable moment." Step by step he was building a reputation with these associates of the belligerent Blackfoot and one which must surely open their doors to his teachings, if only by a crack.

On this occasion he was doing a favour to an ally of the Blackfoot. Before the summer was over, however, he found himself in a Cree camp doing them a favour — in fact, successfully warding off a Blackfoot attack much as he had done about two years previously. And so, now in a Blackfoot, Blood or Sarcee camp, and then in a Cree camp, he seesawed his services back and forth, ever busy and ever mentally bemoaning his lack of ability to do more.

Then for a brief spell he returned to St. Albert to prepare a celebration to welcome Bishop Grandin, who as not only the coadjutor to Bishop Taché at St. Boniface but also the newly appointed Oblate superior of all the missions in the Saskatchewan watershed, was coming for a stay of four months. On his way back through Fort Edmonton Father Lacombe induced William Christie to do him a favour which resulted in the post's journal commenting: "Cath. mission got the loan of one of the Cannons."

Having overseen the preparations for the great event, Father Lacombe hastened back to St. Paul des Cris where he and seven other priests awaited the arrival of the bishop's carts. Then the eight of them, eight priests whose names will ever shine in the history of the Order of Mary Immaculate in western Canada — André, Gasté, Lacombe, Leduc, Legoff, Moulin, Rémas and Vegreville — accompanied him to St. Albert. Three miles before he reached there a cheering phalanx of Métis horsemen surrounded him and then fell in behind to swell the procession.

On October 26, 1868, after crossing Father Lacombe's bridge and ascending the rise, the bishop drove under an arch of evergreens and sheaves erected in his honour. As he did so, salvos of musketry greeted him and undoubtedly Father Lacombe's cannon roaring out its welcome rocked the very valley walls. Never till that time had the mission seen such an exhibition of sentiment, such enthusiasm and such loyalty.

Once the celebration was over Father Lacombe showed the bishop one of his projects which he was still in the process of perfecting — his Catholic ladder. For a long time he and other priests had considered a pictorial method of telling the Bible stories to the Indians. The late Father Darveau, who had lost his life in the service at Le Pas, had taken up Father Blanchet's idea of using a chronological ladder, but little came of it until Father Lacombe focussed his abilities on it. In 1865 he had written Bishop Taché, stating that, "last summer I made a 'Catholic Ladder' which is very popular with the Indians and is of great assistance to me."

Like all of us do, he borrowed ideas, in this case from fellow priests, just as one priest borrowed from others in preparing dictionaries. Any priest struggling to learn one of the native languages made rough notes to aid his memory. With some, these notes assumed major proportions and when another priest came to aid or replace him he gave the newcomer his notes leading to native dictionaries or grammars. Father Lacombe, too, made use of his predecessors' dictionaries, but being of a more assiduous and determined mould than most, he carried his studies on until his linguistic works saw the light of day as printed dictionaries.

Being of that mould he persisted with his ladder. "I could draw a garden with a snake twisted around a tree. For a flood, that would be simple, a ship and a dove. And for the birth of Christ, a manger," and so on. Accordingly, he took a buffalo robe, nailed it up in front of the Indians and, drawing as he talked, he illustrated his Bible stories. By the time he showed it to Bishop Grandin his ladder had become a definite part of his teachings. Later on, as he had time, he drew a careful copy of it and finally succeeded in having it published. For the production of this ladder he was to be justly acclaimed. The acclaim, however, lay more in the persistence with which he followed his idea through to production than in the idea which, after all, had occurred to others.

After a few weeks' stay at St. Albert, the energetic priest, rolling up his ladder and loading up his tent, set out early in December 1868 for a three-months' visit to the Crees. During that period only one major success marked his progress through the camps.

Once, when a guest in Sweet Grass's tepee, he was taken to see a young warrior who to all appearances would fight no more. His hand had been badly mangled and he had cut it off and bound up the stump with a dirty thong. Infection had set in and when Father Lacombe saw him he was aghast at the way in which it had spread up the man's arm from the mass of swollen, rotting flesh bound up so tightly. The very sight of it repelled him and he felt certain that the man's agony would not last more than a day or so before death ended it.

Knowing how much Sweet Grass was hoping that his magic could effect a cure but feeling it hopeless to try, he nevertheless decided to delve into the swollen stump and cut the restraining thong. Carefully studying the anatomy of his own wrist, asking the chief to hold the stump steady and advising the young man to turn his head away, he cut with his razor. Fortunately he aimed well and severed the cord. As blood and matter gushed out, he trimmed the swollen stump, seared the wound with nitrate of silver — one of the few medical aids traders and missionaries usually carried — and covered it with a homemade ointment of balm of Gilead. After he had tended the wound for a few days it healed. Thenceforth another miracle was added to the lengthening list the kindly missionary had performed.

After wandering with the Crees during the depths of the winter, Father Lacombe returned to St. Paul des Cris on February 27, 1869. There he found Bishop Grandin and Father Vegreville discussing the possibility of cutting freight costs by bringing in the supplies needed for the St. Albert mission from the south — by way of the Missouri River. During the preceding four or five years great changes had been taking place in Montana as new mines were discovered and hundreds of men came in to prospect for others. These men and the supplies they required came up the Missouri as far as Fort Benton in steamboats and continued their way west by pack horses or freighting wagons. As a result, Fort Benton grew into an important distributing point.

To it came a number of fur traders who, by making their wares and their liquor easily available to the Blackfoot tribes, began luring them away from the Hudson's Bay Company. Achieving considerable success they pushed their trade north and began rolling wagonloads of whisky over the open prairies to supply Blackfoot camps along the Oldman River. At the time when Bishop Grandin, Father Vegreville and Father Lacombe were sitting in St. Paul des Cris discussing the new idea of sending carts south to the Missouri, some of Fort Benton's traders were talking of following their previous wagon tracks north to establish a trading post near modern Lethbridge. Times were changing and since the forward-looking Oblate missionaries were usually abreast of the times, or actually ahead of them, Bishop Grandin decided to try out this new idea.

He had also decided who was to test the scheme — the enterprising Father Albert Lacombe. For, without doubt, of all the far western priests, he was the most versatile. When any new idea was being discussed he usually had some good suggestions to make. And almost invariably, whenever he opened his mouth to do so, someone shoved a new job into it. Thus it came about that he started out on another trip from which his missions might benefit materially and on which he could work off the wanderlust from which so many of his accomplishments and so much of his happiness sprang. The purpose of this trip, however, was not to bring in supplies but to find out how practical it would be to do that in the future. Not entirely incidental to it was the further inducement that when he reached the Missouri River he could continue east until once more, after an absence of seventeen years, he could visit St. Sulpice.

Before it was time to leave, however, he had several minor trips to make to Indian camps and to St. Albert. Less than a month after he had left the Crees to return to St. Paul des Cris, warfare had flared up again and the Blackfoot had killed their great Chief Maskepatoon. While he was one of the Methodist converts, Father Lacombe had known him as an outstanding leader and regretted his untimely death.

About the same time as he heard this bad news, he and a fellow priest were returning to St. Paul des Cris with a one-horse cart when their horse fell seriously lame. Fortunately John McDougall overtook them and seeing their plight turned his saddle horse over to them and then walked the rest of the way to Victoria. Though the priests and the parsons seldom had a good word to say for each other, they were, after all, men of kindness and integrity, fighting a common battle. The exchange of such courtesies flowed both ways as when, for instance, about three years earlier the missionaries at St. Albert sold McDougall two hens and a rooster to start his own flock at Victoria and when on another occasion he was able to purchase seed wheat from the mission at Lac La Biche.

It was not till the end of May 1869 that Father Lacombe, excited over the prospect of penetrating to the very heart of the prairies, set out south. He was accompanied by three Métis who, like himself, were mounted on good steeds and who took turns leading their one other horse harnessed to a cart. Spring had come and the Indians' "mother earth" was bare and the freshness of green leaves scented the air.

"After having crossed the first valleys, hills and slopes covered today, by the cities, the villages, the ranches near or dotted along the railroad, we made a glorious entry into the sea and ocean of the prairies. Although at a great distance of sometimes 60 miles, we were close to the Rocky Mountains which every day was a magnificent sight to see. . . . The hills, the lengths of the slopes, the shadows in the valleys, the horizon, where huge herds of buffalo appear, are in your imagination the motion of a real ocean. Sitting on my pony, day dreaming as I wound my way every day, I was tempted to imagine myself at sea."

When camping on the prairies, the party had to

"choose a low spot so that the smoke from our fire would not attract the attention of the war parties or of the *coureurs des prairies* who would steal some horses or attack the exhausted traveller by surprise while he slept. We did not have to look for fire wood to cook our food as combustible material did not exist, except the buffalo dung.

"A more important question was to find water for ourselves and our horses. Often we did not find rivers or lakes and sometimes we had to be satisfied with slough water in which case we had an unpleasant smelling liquid. That is why we generally carried drinking water with us, filling a barrel before leaving our camp. One very hot day, we neglected to take this precaution, hoping to find water in the evening. But here is the evening and the darkness! We must camp without water. One of my companions had just killed a buffalo. Our horses seemed to sigh and ask what they could drink.

"Although it was dark, I started to roam the hills and ravines. All of a sudden my feet splashed into a slough where the buffalo had just stirred the mud. With my hand I filled my little kettle. I returned to camp. My men, when they smelled this water, couldn't help but exclaim that it was undrinkable, it was like poison. We tried to make tea, but it was even worse. We go to the carcass of the buffalo which had been killed, to get some blood which my companions drink even though they do so with revulsion. I couldn't swallow this drink which I threw up, even though I tried not to. We had to pass the night suffering from our great thirst. I gather from this experience that death from thirst is certainly much more painful than death from hunger."

After several days the little party found itself passing between the Sweet Grass Hills on their left and what at times seemed to resemble a cathedral, Chief Mountain, on their right.

Finally on the bank of the Missouri River Father Lacombe came to a "sort of village and several steamboats. . . . We had left Edmonton fourteen days ago."

Fort Benton, where I. G. Baker's log store was the largest building, was a busy place filled with shrewd merchants, roughnecks, roustabouts, traders, Métis and some Indians. There Captain Rae of the sternwheeler *Silver Bow* offered him free passage to St. Louis, Missouri. To meet his other requirements several traders, including John J. Healy, presented him with a purseful of American dollars. We do not know whether or not John J. told him that even as he helped the adventurous priest he was on the point of sending off a party to help the Blackfoot by starting the first whisky trading post on Alberta's St. Mary River, which was soon to be known as Fort Whoop-Up.

From Fort Benton he was able to travel by public transport all the way to Montreal. He found the progress of the *Silver Bow* down the river fascinating. For, along all the trip to St. Louis the Missouri River sped them through the heart of the American prairies, the home of endless thousands of buffalo. As Father Lacombe was to say:

"Imagine our boat, steaming into the midst of the bison crazed by the shrieks and whistling of the steam-engine and the reports of rifles and revolvers. Imagine the tumult caused by such encounters! The water was sometimes red with blood, which flowed in streams from the bodies of the poor victims massacred only for the pleasure of killing them."

When the sternwheeler swung around one of the large bends some fifty miles upstream from modern Bismarck, North Dakota, he must have recalled the time in 1851 when he and his Métis had been near this part of the river where the Dogden Butte lay some forty miles to the north. He had been near it when word came of the famous fight to which he had galloped to support the other party.

Shortly before the steamboat docked his fellow passengers passed around the hat and when the money collected was added to what his friends at Fort Benton had given him he found his wallet bulging with $300 — ample funds to take him to Montreal. For a few days, however, he enjoyed the hospitality of the Jesuit fathers at St. Louis and recalled that from this base in

1845 the famous Father De Smet had made his trip to Fort Edmonton.

By the way he had come through the United States, Father Lacombe had been able to use public transportation all the way from Fort Benton. The fact that it was farther west than Fort Pitt, through which he had passed so many times by dog team or Red River cart, indicated how far behind the Canadian prairies were in the matter of public transport. It was no wonder, then, that Bishop Grandin had sent him to see if his missions could not ease their burden by bringing in supplies by way of this American route.

As he left St. Louis to continue east by public conveyance he nevertheless gave little thought to that problem. For on his long trip to Montreal, in contrast to his method of travel west seventeen years earlier, he sped along quickly and easily. In a matter of days instead of months he found himself entering Bishop Bourget's palace.

There, of course, he was met with the extraordinary kindness that was so much a part of the reception of one priest by others. But even then he was unprepared for the welcome they gave him. For they treated him as a hero. Had he not been away in the wilds for seventeen years, had he not worked wonders there, had he not been wounded in an Indian battle and had he not become the very epitome of what a missionary priest should be?

At Fort Edmonton and at St. Albert he had not given the matter much thought. There he had been regarded as a man and as such had taken his place amongst men. Here in Montreal he was acclaimed as a hero. His fame had flown before him.

No man is ever averse to being regarded as a hero and because of that streak in his character which Father Rémas had once noted — his desire to have others like him — he found himself well pleased. Here in Montreal where people and priests clamoured to see him, he found it hard to prevent a touch of complacency from creeping in to sit beside his humility. He had never thought of himself as a hero, but here that role was being thrust on him and it began to occur to him that filling such a role could pay dividends for his missions and for his fellow Oblates in the West. So, even though he fought back the deadly sin of pride, the matter of hero worship was beyond his control.

Moreover, only good could come to the western missions if in all of Quebec his name had become a symbol of all that was devout and good about the work of the prairie priests.

If in Montreal he had become famous, he was much more so in L'Assomption and St. Sulpice. In his old school, of course, his tutors not only greeted him fondly, but held him up as a glorious example. So too did the people of his home parish. For there he was one of their own neighbourhood boys who had returned full of fame.

But it was to his mother that he rushed, his mother who long ago had piled sacrifice upon sacrifice so that he might become a priest. In her arms once more he was her little child she had not seen for seventeen years. As she noted his strong face and observed the confidence of his compelling personality she knew herself to be doubly blessed in this her first-born son.

While she was studying him, he was observing her, white-haired now and in her late sixties. His father had died a year previously. Now that her other son Gaspard had left home and also all her daughters except Christine, her youngest, she was left to keep house in what had once been such a busy home. It was time to relieve her of the cares of the farm which was at the point of passing out of the hands of the direct Lacombe line.

As mother and devoted son discussed her affairs, they decided that it was best for her to retire to the comfort of the Grey Nuns' convent in Montreal. As for Christine, a young woman who in many ways resembled her brother, she rose to the occasion and accepted his challenge to go west with him to teach in one or other of his faraway institutions.

Having settled these domestic affairs and having returned to Montreal for a few days, he soon found its crowds and its busyness tiring and longed to get back to his work with his Indians. On his trip west with Christine he was able to avail himself of steamboat or rail accommodation as far as St. Cloud, Minnesota, and about the end of October after a long cart trip he reached St. Paul des Cris. There he arranged for Christine to stay with a kindly Canadian woman while she became acclimatized. Then he hurried on to St. Albert to advise Bishop Grandin against trying to bring in goods by way of Fort Benton. After that he was free once more to start making the rounds of his many Indian bands.

CHAPTER TWELVE

Smallpox
1870—72

Eighteen-seventy was a bitter year. Displays of the simmering Indian unrest against the white man could have erupted into serious incidents had not intertribal warfare and the nearly inconceivable devastation of smallpox drawn a veil of mourning over its latter half.

Through it all Father Lacombe played a manful part. When, during the fall of 1869, he had returned to Fort Edmonton by way of St. Boniface, it was all too evident that his old Métis friends there were being harassed to the point of oiling their guns. As yet they had not had to dig gun pits as they had done that fearful morning in 1851 when they had humbled the Sioux. But circumstances involving the transfer of their ancestral lands to the new confederation of Canada were driving them in that direction. Moreover, they had communicated their fears and spoken of their unrest to the Crees and Assiniboines as well as to their thinly spread confreres as far west as Lac Ste. Anne.

At Fort Pitt and Fort Carlton and even at Fort Edmonton the Hudson's Bay Company officers were worried when, about the end of 1869, word came that in October the Métis of the Red River Settlement had started their armed resistance to what they regarded as oppression. At Fort Edmonton William Christie sought the advice of Father Lacombe and Father André and of the Reverends George and John McDougall. As a result of these discussions and in an endeavour to keep the Cree and

Assiniboine camps calm, all the missionaries went out to visit various bands. Father Lacombe, for instance, made at least two trips through the country between Edmonton and Rocky Mountain House. To what extent their influence prevailed we can only guess, but the Indians, though muttering all the while, did not join the cause of the Red River Métis. Probably they were too involved in their own fights to take on any more enemies.

For instance, the Fort Edmonton journal for January 15, 1870, reported that:

"two Circees, who have been hanging on here (after two Cree women) since the 23rd Decr. were brutally murdered on Thursday night by 'Takootch' his brothers Mettchinn & chatoose & Big Crow & Ska Pew being present, they persuaded the Circees to go away & pretended to see them safe across & when on the Hill across shot them. The Circees had no arms at all. We had the bodies buried, but they were subsequently dug up stripped & scalped by the Stone Indians & scalp dance performed. The women who were cohabiting with them made to dance with the scalps."

A few weeks after that Father Lacombe, making a circuit of the nearby Blackfoot camps, came to a small band with which he spent three weeks teaching, catechizing and studying the language. When he left to make his way to Rocky Mountain House this little group was on the point of going to Fort Edmonton to trade. Although he advised them against thus taking their lives in their hands, they persisted and carried their pemmican into the fort. Their presence there worried the Hudson's Bay Company men, who, as the Blackfoot left the fort, assembled a large band of Métis to guard them. Their efforts were of no avail as the journal for April 7 explains.

"Four men keeping watch — lots of Indians sneaking about to have a shot at the Blackfoot. Got all the French halfbreeds about with their best men at their head, more than 40 men all well armed to escort Blackfoot safe away. Got a lot of the best Indians, also to promise to stop their young men. They made a start and when the poor Blackfeet were on the hill across, they commenced firing on them rushing them from the bushes and from every side. The halfbreeds did nothing.

They stood to one side and let the Stoneys and Crees and Blackfeet fight away. There were near a hundred Stoneys and Crees and all sorts. They killed only 2 men and 3 women and a child. The rest of the poor Blackfeet escaped, say 6 men and 3 women and 2 boys. There were 13 souls in all came here and 6 were killed, 7 escaping. . . . Murdered, scalped and cut to pieces with all the brutality characteristic of savages and the bodies left naked and exposed . . . these wretches almost ten to one came back as they think, covered with glory."

Unfortunately the Métis had no love for the Blackfoot and as Captain William Francis Butler, who had been involved in the Wolseley expedition to the Red River Settlement and then had come on to Edmonton, wrote, "This guard, composed of French half-breeds from St. Albert, opened up to right and left when the attack commenced, and did nothing towards saving the lives of the Blackfeet, who were nearly all killed or wounded. . . ."

On April 9, Father Lacombe, who was coming in from Rocky Mountain House, met the dispirited remnants of these luckless Blackfoot who had not eaten anything for three days and were floundering along almost barefoot in the melting snow and ice. He tended their wounds, gave them all the food he had and then, lending them his two horses, started afoot for the fort, a tramp of twenty-five miles through the slush.

When the news of this killing reached their main camp, the Blackfoot organized a large force and sent it to retaliate on any Crees, Assiniboines or Métis they might catch. Many of its warriors were also anxious for an excuse to sack the fort. Knowing that such a party would soon arrive, Chief Factor William Christie put the post in a posture of defence, closed all the gates, primed the cannons, ordered all his staff to be ready for an attack and waited.

His wait was a short one. On Thursday, April 21, "the 11 men who left this on Tuesday for the Rocky Mtn House to assist to bring down Returns, came back here in all haste yesterday . . . & gave us notice of their [the Blackfoot] coming & that they had met them & were nearly being killed by them & that they were saved by the interference of some of the chiefs."

About the same time, the Methodists, the Reverend Peter Campbell and George McDougall's trader son David, accompanied by William Rowland, a company man, were coming in from Pigeon Lake. "Before all their things were got across, a large war party of Blackfeet arrived from the Hill & came down to the river & took possession of what property was left on the beach across while the skiff was taking a load across."

That evening while this was going on, William Christie took two decisive steps. First, he sent a messenger hurrying to St. Albert to ask that a large force of Métis be sent to his aid and to request Father Lacombe to come to supplement the fort's guns by exercising his persuasive powers on the Blackfoot. Though it was late in the evening, the father assembled thirty Métis and in the pitch darkness of the spring night galloped across the eight miles to the fort's rescue.

Meanwhile, the corpulent Christie had been taking his second defensive step and was about to gird himself for the fight by donning his wide sword belt, which he had not worn for many a year. Thereby he provided a moment of laughter that helped to cut the tension. Due to his increased girth, it took all the tugging and pinching that Malcolm Groat and Harrison Young could do to squeeze his fat figure into the outgrown belt.

All the while that the Blackfoot were destroying, devouring or otherwise appropriating the goods in the captured carts, they also lobbed many a bullet at the fort across the river. Most fell short, some smashed into the palisades and a few cleared the walls to bury themselves in the muddy courtyard. "All hands were on watch all night. . . . Gates of Fort all closed, bastions manned etc. etc."

That night the gates remained closed except when on three occasions they creaked open to let Father Lacombe through. Splattered with mud from galloping hooves but as cheerful and confident as ever, he arrived about midnight and his entry aroused new courage in the hearts of the defenders. Then, having sized up the situation, he declared that he could do no good cooped up in the fort. He must get out where the Blackfoot across the river or any who would be hovering about would hear him — he would walk around outside to call to them. Had he not done the same thing a couple of years ago when by similar action he had averted an attack on a camp of his Crees?

Fearing for his safety, William Christie, sword and all, let him out and the priest began his lonely perambulations of the river's dark bank. Calling out in passable Blackfoot that he was their *Arsous-kitsi-rarpi,* who had so recently visited their camps and had helped the victims of Cree brutality, he made his appeal. Explaining that he and all the white men in the fort were their friends and that they were enraged at the Crees' perfidy, he asked them to go away peaceably. Eventually after getting no response from the would-be attackers, he re-entered the fort. In the morning the journalist was able to report: "The Blackfeet did not cross last night and none to be seen today."

Thus, due to his courage and the respect in which the Blackfoot held him, he deflected what otherwise might have been a major attack on the fort. His night's work had repaid the Hudson's Bay Company for many of the kindnesses it had extended to him.

By the time that affair was over spring was well on the way and Father Lacombe was eager to be off on another trip. Gladly complying with the request of Bishop Faraud of the Athabasca-Mackenzie diocese, he went to visit Father Tissier at Dunvegan. Being at the extreme western end of that diocese, the isolated priest had not seen one of his clerical comrades for nearly five years. Father Lacombe and his combined guide and canoeman took pack horses to Fort Assiniboine and thence by the same water route and portage he had taken fifteen years earlier finally reached Father Tissier's humble shack on the bank of the majestic Peace River.

We can only imagine the joy the latter must have felt at Lacombe's arrival. It had been a hard winter. He had run short of supplies and altar wine and had journeyed to Carcajou Point, two hundred miles down the river, to obtain more. He had frozen both feet and had lain ill for six weeks in a friendly Indian's tepee, sharing his host's semi-starvation. Then, as best he could, he made his way back to Dunvegan. Happy indeed must these two priests have been on the banks of the Peace, sharing their experiences.

After cheering up Father Tissier for a few days, Father Lacombe retraced his steps to Lesser Slave Lake, where, calling the local Métis to help, he began the erection of what was later to be the mission there. Then in a birch bark canoe he set out for Lac La Biche. "The wind was favourable, and, in spite of a few accidents and some dangers we reached Lac La Biche safely." There his young sister Christine, rapidly adapting to a diet of dried meat and never-ending whitefish, was overjoyed to see her famous brother.

The two Lacombes' joy was ruined, however, by the news that smallpox was raging amongst his Crees one hundred miles to the south at St. Paul des Cris. Cutting short his visit, the priest hurried back to his battle station where, as he said in a letter dated September 2, 1870, to Bishop Taché:

> "None but those who witnessed it can form an idea of the spectacle offered to my view. Upwards of one hundred and thirty families were busily occupied pitching their tents around my dwelling. Hardly alighted from my horse I had to respond to the cries of the poor sufferers calling at me with all their might."

Once more the dreaded killer swept the prairies much as it had done about 1833 and with comparable merciless mortality. This time it came from the American trading posts on the Missouri and swept north over the plains like a prairie fire lashing out at the lodges as it went and leaving bleaching skeletons and stark tepee poles as souvenirs. One after another the tribes fell before it — Piegans during the winter of 1869–70, Bloods the following spring, then the Blackfoot and the Stonies and Sarcees, and finally, by midsummer, it clutched at the Cree camps. By August it was ravishing all the lodges all the way along the Saskatchewan River.

In August 1869, when Chief Factor Christie heard that it had broken out along the Missouri, he wrote to his superior at Fort Garry asking that some vaccine be sent out to the posts along the Saskatchewan River. By the time his letter creaked its way over the one-thousand-mile trail to Fort Garry and the authorities there had time to act and send out vaccine, the winter had gone by, and in April 1870 it arrived at Fort Carlton. There in May it was given to all the traders and passed along towards Forts Pitt and Edmonton. At the same time Christie warned the Cree chiefs to avoid contact with the Blackfoot and told them that if their people did catch the disease they were not to remain in large camps but to scatter. He also suggested certain quarantine measures to them but they failed to pay any attention. As he wrote, "Free and independent as these people are, accustomed from their infancy to do almost as they like, and go wherever they please, without hindrance, any restraint or discipline imposed upon them becomes irksome and unpalatable."

By August when the disease was raging at Fort Carlton, Bishop Grandin was there and, though in frail health, he became the Crees' doctor and nurse, cared for them, washed them and tended their bodies and souls. He was there too to close the eyes of the dead and to prepare the hideous corpses for the graves he dug for them.

Farther west, at St. Paul des Cris, where for two months Father Lacombe struggled, he wrote Bishop Taché:

"Day and night I was constantly occupied, scarcely had time to say mass. I had to instruct and baptize dying infidels, confess and anoint our neophytes at the point of death, minister the different wants, give a drink to one and food to another, kindle the fire during the cold nights. This dreadful epidemic has taken all compassion from the hearts of the Indians. These lepers of a new kind are removed at a distance from the others and sheltered with branches. There they witness the decomposition and putrification [sic] of their bodies several days before death."

Picking his way around the dead, bending over the sick and the dying, feeding them soup and carrying water to those parched with their final fever-thirst, he carried on. At sunrise each day he buried the victims and then for the rest of the long hours of sunlight comforted the stricken.

"The patient is at first very feverish, the skin becomes red and covered with pimples, these blotches in a few days form scabs filled with infectious matter. Then the flesh begins to decompose and falls off in fragments. Worms swim in the parts most affected. Inflamation of the throat impedes all passage for meat or drink. While enduring the torments of this cruel agony the sufferer ceases to breathe, alone in a poor shed with no other assistance than what I can afford.

The hideous corpse must be buried, a grave must be dug and the body carried to the burial ground. All this devolves to me and I am alone with Indians disheartened and terrified to such a degree that they hardly dare approach even their own relations. God alone knows, what I have had to endure merely to prevent these mortal remains being devoured by dogs."

While all this was going on, a messenger arrived from some Catholic Crees camped near the Methodists' Victoria mission who begged their blackrobe to come to them.

"They also were afflicted by the epidemic and thought themselves entirely forsaken. I baptized several at the place, did all I could to relieve the sufferers during the two nights and a day that I devoted to them. I then came back to my Indians, many of whom had expired during my absence, but they had all received the Sacraments before I had left."

Some days after Father Lacombe returned to his St. Paul des Cris mission a messenger from St. Albert arrived to tell how even in that larger settlement the dread disease had dealt death in every direction. Before setting out, he scribbled a note on some ragged wrapping paper and sent it to Bishop Grandin. It read:

"My Lord, I am in the midst of the dead and dying, and am now hurrying to St. Albert where our own men are overcome by the disease. I fear there is not even one priest there able to assist the dying."

At St. Albert the first man to greet him was Father Leduc, pockmarked but recovering, who told him that Father Bourgine and Brothers Doucet and Blanchet were down with the dread malady. He pitched in to help carry the load which had slipped from his stricken brethren's hands. Before long Bishop Grandin also came hurrying along the trail to the mission. As he approached the bridge he met a young man frantic with fear, clasping a blanket in one hand and a piece of meat in the other and crying, "Everybody is dying, everybody is dying." From the moment of his arrival he jumped in to console the dying and their relatives. A few days later he heard of the fate of the

Métis he had met on the way. He too had died and before his body was found it had been severely torn by wolves.

By the end of September the worst was over and the exhausted priests, resting from their frantic toils, tallied up three hundred dead out of seven hundred Métis and Indians who had looked to the mission for refuge.

The deaths at St. Albert were only part of the devastation wrought amongst Father Lacombe's Métis. During the late spring of 1870 his friends from Lac Ste. Anne and St. Albert had to go out for their season's hunt in the vicinity of Buffalo Lake. That year the buffalo were "far out" and they had to travel farther than usual. Since the Blackfoot, usually their sworn enemies, were also suffering from scarcity, they and the Métis patched up a temporary peace during which some Blackfoot came over to visit their camp.

The smallpox came with them but did not break out in the Métis camp until July 26. They were then on their homeward trek and one day's travel out of St. Albert. Amongst them was Virginia Calihoo, a girl at the time who as a bright lady nearing the century mark tried to convey the tragedy of that trip to the writer. The group's arrival infected the St. Albert settlement.

The hunt had been lamentably poor and at St. Albert, with the horrors of smallpox harrying them on the one hand and famine facing them on the other, they were in desperate straits. So once more, this time in August, the healthy set out towards Buffalo Lake to hunt. Father Fourmond went with them and, according to Virginia Calihoo, he took along his four-wheeled wagon — the first she had ever seen.

Not surprisingly, disaster struck. After the epidemic was over the priests estimated that out on the hunt three hundred Métis died. The toll and the agony on this trip is beyond anything we can imagine. As Father Fourmond wrote,

"Every time we changed camps, there were scenes of agony and despair. Frequently there were not enough of us sufficiently well to harness the horses. How the sick suffered as they were jolted over those rough prairies! How they suffered as we passed within sight of the wild beasts which were lying in wait for their next victim to die.

"When we came to a camping ground, we put up the tents

and lighted a fire in each one to warm the sick, to cook food, and to prepare medicine. These tents were only ten feet in diameter and yet I have seen ten sick and dying Indians lying around the fire in one of them.

"I spent all my time tending to the sick in our sixty tents. I cannot describe the revolting stench. When the disease was in the desiccation stage, the victims were masses of putrefaction so that it was impossible to see in them the resemblance of a human being.— And still, beneath that hideous exterior there was a soul, created to the likeness of God, a soul to save!"

When the worst was over at St. Albert, Father Lacombe went over to Lac Ste. Anne where he found forty souls had passed on. Later he hurried out to the parklands where as rapidly as he could he visited nearly thirty camps, many of which Father André had called on. Sometimes he reached them when the worst was over; sometimes he landed during the height of the scabby sickness. Then amongst all his other ministrations he helped to dig graves and often carried to them ten or twelve bodies wrapped in blankets.

One morning he sent a couple of his native helpers to bring the bodies of two children which he had laid out the previous evening and covered with branches. The men came back reporting that the bodies as such were gone; only some portions of them were visible, the remains left by the camp's hungry dogs. Taking his only extra shirt and using some socks and bits of rags which remained in his kit, he wrapped up the repulsive remnants and buried them.

While doing so he saw an old man sorrowing and heard him ask, "Great Father, is it possible that you not only let us die of this horrible sickness but also let us be eaten by dogs?"

By the end of September the epidemic was over. According to an official report compiled by Chief Factor William Christie, about one-half of Alberta's Indians had died of the disease. The official figures for the Saskatchewan District showed that 2,686 of the plains Indians were swept away, while 485 Crees and 373 half-breeds died.

At Lac La Biche where Lacombe's sister Christine was enduring all the hardships and horrors of the epidemic, only thirteen natives died. There her sorrows were compounded by the tragedy which struck the drivers of the mission's Red River carts who had gone to Fort Pitt for the annual supplies. Of the fourteen who had left to make this trip, eight died of smallpox en route or shortly after their return to the mission.

At the Methodist mission of Whitefish Lake, fifty natives died and at Victoria another fifty-five were added to the toll. There, however, all the missionary's family except Mrs. George McDougall caught the disease and two of her children, Flora and Georgina, died. So did her adopted Indian daughter Anna. Then, some weeks later, during his absence, John McDougall's wife became another victim.

But Chief Factor Christie's figures were just statistics. Various writers tried to portray the stark tragedy of the plague. Of these, Captain Butler, who toured the prairies on a commission of enquiry, gave a clear description.

"By streams and lakes, in willow copses, and upon bare hillsides, often shelterless from the fierce rays of the summer sun and exposed to the rains and dews of night, the poor plague-stricken wretches lay down to die — no assistance of any kind, for the ties of family were quickly loosened, and mothers abandoned their helpless children upon the wayside, fleeing onward to some fancied place of safety. . . ."

In the face of the strenuous efforts put forth by Hudson's Bay Company men, priests and pastors, it is perhaps invidious to mention names. Nevertheless, these priests stand out above the others. Throughout all the collective experiences of the Canadian Oblates nothing has ever excelled the devotion and heroism exhibited by this handful of priests working out of St. Albert under Bishop Grandin. The names of these men should be inscribed in large letters: the ailing Bishop Grandin, Fathers André, Blanchette, Bourgine, Doucet, Dupin, Fourmond, Lacombe, Leduc, Lestanc and Scollen. They were a famous band which, drawn together by the bond of this campaign, ever after cherished each other until about half a century later the last one died.

It was not only missionaries, however, who remembered the disastrous epidemic, one of the major turning points in the West's history. The mourning Indians had more reason to remember it than anyone else. Amongst the Blackfoot, Three Suns or Natous, Lacombe's friend, had died, and Crowfoot had become chief of his band. But for them and the Crees life was never to be the same; the Indians' exclusive claim to the parklands and prairies was falling away and their power had passed its zenith. Never again were they to be quite such a problem to the Hudson's Bay Company traders.

As for that company, its power had also waned — but from a different cause. What it had experienced at Fort Garry twenty years earlier and what it had feared for so long at Fort Edmonton had happened. For the last dozen years free traders, French, Métis and its own ex-employees, mainly British, had become established fur buyers. An increasingly large part of their payments to the natives came in the form of liquor. And the more freely it flowed the less controllable and the more lawless the prairies and parkland had become.

After 1869, when the first American whisky posts had appeared in the south and then within a year or two spread north as far as the Bow River and their rot-gut whisky even made its way into Indian camps visible from Fort Edmonton, the Hudson's Bay Company's grip was increasingly weakened. The four-year reign of the whisky posts had begun. During that reign the Indians, and particularly the Blackfoot, were plunged into a disastrous period which woefully reduced their already depleted numbers and irretrievably lowered their morale. All this, of course, Father Lacombe knew and it worried him as he watched white civilization trickling west in liquor kegs and saw what it had done to the Indians who had no more antidote for it than they had for smallpox.

That civilization was not all bad he readily admitted, particularly when he saw what progress his associates were making with their new St. Albert church started in 1870 — 84 feet long and 72 feet wide — a colossal structure. And yet when at Fort Edmonton he saw the logs being assembled for the Reverend George McDougall's residence — the first building to be erected in what is now downtown Edmonton — he must have amended that admission.

Frequently Father Lacombe mentioned the rival sect in such terms as that they were in the "error of protestantism," or filled with the "fanaticism of Wesleyanism," but in none of his writings which the author has seen did he ever let his hatred of that fanaticism go beyond expressions like that.

George McDougall, however, was far less reticent in alerting the world to the dangers of Catholicism, which he considered a papal power "in wakeful exercise, only less pestiferous and Godless than Paganism itself." Writing about his competitors in January 1870 he opined that "the man of sin is powerfully represented in this country. There are five priests to one Protestant missionary; they are anti-British in their national sympathies; and if we may judge the tree by its fruits, anti-Christian in their teachings." In the same letter, however, he had to admit that "these Priests are hard workers; summer and winter they follow the camps, suffering great privations. They are indefatigable in their efforts to make converts."

It was only due to these indefatigable efforts, of course, that any missionaries made any converts. Occasionally, as in the case of Sweet Grass, a high ranking chief of the Crees, these efforts reaped a reward. For some years both the Methodists and the Catholics had hoped to lure him into their fold, but as a man of more than ordinary ability he was not so easily swayed as were the more emotional members of his band. On many occasions Father Lacombe had led up to the subject of baptizing him and each time Sweet Grass had put him off. By the fall of 1870, however, after having witnessed the utter altruism of the priests during the plague, he offered himself to the delighted father as a convert. Thenceforth, he was to be a faithful friend both to the priests and to white men in general.

If Sweet Grass's conversion was a heartening gesture, so was Bishop Grandin's interest in Father Lacombe's Cree dictionary and grammar. Deeming it to be of great importance, he had arranged for Brother Scollen to accompany Father Lacombe to the relative seclusion of Rocky Mountain House where the Irish priest helped him to bring some order out of his voluminous notes and to put it in shape for publication. It should be borne in mind that many priests had compiled lists of Indian words but because of his own painstaking work in this direction and of his great interest in the work, it was left to Father Lacombe, aided by Brother Scollen, to produce a systematic Cree dictionary.

During December the two priests received a visit from Captain Butler. At Fort Garry he had been appointed a government commissioner to cross the prairies and report on conditions. One result of his trip was his classic book entitled *The Great Lone Land* and another was a recommendation that a small body of cavalry be sent to police the area. Writing of Father Lacombe, he was generous but accurate in his appraisal and mentioned the priest's "intense love and devotion to these poor wandering and warring people and his entire sympathy for them."

Being a fellow Catholic he was able to share the priest's dismay over the fact that the Franco-Prussian war, which had been disastrous to France, had also deprived the pope of French support and of the papal states as well. It had also cut off such financial support as had flowed from France to the western missions. Once more as had happened in 1849, the existence of the western Oblate missions was threatened. While he thought about it all winter and found this most discouraging, Father Lacombe could not consider the blow to be anywhere near fatal. Once more as in 1849 the old Oblate spirit was to show itself.

Writing to the Canadian House in May 1871 to ask them to come to the missions' aid, the self-reliant farm boy nevertheless asserts that if necessary he and his fellow priests could get along without it. "Provided I have what is necessary to offer the Holy Sacrifice I do not ask anything else."

Then, as if to emphasize the fact that the priests received very little more help than this anyway, he writes of his plans for the coming season. Once more he is going out to spend the entire season wandering with the Crees. Once more he intends to try to talk them into keeping the peace and to warn them of the dangers of dealing with the whisky traders who had been pushing farther north each year. Fulminating against these he writes that he hopes that the new Dominion of Canada, having purchased the prairies and parklands from the Hudson's Bay Company, will send out a force strong enough to suppress the liquor traffic.

Having got all that off his mind, he and Alexis, as they had done so many times, set out to contact the Cree camps which were fanned out over the huge land of peavine and buffalo grass lying between the North Saskatchewan and the Red Deer River. As usual, Alexis, a servitor of nearly twenty years' standing, deferred to Father Lacombe's every wish. In his devotion to the

father and to the church, he felt himself to be no less a missionary than his patron and, so as to resemble him as much as he
could, he wore a black cassock-type gown. Several times he had
pleaded with Father Lacombe to accept him into the Oblate
order as a brother, but each time he had been disappointed. The
priest, loving him for his loyalty, had difficulty overlooking his
growing eccentricity and began to wonder how it would end
and what would become of his faithful follower.

In spite of that, the two rambled with the Indians all of the
summer of 1871 and whenever Father Lacombe felt himself to
be in Blackfoot territory he realized that he should build a
new mission just for them. As early as 1858, according to Captain Palliser, he had considered building such a mission either
on the northeast corner of Buffalo Lake (near the Buffalo Boss
Hill) or at the mouth of that lake's outflow, Tail Creek. By
1871, however, that was impractical because by then each of
these localities had become rendezvous for the Métis hunters
from St. Albert. By that time he realized that his new mission
should be built along the Bow River and he made up his mind
to make a special appeal to Bishop Grandin for assistance in
starting it. Already he had a name for it. Because year in and
year out he had pleaded with the Blackfoot to keep the peace,
he planned to call his new mission Our Lady of Peace.

When he and Alexis returned to spend the winter at St.
Albert he devoted considerable time and much of his not inconsiderable talent to trying to win Bishop Grandin's approval
of this new idea. But each time he brought up the matter the
good bishop's heart did not seem to be in the scheme. Under the
circumstances, that was not to be wondered at, for not only did
the bishop have another idea up his sleeve, but as well as that,
the recent reorganization of church territory demanded a lot
of his attention.

On September 22, 1871, while Father Lacombe was out along
the Red Deer River, the pope in faraway Rome had decided that
the diocese of St. Boniface should be raised to the dignity of a
metropolitan see. In it St. Albert should become a separate
diocese of which Vital Grandin was to be bishop. The official
news of this change did not reach St. Albert until April 2, 1872,
but it undoubtedly came as no surprise to the new and saintly
bishop of St. Albert.

The change in St. Albert's status probably did little to alter the complexion of the bishop's difficulties. As head of an independent diocese now, he had far more problems than privileges; his missions were expanding rapidly, he needed more schools for his Métis and freemen, and he had to try to start schools for Indians. And where were the resources with which to do these things? For all the work facing him he had only a handful of missionaries and they, like their Indian converts, wore moccasins, ate pemmican, slept in skin tents and at least physically, lived a lean existence.

And here was Father Lacombe trying to wangle another mission out of him. All winter long they had discussed the general situation and had agreed that it was a difficult one. But while the bishop would not yield on the question of Our Lady of Peace, Father Lacombe would not take no for an answer.

About the middle of April 1872 with the matter still deadlocked, Bishop Grandin decided to make an episcopal tour of his territory starting with Lac La Biche. In bidding him bon voyage, Father Lacombe resolved to bide his time and to take the matter up when he returned. A few days later, however, a letter which the bishop had written when camped at the crossing of the Beaver River near modern Briereville landed in his strong-willed priest's lap. Its effective part began:

"I nominate you by these presents my Vicar-General."

"Well," thought Father Lacombe, "that is gratifying — to be appointed as the bishop's deputy in the administration of his diocese."

For a moment he felt a flush of pleasure that in preference to his several outstanding fellow priests he should have been chosen.

Reading more of the letter, however, soon put a different complexion on this new appointment for it continued, "You are begging me to establish the mission of Our Lady of Peace among the Blackfoot; also another among the Crees. . . . It is necessary then to procure resources in some way. . . . It is necessary then, mon cher, for you to abandon your Indians for this year.

"And you, where are you to go? Go I pray you, into your own country holding out your hands to your friends and mine.
"It pains me to impose this onerous mission on you. It is,

I know, an imposition on Canada, which has already shown so much interest in us; but it seems to me that we cannot stand on our dignity — when it is as now a question of life or death — if we would avoid seeing the young Church of St. Albert diocese die at its birth. . . .

"I shall ask one other service of you. It concerns the extreme need for schools. It is the important work, the only real means of civilizing our Indians."

Then having given Father Lacombe his marching orders — not verbally, when he would at least have had a chance to argue, but by letter against which there could be no appeal — the missive concluded: "Bon voyage! dear Father. I embrace you and bless you affectionately."

That was that. The matter was closed. There would be no more argument and there would be no Our Lady of Peace. Even St. Paul des Cris would have to be closed down. That, however, was merely a lesser evil; what with the smallpox and the Methodists — comparable calamities — it had lost much of its reason for existence.

There was no doubt, of course, that the war in Europe had dried up a large part of the bishop's finances — pitifully small in comparison to the need though they were. Nevertheless that part had helped to sustain the work at St. Albert and now that it was missing the western missions would have to rely on donations from the parishes of Quebec. The bishop's letter had asked him to go begging "into your own country," an allusion to the fact that most of the Oblates were from France and in the past had found much of their financing in their mother country. Hitherto the parishes of Quebec had found their hands full dealing with local problems and had enjoyed little time or money to devote to the faraway western missions. Now he was to wander about these parishes — begging! He, who for over twenty years had wandered with the Indian camps holding his head high, was now to bend the knee of humility and to beg!

"Nevertheless," he thought, trying to see the bright side, "after twenty years of taking off my snowshoes to enter uncomfortable Indian lodges, how nice it will be to travel in a carriage from parish to parish and to be welcomed to the easy chairs of Quebec presbyteries and to sniff a good supper cooking in the kitchen."

Moreover, humiliating and hateful though it might be, he would be following in the steps of greater men than himself who had gone begging along the St. Lawrence or in France: Provencher, Taché and even Bishop Grandin himself.

So, as a loyal Oblate and a good soldier, here were his orders — sugar-coated for sure — but nonetheless orders. Straightening his shoulders he set out to obey them. First of all, with an occasional sigh, he went out to close up his mission of St. Paul des Cris. Then pausing at the top of the last hill from which it was possible to look back at it, and at some of his hopes, he slipped down the other side to take the trail to Fort Pitt, Fort Carlton and St. Boniface.

And in any event, it was to be but for one year.

CHAPTER THIRTEEN

St. Mary's Parish, Winnipeg
1872 – 75

Unaware that his one-year absence from the Crees and Black-foot would drag out to ten years, Father Lacombe made his way along the familiar thousand-mile trail to St. Boniface. That the West was on the threshold of an era of rapid change, everyone but the Indians recognized. How rapid or how extensive that change was to be, however, not even an expert like Father Lacombe could guess. As it turned out, the decade of his absence from the West was to pull his native friends far down the ladder of life. At the same time it was to spread his own fame, to lead him towards a position of national prominence and to drape him in the aura of a legendary figure.

New challenges bring out new facets in a man. In the years ahead the Roman Catholic church in the West was to face challenge after challenge and was to drop many of them on Father Lacombe's shoulders. There was no doubt that they were broad shoulders, but Father Lacombe often must have wondered why fame should have fallen to his lot more so than that of a dozen or so of his associates. Many of them had served in the front line of the missionary advance as long or nearly as long as he. Most had spent arduous, dangerous and distasteful years in Indian camps. Most were as devout and as persistent as he. Why then was he destined to make his way step by step up the ladder of popular acclaim while his associates, many of them of equal merit, carried equal loads in the shadows just outside the spotlight's glare?

Perhaps it was that he always happened to be where the action was, just as he had been in Natous's lodge when the bullets had shredded the tepee poles. In this case, when someone was needed to go on a begging campaign in Quebec, he happened to be available when many of his associates were not. When another task succeeded that, it was logical to drop it in his lap. And as his self-confidence fed upon the successful completion of challenges which when first faced made his very knees knock, he went on from one assignment to another. Others of his associates would probably have succeeded in carrying out these challenges but Albert Lacombe was the one chosen to deal with them — and Albert Lacombe won renown for doing so.

His apprenticeship, of course, had been both long and strenuous. For twenty-three years — more than half of his life — with only short interruptions he had toiled on the church's frontiers. Young priests, newly ordained, had not been born when he, bidding goodbye to comfort and civilization, had first made his bed in an Indian tepee. Now a veteran of wars, famine and plagues, a man who could speak Cree fluently and could converse in Blackfoot and a man respected by both Cree and Blackfoot alike, Father Lacombe, though still a comparatively young man, was justly regarded as the church's best authority on matters affecting the prairie Indians. As such and as a vivacious raconteur, he was the logical priest to appeal to the parishes of old Quebec.

After a short stay in St. Boniface he reached Montreal about the middle of July 1872. Thence with his Oblate's cross in one hand and his irksome beggar's staff in the other, he went his way. He hated every minute of it — lecturing to large, smug audiences, seeking support from sleek, important people and always, always, always asking for money! But when facing these audiences he launched into the needs of the St. Albert mission or told of the souls lost during the smallpox epidemic because there had been too few priests to gather them in, his deep conviction swept them along with him. Before long crowds were coming to see this famous priest from the far-flung prairie parish. Soon everyone in Quebec knew who Father Lacombe was and the rugged priest's pilgrimage began to offer the pleasures of a triumphal tour — pleasures he found easy to digest.

After months devoted to the task, he was able to transmit an appreciable sum of money to Bishop Grandin. Equally important from a personal point of view was the fact that his tour had enabled him to meet various moneyed or otherwise influential people and on these he invariably created a favourable impression. Typical of the help that sort of impression produced was the publication of his Catholic ladder. He had persuaded the Sisters of the Congregation to make a presentable drawing of it and the Desbarats publishing house ran off five hundred copies free of charge. Soon his ladder was widely distributed over the missions served by the Oblates of western Canada. He had hoped that he would find a wealthy patron who would defray the cost of publishing his Cree dictionary, but its time had not come.

While Father Lacombe was in the East another problem bothered Archbishop Taché — the preponderance of Protestants amongst the recent influx of immigrants to the Red River Settlement. Louis Riel's leadership of the Métis may or may not have obtained certain rights for his people but it had led to bitterness and to a reopening of the issues of race and religion. When Riel's forces folded up and General Wolseley's army came in with its majority of Ontario Orangemen, conflicts between Métis and Ontario Canadians multiplied. Typical of these conflicts was that which occurred at the old Métis rendezvous along the Rivière aux Ilets de Bois, some thirty miles south and west of Saint-François-Xavier. There, Ontario settlers not only disregarded half-breed claims and squatted where they pleased but they changed the old name of the river to one of highly partisan flavour — the Boyne. In 1871 and 1872, as a result of this sort of treatment, many Métis left the Red River Settlement and moved to places in Saskatchewan or to Lac Ste. Anne and Lac La Biche in Alberta.

With Protestant newcomers from Ontario arriving steadily and Catholic Métis moving out, Archbishop Taché began to have fresh worries about the fate of the Roman Catholic church. If the French and the Roman Catholics were to hold their own, it was imperative that immigrants be brought in from Quebec. Knowing the prairies and parklands of western Canada as few Ontario people knew them, these priests, mainly of French but not often of Quebec origin, could see a day coming when these lands would support millions of immigrants. Was it too much for them to dream that at least half, if not more, of these new-comers might be French and Roman Catholic?

Up until Riel's uprising Archbishop Taché's policy had been to try to protect his Indians and Métis by keeping all white im-migrants out. Now, merely to survive, the church must over-look the effect of civilization on the natives and encourage white people of the right stock to flood the land. The archbishop sent a letter to all the Quebec bishops asking them to promote emi-gration to the West and to help his colonizers, Fathers Lacombe and Proulx. "Work for our colonization," he wrote, "otherwise we are lost."

In any event, while Father Lacombe was in Quebec collect-ing, he and his associates, Fathers Proulx and Beaudry did what they could to induce farm folk to migrate to Manitoba. They had little success because few Quebeckers were impractical enough to leave the security of their old Catholic parish for the dubious material success to be gained by enduring the bullying of a Protestant majority in Manitoba.

Even though Father Lacombe returned from his mission in Quebec with few settlers, his collections had been satisfactory. Having suffered the humiliation of begging for nearly a year, he was impatient to return to the unfettered life in Cree or Blackfoot camps.

But fate stepped in and sent him instead to the sophisticated cities of Europe. Because Archbishop Taché was ill and could not make the trip, Father Lacombe was sent to represent him at the general chapter of their order. Here indeed was a reward for all his years of service. Much as he had longed to look out over the river again from St. Paul des Cris, or to stand on Boss Hill again to watch the sun set over Buffalo Lake, his desire to see Europe was greater. He must have had a hard time restrain-ing his excitement at the prospect of seeing its old cathedrals and shrines where for a thousand years good men had wor-shipped.

Once he arrived there he was able to see Europe from the vantage point of an Oblate who was the guest of brethren who not only were eager to see this famous Father Lacombe in the flesh but equally anxious to ensure that he saw everything there was to be seen. As his travels took him hither and yon across

France he found himself preaching in ancient columned churches and holding forth in hallowed seminaries. His trip was an education. On it he was able to get a quick glance at the cultural riches of England and France. While in Paris, with the blessing of his superior-general, he found another open-handed printer who at very nominal expense ran off some sixteen thousand copies of his ladder.

While there, too, he nibbled at as much of its great many-sided culture as he had time to take in. He was there to witness the glowing spectacle of the government's official reception of the shah of Persia. If in his mind's eye he contrasted it with Bishop Grandin's triumphal entry to his St. Albert cathedral or to the receptions Fort Edmonton extended to Indian chiefs laden with pemmican, or wondered what the money expended by either the Persian or the French government would do if spent on his missions, who can blame him? At the same time as he stood watching the glittering pageantry he would have been less than human if he had not taken some pride in the fact that the farm boy from Father Viau's parish should be standing here in Paris thousands of miles away from St. Sulpice and on the banks of the Seine instead of the *St. Laurent*.

Undoubtedly his sense of achievement accompanied him across the channel. England fascinated him. As the home of the upstart conqueror of his Quebec, he had approached it with trepidation. But London won him over; he delighted in trying all of the city's varied means of transportation.

"I have already commenced to plough London — under the earth and along the streets and over the streets and on the Thames. . . ."

Later on in London this affable priest, never neglecting to seize a chance encounter with someone of political importance and to turn it into an acquaintanceship of potential value, met Sir George-Etienne Cartier and other statesmen. None of his European encounters, however, impressed him so much as his meeting with Archbishop Manning, the one-time Anglican who had transferred his allegiance to the Roman church and who was to rise high in its service. For, when the archbishop spoke of the Protestants and urged Father Lacombe to love them warmly even as he did his Indians, he opened a new window into the world in the Canadian priest's mind.

"For I was one of them once," the future cardinal said, "and I know how they believe in their souls that they are right — so there is no blame for them that they do not see the truth."

Of all Englishmen, Archbishop Manning impressed him most. But England was a surprise to him, for he was

"enchanted with the good manners and politeness of the English of England. How very different they are from our wooden English of Canada and the United States. To your great surprise, doubtless, I shall tell you that not once from Portland to Dover has anyone given me the tiniest trouble nor shown me the least rudeness."

How different it was to be able to travel around in his cassock and not arouse the animosity of half the population. He had assumed that in England, the fountainhead of the British Empire, he would encounter the same hatred between Protestant and Catholic as existed in Canada, but on the surface at least it was not apparent. He knew, of course, that in England the millennium was still far away and that religious intolerance still existed. But to him, a French Canadian and a priest, the absence of anything so bitterly disquieting as the Canadian rift along French-Catholic versus British-Orangemen lines was a revelation of the ideal to which he as a clergyman felt he might well direct more thought.

Regardless of that, long before the summer was out, Father Lacombe was ready to leave all that Europe had to show him.

"It is true that notwithstanding all the beautiful things which I have seen in this France and England I have looked on sights as fine in the beautiful valley of the Saskatchewan or on the borders of some of our fine lakes."

He had had enough. He wanted the feel of crisp snow under his moccasins once more and the crackle of shortribs as they sputtered before the campfire. And when in the fall of 1873, after passing up the St. Lawrence on the left side of the island which blocked the view of St. Sulpice church, his steamship approached Montreal, he felt confident that before long he would look across his bridge again and walk up the slope to the St. Albert mission.

But once more the complications of the world far removed

from his parklands came between him and his camps or his mission. At Bishop Bourget's palace he met Archbishop Taché, the dear friend with whom he had travelled out to St. Boniface twenty-one years earlier and who for all that time had been his kind and understanding superior. The archbishop was in the East trying to pour oil on Métis waters, or, more particularly, on Louis Riel's troubled waters. During the 1869 uprising in the Red River Settlement Taché and his priests, anxious to help their Métis, had been caught in a cruel dilemma. Taking their normal stand in favour of constituted authority on the one hand, and, on the other, torn by their liking for the Métis, by the element of justice in their uprising and by the fact that they were of French blood and religion, the priests had a difficult time. In return for throwing his weight on the government side, Archbishop Taché had been promised — or had every reason to believe that he had — that after the insurrection cooled down an amnesty would be declared which would include Louis Riel.

For years that amnesty and its possible beneficiary, Louis Riel, were to bedevil Canadian politics. With its French-Catholic versus Ontario-Orange overtones no compromise was possible. Archbishop Taché, one of the more honourable men involved in the whole sad affair, justly insisted that the promise of the amnesty be fulfilled. Although John A. Macdonald, the Conservative prime minister, and Alexander Mackenzie, who after Macdonald's defeat formed the first Liberal government, both favoured the amnesty and wished to please the archbishop, their hands were tied by the Quebec-Ontario race-religious hatred which prevented them from taking any action. Also caught in the clutch of circumstances was Louis Riel, who by being elected as member for the Provencher federal constituency (Red River Settlement) on three occasions between October 1873 and September 1874, kept the pot boiling.

Inevitably involved in all this, Archbishop Taché was in the midst of talks with Sir John A. Macdonald and Sir Hector Langevin when in the fall of 1873 Father Lacombe arrived in Montreal. The politicians were hoping that they could prevail upon the archbishop to prevent Louis Riel from complicating an already serious situation by running for office in the Provencher by-election. During these talks, Father Lacombe, still considering himself as an Oblate missionary who by chance had become entangled in these fringes of a high political venture, accompanied and aided his archbishop. Throughout, the archbishop refused to interfere with Riel. Only if Sir John would acquiesce on the amnesty, and promise it in writing this time, would he consider the matter. The prime minister could not promise. So Archbishop Taché refused to take a hand in the affair and returned to St. Boniface.

That October, though Louis Riel was elected by acclamation in Provencher, he dared not risk taking his seat in the House of Commons. His Ontario-Orange enemies, busily clamouring for his head, had made it so nerve-wracking for him that for a time he was sent to the Oblate fathers' seminary at Plattsburg, New York, to try to ward off a mental breakdown. There Father Lacombe and an old friend, Father Poulin, both charged with the responsibility of keeping an eye on him, visited him at Christmas time.

Meantime, Sir John A. Macdonald's Conservative government was defeated and without an election was succeeded by Alexander Mackenzie's Liberals. In short order Mackenzie decided to hold an election and in even shorter order he knew that he had inherited the white elephant of the amnesty and of Louis Riel. Preparatory to the election, but indirectly through his French colleague Antoine Dorion, he also approached Archbishop Taché to try to get him to keep Riel from running. Once more, and quite correctly, the archbishop flared up and refused. Writing from St. Boniface to Dorion, he said in part, "For four years I have been made use of, nominally for the good of the people whom I love, as an instrument to deceive that same people. . . . Allow me to tell you that now, more than ever, my interference in the direction requested (unless there were certain compensations) would to me be productive of pain and difficulty."

The certain compensation which he mentioned was the amnesty. But Alexander Mackenzie was in no better position than Sir John A. had been to agree to an amnesty which would bring forth Ontario's Orange cudgels.

During the last few months the politicians had been watching the performance of the relatively unknown western priest who had been acting as Archbishop Taché's assistant in these recent manoeuvres and had concluded that his good opinion was worth having. When Antoine Dorion failed to move Taché, he and the prime minister decided to see what headway they could make with Father Lacombe and tried to involve him in keeping Louis Riel from contesting the election. But the seasoned priest was too shaggy a buffalo to be shoved into any pound and he turned away from any involvement. Refusing to get mixed up in this very regrettable affair, he wrote turning down the invitation and claimed to be

> "a stranger to all political revolutions and occupying myself only with my poor Indians of the northwest I could scarcely anticipate that men would cast their eyes upon me for this mission. . . . I have concluded that the wisest part for me . . . would be to abstain from interfering in any way in these elections. . . ."

In the same letter he mentioned the fact that Riel had stated that no other candidate in the whole election would be "representing a principle of nationality" as he did. That very principle of nationality, however, with which it is likely Father Lacombe found little fault, was one which the few politicians who were statesmen may well have dreaded. For the local Red River Métis' affair was now being blown up until it had become intermixed with the rivalries of French and English Canada, and no good could come of that.

Like nearly every Catholic in Canada and certainly like every French Catholic in the Red River Settlement, both Archbishop Taché and Father Lacombe felt that Louis Riel's treatment had indeed been a sad business. Ottawa's policy, that of a blind, predominantly British Protestant majority, boded no good for Taché's missions, Métis or Indians. As these priests saw it, their only hope of escaping damage or indeed utter destruction from this new greedy Ontario force was to try to counter it by inviting an offsetting migration of French Catholics to the new lands. Their ancestors and confreres in Quebec had survived the English conquest; now their colleagues must brace themselves to survive the new Confederation which had come to the West.

After working for a couple of months amongst the Quebec parishes with negligible results, Father Lacombe was brought back to St. Boniface. In sight across the river and north of old Fort Garry the new Ontario-oriented town of Winnipeg had been more than doubling its population each year and by 1874 contained some three thousand souls. To cope with it Archbishop Taché needed a strong priest who already had a good acquaintance with such British people as the Hudson's Bay Company traders and who also had a current understanding of the quick shifts of Canada's political vanes, particularly as they affected Louis Riel and his Métis. No other man could meet these difficult specifications half so well as Father Lacombe and on July 22, 1874, he was appointed to serve in the only Roman Catholic parish in Winnipeg, the recently established St. Mary's.

Once more he was kept from returning to his Indian camps; once more he was put to the uncongenial task of being all things to all men. Only this time he was to brave not the ignorance of Indian bands but the intolerance of white men like himself except that their native tongue was English. And he was not only to brave the mud and the crudity of the shack town of Winnipeg, but also the imprecations of a population which in a large measure cursed at the mere sight of his black cassock. Somehow or other, he had to effect a balance between being a hail-fellow-well-met priest whose glad-handing betrayed an inner insecurity, and being an insufferable sniveler who would soon have had everyone's hand against him. Fortunately his long years in the service had made him able to steer between these extremes and had made him both a pleasant companion and a firm cleric.

Winnipeg was now only eight days' travel from Montreal. When Father Lacombe had made his first trip west in 1849, that journey took more than one hundred days. Year by year improvements in transportation had clipped days off that time until now two American railways reached the Red River, the closest being at Moorehead, a mere 250 miles away, and another line was being built north along that river towards Pembina. Moreover, for the last two or three years the Canadian Pacific Railway which Prime Minister John A. Macdonald had promised to build all the way to the Pacific Ocean had been outfitting surveying parties at Winnipeg and sending them west to select a route across the plains and over the mountains. With all that railway activity, Winnipeg had become the jumping-off place for the vast prairies, the gateway to the West.

Settlers, however, had not waited for the railway. Though, after all, there were very few of them, by 1874 their shacks were to be found all the way up the Assiniboine River as far as Portage la Prairie, and a few venturesome pioneers had taken up land along the Carlton Trail for perhaps a dozen miles farther west. To try to be ready for the anticipated rush of settlers, the Dominion land surveyors had been fanning out west from Winnipeg to divide God's grassy oak-dotted paradise into piddling quarter-sections suitable for white farmers. By midsummer 1873 nearly five million acres, or 30,000 quartersections, had been surveyed. It was this rush of white settlers, this rush which all too soon would go roaring across the prairies and parklands like a flood — it was this rush for which Father Lacombe had tried to prepare Sweet Grass and his people and Crowfoot and his warriors.

It was partly to be ready for this same rush that Sir John A. Macdonald had created the North-West Mounted Police, whose advance party had spent the winter of 1873–74 at the "stone fort," Lower Fort Garry. Then, two weeks before Father Lacombe officially took over the parish of St. Mary's, this body of cavalry had started its one-thousand-mile march west from Dufferin on the way to build a fortress somewhere in Blackfoot territory and in sight of the mountains.

As for the pioneer white folks' Catholic parish of St. Mary's, it too had been making progress comparable to that made by Winnipeg. During 1871, Father Joseph McCarthy, O.M.I., had been in the habit of coming over from St. Boniface to serve the Catholics of Fort Garry, mainly of British, Irish or American stock. In September 1872, Father J. B. Baudin had succeeded him and held services in a little convent chapel on Notre Dame Street. Then in 1873, on land donated by the Hudson's Bay Company, a new two-storey church building had been erected. In May 1874, Archbishop Taché blessed it and in July Father Lacombe, as superior and Father Baudin as his curate, came to handle its affairs.

But Father Lacombe was more than merely a parish priest; he was Archbishop Taché's man of all work and St. Mary's church was only his home address to which he could return from expedition after expedition, get his mail and hear what further restrictions were falling on his faraway Cree and Blackfoot friends. He had many things to look after: Louis Riel was still a problem and many Irish and other non-French Catholics came pouring through Winnipeg. The Métis were steadily leaving the Red River Settlement and moving farther west. Their loss weakened the French Catholics' influence in Manitoba and few Quebec compatriots came to replace them.

The church's task in western Canada had begun to take a new tack. Originally it had aimed at restoring the Métis to their ancestral faith and at ensuring that when the Indians died they did so as Christians. For the Indians' souls the Methodists had run the fathers a stubborn race, but regardless of which missionary they listened to, neither Crees nor Blackfoot had been overly responsive to ecclesiastical teachings. In the field of economics they had been even less receptive. As in later life Father Lacombe was to write, "There are certain tribes in this country, especially those who make up the Blackfoot nation, who have given us very little consolation in spite of our efforts to overcome their indifference."

By the time Father Lacombe took over St. Mary's parish, the whole Catholic church in Canada from Archbishop Bourget of Montreal down had begun its campaign to see that French hands tilled a fair share of the prairies' acres now waiting for settlement. Decades earlier the Quebec church, practically abandoned by France after the conquest, had accomplished the near miracle of preserving French culture, religion, language and tradition in the face of the unfriendly conquerors. Now the church, facing a similar problem but in a new land threatened by rapid settlement by Ontario Protestants, roused itself to take on this new challenge. And in the process it roused Father Albert Lacombe and sent him back to his homeland of sugar bush and *tabac* to pick up the gauntlet.

No better man could have been found for the job. Added to all his other qualifications was his intimate knowledge of the West from the point of view of a man who, foot by foot, had walked thousands of miles over its hills and meadows. On top of that, no one could have found a more conscientious worker than Father Lacombe, who, although he disliked this new form of soliciting, nevertheless carried out his orders. In doing so he made the weary trip to Montreal — seven days one way — at least nine times between 1872 and 1876.

Although some success rewarded his efforts, it bore little relation to the amount of work he and two or three of his fellow priests put into the task. By the end of 1877, in their attempt to populate Manitoba with Quebeckers, they were almost ready to throw in the towel and admit defeat. During 1875, sixty had come out to look at the West from the banks of the Red River, during 1876 another 324 souls came, and the following year saw an additional 369.

In spite of various official inducements favouring French immigrants, this poor showing for the three years in question of a mere 750 Quebec French as compared to over 15,000 non-French (mainly from Ontario), did little to cheer the archbishop. Immigration came under the federal Department of Agriculture, which had a French Canadian as minister and Archbishop Taché's brother as deputy minister. Moreover, that department paid most of Father Lacombe's travelling expenses. Then, when it became obvious that few colonists could be induced to come from Quebec, the government and the church focussed their attention on the French then living in the United States. In 1874 the Société de Colonisation de Manitoba was granted a reserve on which repatriated French Canadians could settle. As further assistance, Father Lacombe, who was beginning to learn the government ropes, persuaded the department to pay a grant of $17 per settler for French Canadians brought to Manitoba from the United States. On top of that, the American railway companies showered him with offers to carry his immigrants at reduced rates.

Even this official help did little to increase the proportion of French people in Manitoba. The numbers of English-speaking and French-speaking citizens had been about equal in 1870 but after a lapse of ten years there were four times as many of the former in the province as of the latter. On the whole, the people of French blood were only marginally interested in settling in Manitoba.

There were two apparent reasons for that. The first lay with the habitants themselves; after the Riel outbreak the backlash from the large proportion of Manitoba immigrants who were of Orange sympathies made prospects dim, if not actually dangerous, for newcomers from Quebec. Ontario people, confident of their reception and sure of their large majority, poured into the new pioneering province where they would be the dominant element. The Quebec habitant could see little pleasure in becoming one of a Catholic minority in a predominantly Protestant society.

The second factor retarding French migration to Manitoba was rooted in Quebec itself, where large regions of questionable potentiality remained to be settled. So long as the overflow from the established areas could expand into Quebec's backwoods and thus, so to speak, keep the French family more or less together, they and the government of Quebec preferred such a course. Some government officials who were afraid of depopulating the province tried to discourage any exodus to the West. Indeed, Archbishop Bourget's successor, Archbishop Fabre, tended to that opinion. Then when Father Lacombe, finding his attempts in Quebec somewhat abortive, turned to the New England states for recruits, he soon found resistance against emigration building up there.

Nevertheless, through his efforts, disappointing as he may have found them, several score French families came west and expanded the existing Catholic parishes lying mainly near the Red River. Others who came in 1877 made it possible for Archbishop Taché to set up the three new parishes of St. Jean Baptiste, St. Pie and St. Joseph. About the same time many of Father Lacombe's migrants started another colony in the Pembina Mountains.

But despite all of the church's hard work the results were meagre enough. Of some eleven thousand immigrants who came to Manitoba during the five years ending in 1875, less than two hundred were French-speaking and of the 31,000 who came to settle during the next five years, slightly over two thousand were French. Father Lacombe's showing was not commensurate with his efforts. He and his associates were fighting a battle they could never hope to win.

CHAPTER FOURTEEN

Treaties, Trains and Wheat Exports
1875−80

All about Father Lacombe's St. Mary's parish, Winnipeg was growing apace. New streets and avenues were being staked out, and between spring's thaws and November's snows, whole rows of houses were being erected on them. For a while about this time it seemed that there might be as many newspapers in Winnipeg as streets, but by 1875 the main one, the *Free Press*, changed its status to become the town's first daily paper. By then, of course, this westward-looking gateway to the prairies, boasting a population of five thousand, had decided it needed a formal city hall to add distinction, and a fire brigade to ensure some measure of protection to its hundreds of wooden buildings. By the end of October 1875, with a newly purchased fire engine housed in a still unpainted fire hall, the city officials were able to report that the fire department "was in such splendid organization and the officials so alert that a fire of any consequence would be impossible."

Unfortunately, like so many of the pioneers who paused briefly in Winnipeg, the officials were overconfident. On Christmas morning the engine house and all the fire-fighting equipment became what the *Free Press* called "a $15,000 heap of ashes."

Though not directly concerned with that fire, Father Lacombe kept a wary eye on the aftermath of the Louis Riel conflagration which had disturbed the settlement a mere four years earlier. Since then Louis Riel had been Canada's problem child.

A man venerated by the Métis, revered by French Canada, reviled by Orange Ontario and viewed more dispassionately by Archbishop Taché and Father Lacombe, he was a factor in Canadian political life until some time after September 1874 when for the last time the voters of the Red River Settlement elected him to the federal parliament. After that, fate had dragged him through the shadows of ill health and mental institutions. If possible, whenever Father Lacombe was in the East he went to visit the one-time rebel, but while he felt very kindly towards him, he had to admit that he could see little good in his future. In May 1876, for instance, he wrote, "Poor Riel, I feel so sorry for him. He is worse than ever." Nevertheless, Father Lacombe continued to take a kindly interest in him.

That interest, however, did not go so deep as his concern over the Crees and Blackfoot of the West. He had last seen them in 1872 when he had been called away to serve one year in the East. That year lengthened to five years before he could even plan to return to the land of the foothills so as to be present when his friends the Blackfoot signed a treaty which would turn their lands over to the white interlopers. All the drastic change — all the incredible change — from free, footloose, wellfed Indians to landless, humble and hungry indigents had been compressed into the five years since Father Lacombe had left the St. Albert mission. Had he not followed the situation on the parklands and prairies through reports brought in by Métis, fellow missionaries and Hudson's Bay Company men coming to Winnipeg he could scarcely have believed that disaster could have struck his friends so abruptly.

Many a time he had sat talking with Crowfoot, Sweet Grass or some other thinking man about the day when, inevitably, the white man would take over and when the buffalo would vanish, but none had imagined that it would all happen so soon. Father Lacombe, his associates and his rivals, had tried to prepare the Crees and Blackfoot for a sedentary, agricultural life, but even the wisest chiefs had taken the matter lightly, as something which could happen some day — but that day was far off. And now and almost all at once that day had dawned.

When Father Lacombe had left the valleys of the Battle and the Red Deer rivers his friends had been recovering slowly from the shock of smallpox. For a while they had neither the desire nor the strength for warfare and there had been few intertribal killings. True enough an occasional warrior or horse thief was killed, such as Crowfoot's son, who in 1873 went on a small expedition against the Crees and was slain. It was many months later in Winnipeg that Father Lacombe heard of that incident and at the same time heard of a remarkable young Cree named Poundmaker, whom Crowfoot had adopted to replace his son.

At the time Father Lacombe had set out for Winnipeg the American whisky traders were already selling their liquor as far north as Edmonton and the Crees and Blackfoot who were gleefully buying it were soon feeling its dreadful effects. As that state of affairs continued for two more years, its penalties became increasingly heavy. Indians died in drunken brawls amongst themselves. Freezing to death while drunk, murdering each other and starving because everything they owned had been sold for whisky, all took many lives.

One of the best pictures of this state of affairs is given in a letter written during the summer of 1874 by Father Scollen, who, as Father Lacombe's successor, was wandering with the Blackfoot. "It was painful to me to see the state of poverty to which they had been reduced. Formerly, they had been the most opulent in the country, now they were clothed in rags without horses and without guns."

During 1872 the federal government, spurred on by the missionaries' pleas and by other reports of conditions in the western prairies, sent out Colonel P. Robertson-Ross to study the situation and to bring back recommendations on how best to establish law and order. He reported that:

"The demoralization of the Indians and injury to the country from this illicit traffic [liquor] is very great. It is stated on good authority that last year eighty-eight of the Blackfeet Indians were murdered in drunken brawls among themselves. . . ."

Commenting on the attitude of American whisky traders near Edmonton, he accused them of declaring that "as there was no force to prevent them, they would do just as they pleased."

All the while, working at St. Albert, Bishop Grandin and such priests as Fathers Scollen, Fourmond, André and Lestanc were doing all they could to show the Métis and the Indians the folly of allowing liquor to become their master. Father Lacombe's sister Christine, now a lay teacher, who in 1873 had moved to Lac Ste. Anne, likewise inveighed against intemperance. So too did the faithful Brother Alexis, who was heartbroken when in 1872 he found that he could not go away east with Father Lacombe.

Unfortunately his separation from the master he had served so devotedly for twenty years increased his eccentricity. At the same time it had intensified his piety and, knowing how much Father Lacombe had wanted to start a mission to be called Our Lady of Peace amongst the Blackfoot, he went alone during the summer of 1872 and built a shack on the Elbow River some twenty miles west of modern Calgary. The next year Fathers Scollen and Fourmond used it as a convenient mission from which to deal with the Blackfoot and the year after that enlarged it.

Meanwhile, in 1873 the Methodist McDougalls started their sojourn amongst the Stoney Indians at the spot they named Morley, some 200 miles south of Edmonton. This venture became a combined ranch and religious institution, for the missionary McDougalls, father George and son John, had found in ranching the only means by which they could support their primary interest, their mission.

That Fathers Scollen and Fourmond and the McDougalls were able to take such daring steps and advance so far south as the Bow River not only indicates the hold the missionaries were gaining on the prairie Indians but also how much the Blackfoot hold on their native land was slipping. This, however, was also demonstrated by the manner in which about the same time the Métis had begun to set up establishments in the parklands, and in a different way by the increasing numbers of American whisky posts which had begun to dot the prairies from the Bow River south.

As well as reporting on their own successful penetration into Blackfoot territory, Protestant and Catholic missionaries also wrote decrying the debauchery caused by these whisky posts and begging the government at Ottawa to send in a police force. Eventually the government acted, but before sending the newly-created North-West Mounted Police to the banks of the Bow and Oldman rivers in 1874, the Northwest Territories Council asked the Hudson's Bay Company men and the missionaries to explain the reason for the creation of this proposed force to the Indians. Since Father Lacombe was away in Winnipeg, the Reverend John McDougall happened to be the main missionary who went to see Crowfoot, by now the leading Blackfoot chief.

Crowfoot acknowledged that his people were utterly incapable of resisting the temptation of liquor. Aware of how rapidly it was destroying them, he expressed extreme satisfaction at the news.

Far less satisfactory to Crowfoot and the Blackfoot was the fact that about that time the Métis of Lac La Biche and St. Albert were building villages around Buffalo Lake. In the fall of 1874 Father Doucet stayed with them in a shack village where "they had built their little winter houses in the woods right next to the beautiful Buffalo Lake."

This village of typical half-breed shacks scattered along the shores of the lake had been the outcome of the St. Albert Métis' need to have a base closer to the diminishing buffalo herds. Entering into their decision to build it was also the fact that for the previous two or three years there had been an exodus of Métis from the Red River Settlement, mainly to such places as St. Laurent, Duck Lake and Buffalo Lake. After 1870, when their first fight with the white man had made them sullen and suspicious and when this was followed by the obvious contempt in which the increasing influx of white immigrants held them, they decided to move west.

In any event, when in April 1875 Bishop Grandin wrote the minister of the Interior at Ottawa, he stated that out of the seven hundred Métis who had recently resided at St. Albert, three hundred had now moved more or less permanently to this new colony near the Boss Hill and that they had been joined by other recent Métis immigrants to the West. During the winter of 1875-76, Fathers Lestanc and Fafard ministered to them. In a letter the latter wrote in the fall of 1876, he stated that some eight hundred Métis were wintering in this one community while there were at least two other smaller camps within thirty miles and another "little camp at Tail River." By this time, of course, the North-West Mounted Police had established themselves in the West and visited the Métis settlements near

Buffalo Lake and thereby severely restricted the flow of liquor into them.

Fortunately when these red-coated soldiers arrived and built Fort Macleod in 1874 they proved to be of the calibre Reverend McDougall had predicted they would be, and almost immediately the sale of whisky stopped. Within two years some measure of the Blackfoot's former prosperity returned to the lodges. The police had built additional posts: Fort Walsh near the site of the Cypress Hills massacre, and Fort Calgary, which had previously been the scene of some of the drunken orgies of Crowfoot's people.

The site of the Mounties' Fort Calgary had not only felt the tramp of whisky traders but also the tread of Father Lacombe's associates. A year before the police had decided to put their post there, Father Scollen had planned to establish a mission right at the mouth of the Elbow River. In October 1874 he and Father E. Bonnald had returned to Alexis's Our Lady of Peace mission which appeared as though it would be the church's headquarters for the Blackfoot. As well as its three priests, Fathers Scollen, Doucet and Bonnald, it was served by three remarkable laymen: Father Lacombe's Alexis, Jean L'Heureux and Louis Daze. Unfortunately, the next spring Louis Daze went out hunting, was caught in a blizzard and froze to death. When his body was found Father Bonnald and Alexis took it to St. Albert for burial.

That summer Father Scollen visited the North-West Mounted Police at Fort Macleod while he left Father Doucet to build the proposed overnight sleeping hut, about eight feet square, at the junction of the Bow and the Elbow. By September when the police arrived and chose to build on the same site, he had not made much progress but by then Father Scollen had decided to move Our Lady of Peace to the site of modern Calgary. Within a month or so Brother Alexis had pretty well completed its combined residence and chapel about a mile up the Elbow from Fort Calgary.

About the same time, John McDougall, feeling it necessary to have an outpost from Morley, started building a small log chapel a short distance west of the police detachment. Within a few months — in the spring of 1876 — his father, the Reverend George McDougall, perished in a storm near Nose Hill in the same general area that Louis Daze had frozen to death the year before.

While the police were building Fort Calgary, Crowfoot went to visit John McDougall, expressed his pleasure at the police's performance and was anxious to talk over a problem which of late had been worrying his people. At last they could understand what the missionaries had tried to make them see all these years. "When thousands of white men come pouring in and the buffalo are all gone," Crowfoot asked, "what will become of us?"

This gave McDougall a chance to discuss the subject of farming and to lead up to the fact that the government was anxious to make treaties under which the Indians would formally give up their lands in return for certain reserves set aside for them and certain rights guaranteed them. Some weeks later in a large meeting of important chiefs attended by Jean L'Heureux, Crowfoot sought everybody's advice and L'Heureux wrote to the government setting out the tribe's problems.

After similar discussions among themselves, the Crees and Blackfoot gradually adopted an attitude which set the stage for Treaty No. 6 which was signed at Forts Pitt and Carlton in 1876. By its terms, most of the Cree lands in Alberta and Saskatchewan, 121,000 square miles, were ceded to the white man represented by Alexander Morris, lieutenant-governor of Manitoba and the Northwest Territories. At the main gathering at Fort Carlton some three thousand Indians, guided and advised by Bishop Grandin, John McDougall and representatives from Anglican and Presbyterian churches, authorized their chiefs to enter into the treaty. With the exception of a few like Big Bear, all the Cree chiefs signed, including Father Lacombe's friend Sweet Grass, who did so at Fort Pitt.

The following year at Blackfoot Crossing the Blackfoot and a few of their associated tribes gave up the rest of the arable land in Alberta. Whereas at the signing of Treaty No. 6 Bishop Grandin had been present on behalf of his church, at Treaty No. 7 it had been intended that Father Lacombe would substitute for his superior. Shortly before the date fixed for the gathering at Blackfoot Crossing he had been in Ottawa and the government officials, knowing him well by this time, had asked him to attend the ceremonies as one of the Indians' counsellors. Unfortunately, on his way from Ottawa to Fort Benton, whence he was to proceed to Fort Macleod, he fell sick at St. Paul, Minnesota. After a long, severe illness during which the gathering had taken place without him, he returned to St. Boniface.

By a stroke of bad luck, he, who for so many years had advised the Blackfoot and had long forecast this day when the Indians would have to settle down and begin to farm, had missed the opportunity of standing at their side when they signed the treaty document. His place, however, was taken very ably by Father Scollen, who since Father Lacombe's departure for Winnipeg had been an assiduous visitor to their camps.

At the signing of Treaty No. 7, when the Indians gave up some 50,000 square miles of grasslands, it was pointed out that white men were to be allowed to move into the lands they were ceding. The plains Indians were to be free to hunt over their old lands as long as the buffalo lasted, but since that animal's extermination was a foregone conclusion, the Indians were to be assigned reserves of their own choosing on which they were to live when the time came. It was expected that then they would support themselves in much the same way as white men did, by cultivating the earth.

The terms of the treaty, of course, were conceived and written by white men, men who, seeing no practical alternative but for the Indians to turn to agriculture, tried to ensure that they got off to a good start in this direction. As it turned out, the Indians were not practical in the white man's sense. Physically they could have tilled the soil or tended cattle; psychologically they could not.

Knowing that the buffalo could not last many more years, most of the Indians were of the same mind as Crowfoot and, making the best of the bad bargain which was their lot, signed the treaty.

At a colourful gathering at Blackfoot Crossing in 1877 the last of the natives' arable land passed to the white men. The Indians' reign on the prairies was over. When five years earlier Father Lacombe had taken what he thought to be temporary leave of the Blackfoot camps he had forecast such a destiny for his friends, but neither he nor they could have dreamed that his prophecy would be fulfilled in so short a span.

Though both natives and interlopers had failed to realize how sudden the Indians' transition from dominance to dependency was to be, the whites had been preparing for it. Most of the preparations involved either surveying in one form or another or establishing communications of various sorts between the prairies and parklands and the rest of the world. Starting about the time Father Lacombe closed up St. Paul des Cris, the surveyors for the CPR sent scores of parties hither and yon over the prairies. By the time of Treaty No. 7 they were still far from pronouncing one route better than all the others but they had gathered a great deal of detailed information about the terrain which, of course, Father Lacombe knew by the soles of his snow-shoes, so to speak.

At the close of 1877 the land surveyors had staked out some 70,000 quarter-sections in Manitoba. This was a mere fraction of the available arable land but enough for 70,000 individual holdings or nearly 300,000 white souls as compared to the 50,000 Indians in all who had recently owned the western prairies.

Working in conjunction with the railway instrument men came another group surveying and building a telegraph line towards the Rocky Mountains. When in 1875 they established a camp at the mouth of the Battle River, they founded a new town which, in the year Treaty No. 7 was signed and under the name of Battleford, became the capital of the Northwest Territories. By November 1877 the telegraph line had been extended to within a few miles of Edmonton and thenceforth the few people in that growing hamlet were able to send messages back and forth to Winnipeg in minutes.

To speed up communication between Winnipeg, the gateway to the prairies, and the far West, the sternwheeler *Northcote* was put into service on the North Saskatchewan River. It made its first trip from Grand Rapids to Fort Carlton in 1874 and the next year went on to tie up at Fort Edmonton. She was eighteen days on the way from Grand Rapids where her cargo of 130 tons had been trundled across the portage. Thirty-four days had elapsed since her freight had been loaded at Lower Fort Garry. Her trip had cut to half the average time of delivery of freight to Edmonton — a large step forward from Father Lacombe's 1862 brigade of thirty carts.

The *Northcote* was not the only steamer in the news during those exciting years of Winnipeg's and Father Lacombe's careers. In 1876 one of her sister craft plying the Red River, the *Min-*

nesota, thrashed her way upstream from Fort Garry with a much more portentous load than the *Northcote* had borne. For the *Minnesota* carried the first export shipment of wheat ever to leave the Canadian West. It was bound for Ontario, and to make up such a large order — $857\frac{1}{4}$ bushels — the very bottom of many a Red River settler's bin had to be scraped. Moreover, just as the *Minnesota* had marked a most important milestone in the West's history, so in the fall of 1877 the *Selkirk,* also swinging around the bends of the Red River, brought in the first locomotive ever to puff its stack in Manitoba. As W. F. Luxton's *Free Press* elated:

"THE FIRST LOCOMOTIVE"
"At an early hour this morning, wild, unearthly shrieks from up river announced the coming of the steamer *Selkirk,* with the first locomotive ever brought into Manitoba. . . . A large crowd of people collected on the river bank and as the steamer swept down past the city, the mill whistles blew and bells rang out to welcome the arrival of the iron horse. . . ."

Whether or not Father Lacombe had recovered from his illness in time to return from St. Paul, Minnesota, to watch this very first locomotive arrive, he was probably on hand in December 1878 to witness another important event in the history of the West's transportation. That day a crowd boarded the train at St. Boniface and was taken south to a point near today's Dominion City to watch the last spike driven on the Pembina branch of the CPR. When that was done, although Canada's great transcontinental railway, the main line of the CPR, was still a somewhat vague dream, Winnipeg at last had a connection to the outside world. At last Winnipeg, the gateway to the West, had the world by the tail on a downhill pull.

Such a bustling young city was certain to attract interesting and aggressive men. Being an interesting man himself and filling such an influential niche in the community, the priest of St. Mary's parish soon came to know them. No important man came to Winnipeg looking for information, intending to start a business, or hoping to use the city as a springboard to political life, without seeking his advice. As a result of his several years' residence there, he met all the men who were, or were to become, prominent in the political or commercial life of the West.

Quick to sniff out the scent of distinction in other men, he never lost an opportunity of burnishing their mutual friendship.

For the vigorous priest, now a man in his fifties, at the height of his persuasive powers and beginning to relish the feel of responsibility thrust on him, found Winnipeg an ideal training ground. For there he was emerging — not entirely unwittingly — as one of the West's influential men. If his years of wandering from camp to camp had earned him his reputation, his years in Winnipeg set the seal upon it and spread it abroad. It was during his decade in Winnipeg that men in all walks of life began asking favours of him and in turn found themselves doing some for him.

Interestingly enough one of the transactions of his Winnipeg days concerned the bridge he had first built over the Sturgeon nearly fifteen years earlier. All his life he was to be a man of high ethical convictions who in a personal sense was utterly unselfish. Nevertheless his years of collecting for his church and of coming into contact with politicians of the day had begun to impress on him the fact that there were many angles from which he could approach the problem of raising money for the church. One of them which crossed his mind in 1875 was to ask Lieutenant-Governor Morris for permission to allow the church to collect fees from all travellers who crossed his bridge over the Sturgeon or else to have the government buy the bridge.

But the question of some recompense for the bridge was only a minor problem compared to many others which Archbishop Taché turned over to him. In the eyes of his superior, Father Lacombe's abilities were far more versatile than those possessed by any of the rest of his priests. And when it came to the church trying to hold its own in this land which was rapidly filling with Protestants and being governed by Ontario or British officials, there could be little question but that Father Lacombe's characteristics made him the best priest to ask for justice or even for concessions. As a result, the challenges and the opportunities to engage in new negotiations which Archbishop Taché threw his way all helped to broaden his already wide experience.

In 1879, one of these opportunities enabled him to represent the archbishop at the general chapter of their order in France. On that jaunt, which was somewhat in the nature of a holiday, he was able to go all the way to Montreal by train. In contrast to his trip in the other direction thirty years earlier, a trial which had occupied a hundred days, he reached Bishop Bourget's palace in less than four days' time. Locomotives, railway tracks and civilization were reaching out west at a fantastic rate. How long before they swept on over Father Lacombe's old stamping grounds was as yet uncertain but the months of the prairies' untrammeled freedom could undoubtedly be counted on a few fingers.

In any event, on that trip he was able to visit Rome where he presented a copy of his Cree-English dictionary to the pope. On his way back he went to see his publishing benefactor in Paris and arranged to have a run of a new and nicely illustrated Cree catechism turned out. Then, early in 1880, stopping off in Montreal long enough to arrange a loan of $20,000 towards the construction of a college at St. Boniface, he returned to his growing St. Mary's parish. It, too, required money to be directed into beneficent works, and between his efforts and those of his parish associates, the stone church which still stands as one of their memorials was commenced. Wherever he turned, some worthwhile work emerged from his labours of hand or brain.

Although he tackled all of the multitude of problems laid at his door by his superior or his parishioners, he found the duties of a parish priest in Winnipeg little to his liking. He still longed to get out to the far West and to get away from Winnipeg's "modern civilization. More than ever I long for the Indian missions. . . ."

CHAPTER FIFTEEN

A Role in CPR Construction
1880–83

On December 29, 1879, a few days before Father Lacombe returned from his visit to the pope, the first locomotive ever to enter Winnipeg under its own steam crossed a set of rails laid on the ice of the Red River. She was owned by John Ryan, who had taken a contract to build the first one hundred miles of the CPR's railway grade west from Winnipeg. Before setting out on more strenuous duties the next day, this locomotive spent its first night in the prairies parked on Winnipeg's main street.

At last the Pacific railway which for so many years had been bogged down in the muskegs and mountains of northern Ontario appeared to be on the move again. Already the line from Emerson to St. Boniface provided a rail connection to the East by way of the United States. What was needed, however, was a direct all-Canadian link with Ontario to the east and above all an entry to the rich farm lands out west. At last these railway lines appeared to be actually under construction and Winnipeg was jubilant.

For a while, as parish priest at St. Mary's, Father Lacombe had his hands full ironing out the kinks so that the construction of his new stone church could begin. But in the fall of 1880 Archbishop Taché felt he should assign one of his strongest priests to attend to the spiritual needs of hundreds of drinking, fighting and blaspheming construction men, and it came as no surprise to his religious community that he turned this task over to Father Lacombe.

Thus it was that on November 2, 1880, Father Lacombe,

changing jobs again, took on another assignment which was to add another type of experience to his repertoire, another accolade to his collection and to spread his fame across Canada. And in typical Albert Lacombe fashion he opened the first scene of this new drama by heading for the construction camps in company with no less a person than Sir Charles Tupper, the recently appointed minister of railways in Sir John A. Macdonald's cabinet. In his entry to the western fur-trade domain nearly thirty years ago he had travelled with the doughty John Rowand. When later on he had visited Cree or Blackfoot camps, he usually stayed with some of the head chiefs, Sweet Grass, Natous or Crowfoot. Now, to launch his career among the construction camps, he travelled to Rat Portage with the one man in Canada who had control of the country's railways.

Rat Portage, which in later years was to change its name to the more elegant Kenora, was a focal point for some thirty construction camps temporarily dotted along the right-of-way and to it as far as Father Lacombe could see flowed all the sins of civilization. From immorality as he was to see it on railway construction he had hitherto been almost totally shielded. At times his Métis had misbehaved but at the shake of his finger came fawning for forgiveness. In Indian camps he had seen physical filth and the suffering brought on by liquor. But here for the first time he found many of the almost unbelievable refinements with which white civilization had elevated sinning to a professional status.

For the first time in his life drunkenness, blasphemy, brutality and lechery far worse than he had seen in Indian camps were openly flaunted before him. As ceaselessly he travelled on foot, by hand-car, freighter's wagon, construction train or tug, or indeed by canoe or snowshoes, he found the men to be well-disposed and respectful. When in a cookhouse or in a bunkhouse reeking with sweat, socks and tobacco, he could sit and talk to the men — Catholic or Protestant — he found them fine fellows. But under the influence of bootleggers, gamblers or madams he found their conduct unfathomable. *"Que c'est triste de voir l'etat des choses ici!"*

His diary, so often filled with exclamations about the scenery or *beau temps*, frequently had entries indicating worries about his health.

"Feb. 11 — Sick; like pleurisy. I am paid for undertaking this trip.

"Feb. 12 — I continue to suffer.

"Feb. 16 — My God, I offer you my sufferings."

More frequently they reverted to the condition of the hell hole of some construction camp. "I am convinced more and more that the sins committed in this little corner of the world are enormous. Since I cannot stop all the evil, at least I have the power to pray for these sinners and withhold Divine anger."

Father Lacombe was not long in coming to grips with the flagrant wrongdoing of Rat Portage. He had left Winnipeg on November 2 and by November 8 was writing:

"What disorderly life of all kinds goes on in this place! Drunkenness, debauchery, and the infamous houses! The defiance of not keeping the Lord's Day! My God, what must I do to have your laws kept? Inspire me!"

A day or so later, while a dance was going on two or three doors away, he was kept awake by the loud ribaldry of drunken men and women. Next day he called on Mrs. G., the madam, to reprimand her for the evil she was doing and to demand that she shut up her bawdy-house.

He got the surprise of all his thirty years of missionary life. With insults and jeers, Mrs. G. flared back at him and ordered him out of her house. Never had he been so surprised, insulted or humiliated.

Two days later still he happened to drop into the telegraph office where the operator showed him a copy of a message he had just sent to Winnipeg. The good father was evidently so exasperated that he wrote his diary entry in English. It read:

"Always the same way at Rat Portage. That G——— woman is a very bad caracter [sic]. It appears by a telegraphic communication that she called for more women — 'Business is good' she says!"

If, however, Father Lacombe had many things to disturb him, he nevertheless derived some pleasure out of his vigil along the new grade. The working men after all were a good lot, and when they were sober he was able to strike up worthwhile friendships with many of them. He found them glad to contribute towards the construction of his Sacred Heart of Jesus chapel which he started at Rat Portage in the Spring of 1881. Using it as a base, he kept up his unending patrol of the railway grade from Thunder Bay to Winnipeg. Time after time he made his way to Whitemouth, Stuart Lake, Eagle Lake, Camp S, Camp M, Trout Lake, Cross Lake and all the other temporary camps and, for a bit of relaxation, managed to get to Winnipeg now and then. Though his means of locomotion were often crude, his very travelling satisfied an inner urge.

It was this propensity for travelling and his dramatic flair that made him enjoy taking part in the Indian ceremonial with which the governor general, the Marquis of Lorne, was received at Rat Portage during that spring of 1881. On another occasion he was delighted to meet the man who had come to Canada to breathe life into the whole CPR concern — W. C. Van Horne. The general manager of the CPR was so impressed with the rugged priest that then and there he took time to paint a picture of him. As he wrote later,

"I saw a priest standing on a flat rock, his crucifix in his right hand and his broad hat in the other, silhouetted against the rising sun, which made a golden halo about him, talking to a group of Indians — men, women and pappooses [sic] — who were listening with reverent attention. It was a scene never to be forgotten, and the noble and saintly countenance of the priest brought it to me that this must be Father Lacombe of whom I had heard so much; and it was."

This must have been Van Horne's first visit to this stretch of construction. Otherwise, like all the lesser lights of his company down through the contractors and the labourers, he would have known the sturdy priest who was apt to show up at any place at any time.

Ever mindful, however, that some nine years earlier he had been forced to forsake his Crees and Blackfoot far out on the prairies "for a year only," Father Lacombe kept comparing their simplicity and sincerity with the scandalous behaviour in the construction camps and wishing he could go back to them. Frequently he had confided his wish to his diary. "My God, send me back again to my old Indian missions. I am longing for that."

Both his superiors, Bishop Grandin of St. Albert and his life-long friend Archbishop Taché of St. Boniface, would have been happy if they could have acceded to his desire but they could not find anyone of nearly comparable ability to replace him. As Taché wrote to Grandin, "my responsibilities as a Bishop do not permit me to send away an individual who does so much good."

Nevertheless, he fell in line and wrote asking the Canadian provincial of the Oblates to send him someone to step into Lacombe's shoes. That official evidently promised to secure someone as soon as possible. The displeasure in Archbishop Taché's reply to this offer indicates the high esteem in which he and everyone else held Father Lacombe.

"You say you have no one to send me at present; but after an ordination you may have perhaps a newly-ordained priest to give me to replace — my premier counsellor, my advisor, my Vicar-General, a missionary who speaks four languages, one who has thirty years of experience! Confess, mon cher, that this is not generous. . . ."

Well aware of his superiors' tug-of-war over him, he had to wait till March 17, 1882, before permission to return to St. Albert was granted. That day his diary recorded his gratitude. "Monsignor told me that the Superior General has decided to approve my going to St. Albert. *Deo Gratias.*"

Perhaps his joy might have been more constrained if he had realized how much the foothills country had changed during his absence. It was true that his Indians were still out there and needed him, but it was perhaps not so obvious to him that the church and the priests could no longer afford to commit their services wholly to the Indians. A number of white people were already in the West, more would soon rush in and the church would have to spread its limited resources over natives and new-comers. He daydreamed of ministering to the Blackfoot and at this stage could have been unaware that Bishop Grandin wanted to make him parish priest of the new hamlet of Calgary which had not existed the last time he had seen the Bow River.

Though he may have been delighted with the prospect of leaving the gambling tents and the log brothels along the CPR line, many a man was sorry to see him go. Amongst these were some of the railway engineers and the contractors who expressed their regret with a parting gift to the priest who for nearly two years had passed up and down the line blessing, rebuking and exhorting. At a little gathering they presented him with what he must have considered a magnificent gift, *"une cheval, une voiture, une tente"* and various associated bits and pieces and bid him godspeed in the many years of work which they hoped lay ahead of him.

Then on May 15, 1882, pleased as punch with his new horse and buggy and bubbling over with the anticipation of the sheer joys of the two-month trip across the prairies and parkland, he set out for St. Albert. For ten years he had looked forward to this trip back to the land of the Cree and the Blackfoot — back to the land of his youthful hardships. He knew, of course, that it would have changed in many respects but because of these very changes his native friends had all the more need of his help.

The most apparent change was that CPR trains were running as far as the new town of Brandon. From there to the vicinity of old Fort Qu'Appelle men were busily laying ties or rails or merely banking up the grade. With his new buggy and cayuse Father Lacombe jogged along beside the grade for some three hundred miles to the site of modern Indian Head, spending the nights camping out or else in a construction camp where someone was sure to recognize the bronzed missionary.

The second change was that in all that distance he never saw a buffalo or a more recent sign of their presence than their stark, white bones and skulls lying scattered all over the prairies. Thirty years ago when he had thrilled to the Métis' charges into the herds, the shaggy beasts would have been met at almost any point along the route he had come. Instead of buffalo, however, signs of settlement had crept west along the grade as white men, bent on using the rich soil, had come pouring in to take up the land. Father Lacombe had heard that in 1881 twenty-five thousand settlers had flocked into southern Manitoba and it appeared that in 1882 four times that many were moving in — some of them into modern Saskatchewan. Thinking this over brought a twinge to his heart — so very few of them were of French descent.

Savouring the pleasures of the trip, Father Lacombe took two weeks to travel as far as Fort Qu'Appelle. Eight days later he found himself crossing the South Saskatchewan River at the new Métis settlement of Batoche, where he met his old and "always agreeable" friend Father Vegreville. A couple of days later at the Duck Lake Métis community he found Father André — "a pleasure to see an old friend again." At Fort Carlton he noted little change but when on June 14, nearly a month after he had left Winnipeg, he reached the mouth of the Battle River, he found a thriving new town aptly named Battleford.

It had been built during the previous three or four years. Its first real importance had come about when as a result of Treaty No. 6 a large number of Indian reserves had been created nearby. Its future seemed assured when in 1877 it had been chosen as the capital of the Northwest Territories and many new buildings were erected to house various government offices. By the time of the priest's arrival it even had a newspaper run by Patrick G. Laurie, who, during Father Lacombe's residence in Winnipeg, had worked for W. F. Luxton's *Free Press*.

In Battleford, Father Lacombe relaxed for three or four days while he rested his horse and obtained a first-hand account of the state of affairs amongst the Indians. He talked to mounted policemen and various government officials who all gave him similar accounts of the rapid decline in the Indians' morale. Everything the father and his associates had feared and forecast before he had left for Winnipeg ten years previously had happened, but neither Indians nor whites had been allowed any time to adjust to the new order of things.

That new order could be attributed to a single fact: the buffalo had been wiped out.

Whereas in 1874, the year the NWMP had reached the prairies, great herds had grazed in every valley, by 1879 — a mere five years later — they had been virtually exterminated. In 1874, Father Leduc, writing from St. Albert, had said the buffalo would soon disappear. The next year Father André at St. Laurent had prophesied their demise within five years. In 1876 Crowfoot said, "We all see that the day is coming when the buffalo will all be killed. . . ." During 1877 and 1878 the fur traders had reported a rapid falling off in the number of the great beasts. Then during 1879 the Hudson's Bay Company's chief commissioner was virtually correct when he wrote of the "total disappearance of the buffalo."

By 1879 indeed the impossible had happened; the buffalo were really gone and utter disaster stared both Cree and Blackfoot in the face. In the space of the three years since they had signed Treaty No. 6 they had lost not only their land but their livelihood.

During the next three years Crees and Blackfoot, as well as Assiniboines, following the scanty remnants of the herds which had vanished from their own lands, had crowded into the Cypress Hills — thousands of Indians seeking a few hundred fleeing buffalo. During 1878, 1879 and 1880 they endured the worst starvation in their history.

At Fort Carlton in July 1879, Chief Factor Clarke wrote:

"The winter has been most trying to us, the whole of the Indians on the five reserves about Carlton have been in a state of semi-starvation, causing me great care and anxiety at times. The summer is now upon us and instead of our prospects improving the outlook is still more gloomy, and the future really looks desperate. . . . I foresee that this is only the beginning of the end."

That year the destitute Indians had flocked into Battleford looking for what help the hard-pressed officials could give them. Far out onto the wind-swept prairies the hunters searched in vain. Amid the snowdrifts in copse or coulee Indian mothers waited, boiling bone scraps, moccasins and shaganappi, watching in vain for the return of the hunters; in tent and tepee Indian children, weak and empty, whimpering for food, cried in vain, and died.

At Blackfoot Crossing many old people and children suffered until finally, abandoned by their starving families, they perished. At Fort Macleod, every other day the police fed seven thousand famished Indians. "What a change from the previous autumn," wrote Father Doucet of the Blackfoot. "It is hard to recognize in the victims of the famine, thin and emaciated, without vigour in their voices, the magnificent savages which I have formerly seen. They are no longer men but walking skeletons."

The worst starvation was in the south and the government rushed extra food supplies to Fort Walsh and Fort Macleod.

In order to keep abreast of the grim situation, it appointed Edgar Dewdney as Indian commissioner. One of his jobs was to point out to the natives the necessity of going to live on the reserves and growing their own food. But when stories of buffalo herds alleged to be grazing in their thousands in Montana came in, Canadian Indians hurried off south. Even Crowfoot led his people south and it was while they were there that, in an effort to stir up trouble, Father Lacombe's old charge, Louis Riel, went to see that great chief. Having spent most of 1877 and 1878 in a mental hospital, Riel had moved to Montana after his release. There he dreamed his dreams and imparted them to Métis and Indian alike.

With all these influences dissuading the Indians from settling on their reserves, Commissioner Dewdney had to report that at the end of 1881 less than half were on the lands set aside for them. Early in January 1882, however, the various bands, finding their hopes of living on buffalo in Montana illusory, began to drift back to Fort Walsh. They returned in a state of utter starvation.

This then was the situation when Father Lacombe paused in Battleford for a few days during the summer of 1882. What he had tried to warn the Crees and Blackfoot about had happened. What he had hoped to set up to shield them from this disaster had failed.

Determined to aid them where he could, he turned his horse's head west once more. Through springing grass and new leaves he made his way across the Turtle River valley, past Horse Hill, through Red Deer Creek, around Frenchman Butte and on June 23 reached Fort Pitt. Now that the tall prairie grass was no longer cropped by the wild herds and now that most of the Crees were either on reserves or far to the south, he could at times go fifty or a hundred miles in any direction without meeting a soul.

Trotting along through jackpine groves bright with the lanterns of tiger lilies, Father Lacombe's horse kept on its way to Long Lake where Chief Kehewin greeted his old friend gladly. Across the wide Dog Rump valley, around Egg Lake's north shore, where several years later his St. Paul des Métis was to bloom and fade, he and his horse pressed on. As the miles rolled by, punctuated by the tinkle of heel chains, the father, dreaming of the future of this rich land or dwelling on fond memories of his St. Paul des Cris, felt the presence of his faithful Alexis with whom so many times he had trodden this trail. Poor Alexis!

Year after year during Father Lacombe's long absence from the West, Alexis, ever lonesome and ever loyal, had tried to serve as he felt his chief would have done. When four or five years had slipped by and his mentor was reported to be still in Winnipeg, he decided to leave Father Doucet's Calgary mission and to seek out his first master and serve him once more. But instead, poor Alexis went wandering, physically from camp to camp over the prairies, and mentally from one hallucination to another, until he fancied himself to be filled with a divine mission. Once the fathers at St. Albert brought him back to the comfort of the home there, but he had soon stolen away. On his final trip along the trails he knew so well, still hoping to find Father Lacombe and still groping towards his destiny, he set out for Cold Lake more or less by the route Father Lacombe was now travelling. Somewhere along it and about a year before his sorrowing friends found his skeleton, the faithful Alexis reached his earthly destination.

Stopping overnight at the home of his friends the McGillivrays in the Victoria settlement, crossing Namepi Creek the next day and then wallowing through mud for three or four days, Father Lacombe crossed the Redwater River and finally reached St. Albert on July 18 — sixty-four days outbound from Winnipeg. *"Enfin me voila arrivé. C'est bien change."*

Everywhere he went people rejoiced to see him, Indian, Métis or white, communicant or Protestant. For if they were old-timers of ten or more years' standing they knew him and were glad to see him; if they were newcomers, they had heard of him and now saw this almost legendary figure in person. Included with them, of course, was Leon Harnois who two or three years previously had married Father Lacombe's sister Christine.

Amongst the groups of Indians still coming to Edmonton to trade he found the most change. All of them spoke of living theoretically on such and such a reserve and of supplementing the produce of their hunts with government handouts. All of them spoke of humiliation and hunger. Their unenviable lot was reflected in their thin frames and pinched faces but much more so by their lack-lustre glances — much of their old devil-may-care pride had slipped away. Their looks alone told him that even that early they had become the unwanted skeletons in the white man's closet. Although he knew it was late in the day, he nevertheless resolved to continue his efforts to help them back to the high road of independence and respect.

The hamlet of Edmonton exhibited change of a different sort. The fort was still standing but much of its vigour had seeped away. John Rowand's Big House had been torn down. Its successor, Hardisty's Big House, had been built outside the palisades and a little farther up the hill. He was jarred by the discovery that his old St. Joachim chapel, the one William Christie had built expressly for him, had been moved away in 1876 when Hardisty had told the priests to find themselves new quarters. Richard Hardisty had been and was still his good friend. Would St. Joachim have been moved if he, its first priest, had remained in the West? The fact that Hardisty's wife was the daughter of the Methodist preacher, did that have some bearing on its removal?

Perhaps it was just as well, because Malcolm Groat had come to the church's rescue and helped to see it rebuilt on a piece of his land out along the trail to St. Albert. In doing so, however, he had showed no special favouritism towards the Roman Catholics; he had made a similar gift to the Reverend Canon Newton, the Anglican who had arrived about this time. The Methodists, of course, were fairly well established up at the tip of what people were beginning to call McDougall Hill, where their church formed a focal point for the emerging town of Edmonton. Moreover, at the time of Father Lacombe's arrival a fourth denomination, the Presbyterians, had entered the competition for the settlement's limited number of souls and the Reverend A. B. Baird was busily building their new church.

By this time Edmonton, with a population of about 275, had become a definite entity and for a couple of years Father Lacombe's old acquaintance, Frank Oliver, who had worked for W. F. Luxton's Winnipeg *Free Press,* had been publishing his Edmonton *Bulletin.* At the time the father went to see him, Oliver's optimism had received a jolt — the CPR, which had been slated to come through Edmonton, had recently been diverted so as to pass through the southern fringe of the prairies.

That bad news, however, did not prevent one great man from paying respect to another and the next issue of the *Bulletin* reported that, "Rev. Father Lacombe is an old pioneer missionary of this country and is well known throughout the northwest. It must have been very pleasing to the reverend gentleman to see his old mission of St. Albert . . . improved so much in appearance and in such a flourishing condition."

On August 14 Father Lacombe headed south to visit the two North-West Mounted Police posts and their surrounding hamlets of Forts Calgary and Macleod. Calgary with its seventy-five people counted for little, but including nearby ranchers, Fort Macleod could muster five hundred white adults.

The father's trip followed the same route which he had taken thirteen years previously when he had been on his way to Fort Benton. This time, travelling the execrable new Edmonton-Calgary Trail in a four-wheeled buggy, the miles did not slip by as swiftly as they had done when he had used pack horses. On his second night out he stayed at the new government farm on Bigstone Creek. It, like other such farms, had been operating only two or three years and was intended to demonstrate the virtues of agriculture to the Indians on the Ermineskin and Samson reserves in what had once been called the Peace Hills area. His next day's travel took him to Father Beillevaire's mission on the Battle River where once more one of his associates brought him up to date on the Indians' new and discouraging status. Four days later saw the concerned father looking across the Bow River to the settlement of Calgary.

It is doubtful that he had ever been at the exact junction of the Bow and Elbow rivers before. If he had not, Alexis had been and seven years earlier and a mile or so up the Elbow River from the spot where the NWMP were putting up their Fort Calgary had erected Calgary's first Catholic building. For the next few years a number of devoted priests served the Indians out of this mission, as well as the small half-breed settlement on the Highwood River and even the white people of Fort Macleod. When Father Lacombe arrived at the mission on August 25, 1882, he came in the capacity of father superior of the establishment. By the following Sunday word of his return had gotten around and when he preached in three languages the little chapel could not hold a quarter of the crowd.

Having spent a few days sizing up the needs of the hamlet of

Calgary and of Our Lady of Peace mission, Father Lacombe took off for the south and on September 1 reached Fort Macleod. It was a most important station of the NWMP whose presence had made it possible for a few ranchers to start grazing their herds in the area. Already it had become a commercial centre which was growing more rapidly than Calgary. About the time Father Lacombe visited, Kamoose Taylor aided the cause by launching the Macleod Hotel. And, under the circumstances, launched is undoubtedly the proper verb, for he notified one and all that, "The Bar in the Annex will be open day and night. All Day drinks, 50 cents each; Night drinks, $1.00 each. No Mixed Drinks will be served except in case of death in the family."

Two months earlier, in July 1882, ex-Mountie C. E. D. Wood's Macleod *Gazette* had become the second newspaper to be published in Alberta, and the world began hearing more about the wind-swept town in the heart of the grasslands. Like Frank Oliver at Edmonton, Wood was anxious to pay his respects to Father Lacombe and commented, "We are glad to hear that the health of the Reverend Father is good notwithstanding the hardships which he has faced. We extend a hearty welcome to him in Macleod."

Father Lacombe made the most of his welcome to preach a sermon begging for money to build a chapel. He appealed so effectively that a week or so later he was able to buy a small log building from the NWMP which he dedicated as Fort Macleod's first Roman Catholic church.

But no matter what ideas Bishop Grandin had about Father Lacombe taking charge of rapidly developing towns and ministering to the white folk who were beginning to trickle in, his heart was still with the natives. From September when he reached Fort Macleod till the spring, he and Father Legal divided their time between a shack on the Blood reserve and their sod-roofed Fort Macleod home.

It was during this period that Father Lacombe received the only letter from his mother that remained amongst his papers. It was dated L'Assomption, November 4, and expressed her joy that at last God had granted his request to return to his Indians. She pointed out that though she was now over eighty years old she still hoped to see him once more and recalled the days of "fifty-six years ago when I rocked you on my knees." In the meantime she declared that her life with the Sisters of Providence was a happy one.

Cheered by her letter, Father Lacombe spent much of his time working on his Blackfoot dictionary and was on the reserve as the new year opened. "Jan. 1st: New Years Day with the Bloods. We offered them tobacco and tea. It is very cold. Time flies. The poor Indians, how I pity them."

Somewhat later he was to reiterate, "Thank you, oh God, for having me return to my poor Indians. Have pity on them! My only wish is to bring them into the folds of Your religion."

But they needed help on the material plane as well as on the spiritual. This was obvious from the typical position in which Crowfoot and his people found themselves that winter on their reserve at Blackfoot Crossing. The previous July they had struggled back from their near futile expedition to the United States in search of buffalo. Then, according to official correspondence, the chief's 1,064 followers were "all in a most destitute condition. A large proportion of them consisted of old men, women and children. They were nearly all on foot."

The police had given them what food they could find and sent them on their eighty-mile trip to Blackfoot Crossing. On September 6, in the course of his western tour, Lord Lorne, whom Father Lacombe had welcomed to Rat Portage some months earlier, called on Crowfoot. He was accompanied by Commissioner Dewdney and the whole party was guided across from Battleford by Crowfoot's adopted son, the Cree chief, Poundmaker. At that meeting the Blackfoot chief pleaded for more provisions. As the Reverend James MacGregor wrote:

"I have rarely seen a more touching sight than the poor infirm chief, with his finely chiselled countenance and bright smile, as, leaning heavily on his staff, and worse clad than any of his followers, he moved forward to his place; the shabby clothes, which the poorest artisan would be ashamed to wear, contrasted sadly with the Victoria medal which he wore on his breast."

Unfortunately, little but sympathy resulted from that meeting. That winter Crowfoot and his people suffered dreadful privations and endured unnecessary humiliation. His genuine friend Colonel Macleod had left the NWMP and one of the few other officials he trusted, Inspector C. Denny, had been assigned to other work. The desperate chief had no one to whom he could turn to help him counter the inexperienced and biased political appointees who had been sent by a blind government to lord it over the Indians. All through 1882 and into 1883 the bitter injustice laid on them by uncaring or ignorant men rankled the Blackfoot. Within a few months these men destroyed the faith the Blackfoot had reposed in the mounted police and the white man's justice and they began to regard every white man's move with distrust, even Father Lacombe's church.

By the time the priest returned to the West Crowfoot had become a leader amongst those who had signed Treaty No. 7. By that time also Father Lacombe had become a man of wide report and although neither chief nor catechist had paid much attention to the other in the past, they now met as two famous men who, perforce, must deal with each other. Fortunately each had come to respect the other.

During the first week in May 1883, Father Lacombe set out for Crowfoot's reserve. An interesting note in his diary for May 7 tells of meeting some settlers on their way to look for land. The priest noted that they were Ontarians and grumbled that "Truly they have more courage than our *Canadiens Francois.*" On May 8, after urging his horse and buggy over the prairie gopher holes, Father Lacombe reached the Blackfoot reserve. His reception was cordial enough that, although Crowfoot regarded the project with a cool eye, within a few days with Blackfoot help he started building his chapel.

However much wishful thinking may have deceived the Reverend John McDougall or Father Lacombe, Crowfoot was never more than a moderately religious man. He had paid only the necessary minimum of attention to the mystic teachings of his fathers and merely listened courteously to the preachings of Catholic or Methodist missionaries. All of these he recognized as honest, unselfish white men trying to help his people and to all of them in roughly equal but noncommittal portions he extended his friendship. In this way when he found that Father Lacombe had come to visit him and wanted to build a church, he permitted it but did not attach earth-shaking importance to either the structure or indeed to Father Lacombe.

Some weeks later, however, after the railway surveyors had passed through his reserve and Crowfoot was becoming increasingly irritated, the Anglican missionary was refused permission to build his church near Father Lacombe's. Crowfoot is reported as saying that "since one Church had been built all the old men & women & children had died & if another Church was built, all would die. They had too much church."

But if Crowfoot had little use for churches, he was friendly enough with Father Émile Legal who was glad to welcome Father Lacombe to the reserve. A few months earlier, in December 1882, he had written, "For us this year the most important event has been the arrival of Father Lacombe in our district. . . ." Then with a scarcely noticeable contradiction he added, "Another event of equal importance to our missions has been the construction of the Canadian Pacific Railway . . . [whose] terminus is now a distance of only 180 miles from here." The approaching railway was never far from westerners' minds.

On the one hand, because of what it would do to the Indians, Father Lacombe disliked the railway. On the other, because it would make the rich soil of the West available to millions of settlers, he was eager to see it come. Either way he looked at it, however, he found himself inevitably caught up in its affairs.

On May 19, 1883, slightly more than a week after he arrived at Blackfoot Crossing, he wrote to the absent Father Legal. "The advance party of the railway will be here in twenty days levelling the ground for the road which will pass about 4 miles from this reserve." Writing his friend again a week later he states that he is going to leave in three or four days to go east along the right-of-way and that he expects to meet the first workmen about fifteen miles away. Knowing the Blackfoot as he did, he was worried about a clash between them and the labourers. Some weeks earlier blood would have been shed but for the intervention of the mounted police in dispersing a party of angry Crees which under their notable Chief Piapot had recently camped right across the right-of-way between Maple Creek and Walsh.

The prairie Indians dreaded the coming of the railway

which was going to permit white people by the thousands to enter and occupy their ancestral lands. Perhaps nothing could convey to white minds the pathos of the Indians' situation more than an occurrence witnessed by some of the railway contractors on the prairie east of Medicine Hat. There, late one afternoon, a native rode his horse to the crest of a nearby rise and sat immobile watching the grading crew eat their way west into his area. With a few eagle feathers scarcely stirring in the breeze he remained for an hour or so silhouetted against the reddening sky and then as if in a gesture of unspoken desperation disappeared with the setting of the sun. For him the end was at hand.

From the white man's point of view, however, this railway was only the beginning of greater things as across the prairies some 5,000 men and 1,700 teams worked incessantly to drive the road onward. The prairies which so recently had rumbled to the rush of the buffalo herds now felt a new rumble as graders, track-laying men and steam locomotives pushed the rusty new rails west. Young Canada's greatest accomplishment was on its way.

Keeping up with the railway, settlers started to pour in to the prairies — over twenty-five thousand in 1881, about a hundred thousand in 1882 — and the rush was merely starting. In February 1883 immigration sheds were built at Qu'Appelle to shelter the throngs of settlers. By March, Regina was incorporated; in May, Moose Jaw sought incorporation; in June, Swift Current flashed into existence. Medicine Hat was soon to follow, then some town to be built near Crowfoot's reserve, and then Calgary would be next.

So, from Blackfoot Crossing on May 29 the father, worrying about the possibility of *"desordes"* amongst the Blackfoot, set out to meet the advancing railway head on. Day by day his diary keeps us in touch with its progress as he headed east to confer with Lieutenant-Governor Dewdney. On the first night he camped with an advance party: *"au camp des Canadiens — Comme ils sont heureux."* Next day he marvelled at the hundreds of workmen all along the line. On June 1 he reached Medicine Hat and met up with locomotives. *"Quel train et quel commerce! Nombre de chars de construction."*

June 4 found him at a great camp of Crees near Maple Creek. He evidently stayed to visit until June 9 when

Lieutenant-Governor Dewdney came in an endeavour to get them to move north to their reserves in the watershed of the North Saskatchewan River. By June 11 he was at Swift Current where he met Mgr. Thomas Duhamel, bishop of Ottawa, and a special train of touring priests. On June 17 he was back at Blackfoot Crossing awaiting the arrival of Dewdney. By that time a gang of workmen were camping near the point where the railway would cross Crowfoot Creek some five miles away.

It is hard to tell from the priest's brief and modest diary entries what was the sequence of events during the touchy few days which began when the railway construction crews were about to enter the reserve. When Father Lacombe intervened the Blackfoot were standing glaring at the men, ready to attack them. He was able to prevent that and at a later meeting made promises which were afterwards confirmed by Lieutenant-Governor Dewdney. While the father's diary does not say much of this episode, nevertheless Van Horne and the railway officials felt that his pacification of the angry Indians had not only averted bloodshed but had been a major contribution to the railway's construction.

In general, the grade was run near the north boundary of the Blackfoot reserve. Adjacent to that, however, were the lands originally intended for the Bloods and Sarcees but which they had not accepted. When the railway surveyors began encroaching on these lands, which they had every legal right to do, the Blackfoot, still mistakenly considering that they were Indian lands, objected. At times the railway did cut across small portions of the actual Blackfoot reserve. Once Father Lacombe intervened and received Dewdney's backing, Crowfoot agreed to accept other lands south of the Bow River in lieu of these and eventually the Blackfoot's boundaries were changed so that from Crowfoot station to Gleichen the railway forms the northern boundary of today's reserve.

Such transactions, however, all lay in the future when the surveyors approached. According to the *Codex historicus* of the Cluny mission (copy made in 1908), which does not correspond exactly with Father Lacombe's diary:

"When the Indians saw such large numbers of surveyors put in stakes, mark the CPR road and cutting off a corner of the reserve, they stopped the workmen violently. . . . Father Lacombe heard all the grumblings which were rumoured at camp, he was afraid his land surveyors would be massacred and he wired the Indian Commissioner at Regina immediately, to come as quickly as possible. He sent wire after wire, and, as the Commissioner did not come and as there was no time to waste, the Indians getting more and more excited, he went to see Crowfoot, the head chief of the Blackfeet at this time, and convinced him as well as the other chiefs to hold a large meeting at the mission."

To this meeting held on June 19 the father took two hundred pounds of sugar, as many of tobacco, as well as tea and some sacks of flour. Having distributed these as a preliminary, he is recorded as saying:

"Well, my friends, I have some advice to give you today; let the whites pass on your lands; firstly these whites who are on your land are only workers who are obeying their chiefs, and it is with these chiefs that you must settle your difficulties. I have told them of your dissatisfaction and in a few days the Lieutenant-Governor himself will come. He will listen to your complaints, and, if the agreements he offers you, do not please you, it will be time enough to guard your land and to drive out the workers."

Continuing with the narration of events the *Codex* adds:

"A few days later, as Father Lacombe had announced, Dewdney actually came to visit the Indians and told them: 'You did well and I thank you for it. Here is what I come to suggest to you now: in exchange for the land which the railroad is taking from your reserve, I am going to give you much more on the other side of the river: and if you do not want this, we will undo the work which is started and lay it out on the outside of the reserve.'

"Thanks to Crowfoot, they all declared they were satisfied, and, the reserve had since then the railroad on the north and east as their limit. The reserve was enlarged by the actual parcel (1908) of the reserve situated on the other side of the Arcs River. However, on the north side the Indians kept a corner beyond the line. . . ."

Once the issue was settled Dewdney invited his friend the priest to accompany him on a visit to the Stoney reserve west of Calgary where they were guests at the McDougall mission. Later on the two men went to visit the Sarcees just outside of Calgary. For about a month during the long hours of the summer's daylight the itchy-footed priest was always on the move, appearing from time to time anywhere from Fort Macleod to Calgary and as far east as Regina. On August 20 he met with the lieutenant-governor and his council at the new capital of the Northwest Territories, Regina. There he joined forces with Archbishop Taché and Father Maisonneuve. All of them were interested in their proposed industrial schools which they hoped to build at Qu'Appelle and at the mouth of Alberta's Highwood River. On August 22, Lieutenant-Governor Dewdney finally gave his approval to starting the Highwood River school.

Having been honoured at Regina and also having advanced the prospects of his school, Father Lacombe returned to Calgary on the evening of the 24th. "The next day I relaxed more or less." A day or so later he received a wire. It had been filed at Winnipeg a couple of hours before it was handed to him and in that time the message had flown across the nine hundred miles to Calgary. What a marvel!

But its message was no less astounding. It came from George Stephen, the president of the CPR, and it read, "Come to lunch with me tomorrow in my car at Calgary." And it was intended for him, Albert Lacombe, the farm boy from St. Sulpice!

His diary entry for that tomorrow was perhaps an indication of how his modesty tried to cover up his pride, for it said simply, "This evening most of the officials of the Syndicate [CPR] arrive. Messrs. Stephen, Robitaille and others. I dine with them. Their courtesy to me."

In a letter he wrote to Archbishop Taché he elaborated a little more: "The famous excursion arrived in Calgary in a royal manner. Seven palace cars with a large staff. Two hours after its arrival, on the invitation of Mr. Stephen, President of the CPR, I supped, or rather dined with princes, lords and counts, etc. The champagne flowed like the clear water of our river. I obtained many favours of these gentlemen."

Father Lacombe did indeed obtain many favours from the executives of the CPR, but, on his part he had conferred favours. As well as the president and the presidents of three American railways, this group of men having lunch together at the end of steel at Calgary included Donald Smith, R. B. Angus, William Van Horne and Count Hermann Von Hohenlohe, after whose German estates the railway station of Gleichen was named. Some of them he had known for some time, such as Donald Smith, who had been sent to the Red River Settlement to out-manoeuvre Louis Riel, and George Stephen and Van Horne whom he had met during his Rat Portage days. Now these great men, jubilant that the CPR was making such good progress, and aware of the father's role at Blackfoot Crossing, were eager to meet this other great man, the legendary Father Lacombe.

If these men admired the black-cassocked priest, he also admired them and on many occasions wrote or remarked that he considered the directors and organizers of the CPR a great boon to Canada and the West. As he explained his feelings to his biographer Katherine Hughes,

> "I would look long in silence at that road coming on — like a band of wild geese in the sky — cutting its way through the prairies; opening up the great country we thought would be ours for years. Like a vision I could see it driving my poor Indians before it, and spreading out behind it the farms, the towns and cities you see today.
>
> "No one who has not lived in the west since the old-times can realize what is due to that road — that CPR. It was magic — like the mirage on the prairies, changing the face of the whole country. . . . But I say to you of the men I met those first days of the road — there was more than money-making in their heads.
>
> "There was courage; yes, and daring. . . . How we admired that man Van Horne."

Unlike a generation of farmers whose comfortable entry to the West was made possible by a two- or three-day trip aboard a CPR train and who then proceeded to complain of a CPR monopoly, Father Lacombe had a different viewpoint. On several occasions he had spent two months walking from Winnipeg to Fort Edmonton urging his Red River cart along, and he could appreciate what a nearly inconceivable luxury it was to travel from Winnipeg to Calgary in less than two days.

It was, then, with mutual respect that these men seated Father Lacombe at the chairman's right hand and began passing goblets around the table. To this priest they owed much. And now, amid many speeches and toasts, the directors adopted a unique way of showing their gratitude to the tireless pioneer. They convened a directors' meeting and President Stephen rose and temporarily resigned his position. Then, to the blackrobe's bewilderment, upon motion by R. B. Angus, a motion received with applause and carried unanimously, Father Lacombe was elected president of the CPR. Thus these men, as great in their way as he was in his, acknowledged their debt to the missionary; for an hour he remained the president of the CPR and for a lifetime they allowed him a free pass over their railway.

With a spirit no less courteous than theirs, he accepted the office and in return mischievously nominated George Stephen to the rectorship of his Calgary St. Mary's parish. Amid more laughter and applause the ex-president accepted his new dignity, but with a glance out the car window at the village, he exclaimed, "poor souls of Calgary, I pity you!"

With this luncheon and pass the company and the priest cemented an alliance which, beginning a couple of years earlier, had now ripened into friendship. If, however, now that the railway ran into the heartland of Father Lacombe's decades of endeavour, the company imagined that by means of this meal and this gift, it was making the last instalment on its debt to Father Lacombe, it was mistaken. For decades after this luncheon both Father Lacombe's church and his enterprises were to collect many a welcome dividend.

CHAPTER SIXTEEN

The North - West Rebellion
1883 – 86

As Father Lacombe left the luxury of George Stephen's private railway car to hurry home through Calgary's newly scratched out streets, thoughts raced through his head like the bubbles which so recently had risen in his champagne glass. The railway across the prairies and parklands was now a fait accompli; he had played a part in that accomplishment and his part had been noticed and rewarded.

Now the band of steel stretching nine hundred miles from Winnipeg to Calgary would make his western prairie areas accessible to all who cared to come to caress them. Thousands of settlers would pour in to claim this rich soil and to fall in love with the many valleys like those of the Battle and Red Deer rivers in which with his Blackfoot he had camped so often. In a land now almost entirely empty of buffalo and Indians a new civilization would arise having plenty and contentment as its watchwords.

Plenty for whom? For the Métis who had rearranged their economy when the buffalo had disappeared so that much of their living came from freighting for the little frontier settlements and now had lost most of this work to the railway? Which way would they turn when the waves of white settlement came splashing up the valleys and washing over the prairie ridges?

The Indians, too, which way would they turn? The buffalo were gone and the government had nearly completed the operation of impounding Cree, Stoney, Sarcee and Blackfoot on

264

their piddling reserves. Edgar Dewdney, lieutenant-governor of the Northwest Territories, was optimistic that by settling them and encouraging them to be farmers they would soon be self-supporting. Father Lacombe was dubious. There was little obvious reason, however, why Indians and Métis could not live off the soil as white men did. Moreover, to make some allowance for their inexperience the treaties had provided that each Indian family had available to it four times the area of land which a white homesteader would be allowed to claim.

And yet as it turned out there was every reason why the Indians of the time could not live by agriculture. The white man knew how to farm or could learn quickly and was eager to do so, whereas it was too much to expect the Indians to make the abrupt transition to agriculture. Nevertheless, the vision of the time could perceive no other course for the natives to follow. This was the vision which, although Father Lacombe felt it had many weaknesses, was the only solution to the problem which he and everyone — Protestant or Catholic, Mountie or government employee — who wanted to help the Indians could offer.

As on the August day in 1883 he made his way back to his mission, these were the questions to which he could see no clear answers. By one of life's contradictions, having spent most of an ordinary man's working life trying to protect his natives from the inevitable corrosive effect of white civilization, he now found himself not only welcoming a railway but helping it to make its way into the West. Moreover, he had even welcomed the new interlopers which at one time he had hoped would never come in. Nay, he had done worse, and had gone to plead with white settlers to come in and populate the former Indian lands and he would continue to do so. How different life is to what one plans.

For twenty-three contented years he had been a missionary to the Indians, for ten long not so contented years he had been a parish priest, collector and colonizer. During that decade his superiors had continued to pile new responsibilities upon his shoulders and to delegate tasks to him that were to see him rubbing shoulders with the crafty of the country and matching wits with the mighty of the land. When at its end they had allowed him to return to his Crees and Blackfoot, the aura of being a national figure had clung to him.

But life pushed him around too. He wanted to continue his mission to all Indians, but had to give up much of that work in favour of serving the whites who were flocking in and in favour of taking further time off to go on the church's many errands. He compromised by dividing his time between Fort Macleod, Calgary and camps on the reserves. When other tasks were entrusted to him he bore them by absences of varying length in the East or by making side trips as far afield as the New England states. Thus in a purposeful and busy round of duties nearly ten more years slipped by while the land which ultimately became Alberta lay more or less fallow waiting for the influx of settlers which did not begin until about the latter half of the decade.

A whole month elapsed before he was able to use his CPR railway pass but since he went by pack horse to St. Albert for a retreat during that time, the long, idle interval is perhaps understandable. Then in a delightful, hurried trip to Medicine Hat, Regina and back, travelling by day, and, miracle of miracles, at night too, he enjoyed the speed of his effortless passage over the empty prairies. Having completed that errand, he decided to build a small chapel in east Calgary, worked hard at it himself and opened it on Sunday, December 2, 1883.

Then he was off again. On December 6, with his bag full of papers and his head buzzing with projects, he set out for the East. His journal records his departure at eight o'clock in the morning. Next day it shows him as being *"Trés comfortable* in a Pullman car — *Quelle difference,"* while on the third day he reaches St. Boniface. But that was only a start. With flashing pass and clacking car wheels he headed for Montreal. Leaving St. Boniface on December 13 and touching bases at St. Paul and Chicago, he and his pass rattled into Detroit on the 15th. He was finally received by the bishop at Montreal on December 17. *Bien!*

Two days later he was making a whirlwind tour of government offices in Ottawa where he had many successful interviews concerning the current crop of concessions he felt he should have. He called on Sir Hector Langevin, Sir Adolphe Caron and other senior officials — *"comme toujours, beaucoup de politesse et de promises."* If Father Lacombe was becoming well known to the highest officials of the federal government and was making his impression on them, he was also beginning to learn how successfully they could retreat into their invulnerable shells of politeness and ambiguity.

He spent New Year's Eve at his old college at L'Assomption happily recalling the days forty years earlier when as a student he had paid rapt attention to great clerics who came visiting. Now, although it gave him little emotional uplift, he stood before the students as one of the great of the land — the famous Father Lacombe. During his few days there he spent all the time he could with his aged mother, now living with the Sisters of Providence. Never one to miss an opportunity, he tried at the same time to talk them into sending some sisters to serve in the Indian school he proposed to build that fall.

After winning only a noncommittal answer, he went visiting some of his relatives on the rich, flat farms of St. Sulpice parish. One he missed seeing on that trip was his sister who had married a Foisey and later had crossed the United States boundary to live in Providence, Rhode Island.

For the next four months his diary reads like the record of a whirling dervish as the tireless priest swirled all over Quebec and the northeastern states, begging, colonizing, preaching and at times returning to Ottawa to stir up the politicians to making more concessions and going back to L'Assomption on two further occasions. Back at St. Albert, reading the letters he wrote explaining his accomplishments and his failures, Bishop Grandin marvelled. From a diary entry for February 18, when he received a letter from that bishop, who evidently had failed to appreciate some of the complexities of a situation, Lacombe allows his frank opinion to overreach his caution, for he confides to his little black book, *"Pauvre Eveque! Comme il est näif!"* — "Poor bishop, how artless he is!"

So involved were his own objectives and his travels that one can only wonder that even with his railway pass and another he obtained from William Wainwright, vice-president of the Grand Trunk Railway, he was able to accomplish them all. Without attempting to do so in sequence, we can mention some of the outstanding men he met and summarize the main features of his winter's stay in Quebec.

Amongst those leading men were the governor general, the Marquis of Lansdowne, and of course his old acquaintance the prime minister, Sir John A. Macdonald. Along with theirs he added several other calling cards to his collection, including those of Sir Mackenzie Bowell, J. A. Chapleau, Senator L. F. R. Masson, Edward Blake, Sir Joseph Pope and Sir Charles Tupper. Most of them met him because of mutual problems they had to iron out. Some, of course, met him first on a casual basis or out of curiosity, but having talked with him soon decided that he was no freak from the West, but that behind the gentle smile and the easy wit lay a purposeful intellect well worth cultivating.

With all of them he had some special need he wanted to discuss: his homestead in Calgary, his dictionary, the industrial school, a French colony for the Qu'Appelle valley or perhaps a hospital. Everywhere he went they watched him intently because he always wanted something and they knew that inevitably he would wangle at least part of it out of them. For never was there a more charming, proficient or praiseworthy beggar.

Indeed, it was in this guise that Donald Smith invited Father Lacombe and Archbishop Taché to dine with a select CPR-tinged group on January 9 when, as the diary says, "Stephen, Angus, Van Horne, Norquay *et autres*" were present. That same diary entry wasted no time summarizing the chit-chat or listing the courses or the wines, but went on quickly to the meat of the matter, saying that everything passed off agreeably "to the advantage of our missions. I expect that I shall obtain several more favours."

One of these prospective advantages concerned bringing in French Canadians to settle a block of 200,000 acres (1,250 quarter-sections) which had been set aside in 1883 for the church's Société de Colonization. It was to be in the lower Qu'Appelle watershed some seventy miles west of Brandon. About ten days after the dinner, George Stephen wrote the father, saying, "I will be ready to expend the sum of $500 on the homestead of each of the 50 families it is proposed to settle, taking a lien on the homestead for the repayment of the money...."

His winter spent in the East was surprisingly successful. First of all, it put him on first name terms with all the great men of Canada. Then it cut through red tape to concessions affecting his diocese, French immigration to the West and many other matters.

Not the least of the advantages which that winter and his powers of persuasion brought Father Lacombe was his luck in convincing his niece, Georgiana Foisey, to leave Rhode Island to come out to teach another of his schools near St. Albert in much the same way his sister Christine had done fourteen years earlier.

Finally on May 18, 1884, he and his niece boarded a steamboat at Lachine for their long trip west just as in that same month thirty-two years earlier he had set out for Fort Edmonton. On this occasion, however, after short visits in Toronto, Rat Portage and Winnipeg, he reached Calgary thirteen days after leaving Montreal — one-tenth of the time his 1852 trip had taken.

Everything had been speeded up. As the diary jubilantly reports, "Great changes in the new town." Nevertheless, he is happy to look upon and enter his *"pauvre cabane de Notre Dame de Paix."*

As Father Lacombe had noted, great changes were sweeping not only the urban centre but the whole area. The town of Calgary had been incorporated recently and already contained some five hundred people. Edmonton with about 250 was not doing so well. Fort Macleod continued to grow and to attract men of high calibre and so did the rival coal mining town of Coal Banks (soon to be known as Coalhurst and later as Lethbridge) some thirty miles away.

By 1884 Edmonton, Calgary, Fort Macleod, Coalhurst and Medicine Hat were the cardinal points of the framework of the future Alberta. As yet it had barely started to flesh out. A smattering of white people growing a few vegetables and milking a few cows occupied the various missions. Along the CPR sidings at Gleichen, Canmore, Banff and Silver City, a handful of railway employees prodding with their picks tried to keep the recently laid rails in alignment. Along the trails at various places, later to be known as Wetaskiwin, Red Deer, High River, and others, a few optimists had come in to keep stopping places. Scattered here and there south of the Bow River from Medicine Hat to Morley, several ranchers were becoming bitter because starving Indians killed their cattle.

That year near the mouth of the Highwood River Father Lacombe's efforts had successfully channeled federal funds into the construction of St. Joseph's Industrial School, popularly known as the Dunbow School. Like the other Indian schools that came into being about the same time — the one operated by the Roman Catholics at Qu'Appelle and the other run by the Protestants at Battleford — it had a slow gestation. After some experience all missionaries came to the conclusion that the only way to assimilate the Indians would be to operate such schools where the children could be isolated from their parents and taught the skills necessary to ensure their success in the white world. The Methodist McDougalls had thought in those terms and as early as 1872 Bishop Grandin had written Father Lacombe asking him to orient his thinking in that direction. In turn, the good father, with his understanding of the political ropes at Ottawa, kept urging such a development.

Finally on October 1, 1883, Prime Minister Macdonald wrote to him saying that "all difficulties have been overcome and three Industrial Schools are to be established." During his long sojourn in the East the following winter the priest pulled a number of strings which resulted in various concessions from the CPR and in a promise from the Sisters of Charity to teach in his new institution. On October 17, 1884, the Dunbow School celebrated its official opening with Father Lacombe as the resident principal assisted by a staff of two lay brothers and two sisters.

It had never occurred to the unilateral do-gooder, Father Lacombe, that the Indians would hesitate to send their children to his school. Only after his almost single-handed effort had brought it into being did he come to realize that, regardless of their friendship for him personally, the Blackfoot parents did not want to part with their children and exile them to his school. Finally, with a great deal of difficulty and with the active support of Jean L'Heureux, he rounded up seventeen boys between fifteen and seventeen years old and herded them through its gateway. Before a long day was over he had seen them bathed, had their long hair cut and put new clothes on them.

They led the patient father and his small staff a merry dance. Running away, breaking all his rules and thinking up scores of new varieties of mischief, they overtaxed even his deep reservoir of geniality. Overwhelming all other entries in the records of the school's progress were such comments as, "Our boys are getting more and more difficult to manage — pupils turbulent — trouble *avec les enfants.* Some of the boys appear too big . . . to remain in an institution like this."

And indeed the boys were too old to be broken to school ways, and by the next spring when Father Lacombe took on another task and Father Claude replaced him temporarily, only three students remained at Dunbow. That day one of them ran away, and another had to be expelled. The school's first year had been far from propitious. But Father Lacombe's persistence never wavered and, leaving alone the Blackfoot children for a while, he recruited younger Cree and Métis pupils from up north. Eventually the Blackfoot, Bloods and Piegans came to see some value in his school and permitted some of their children to attend.

Thus in the hands of various religious denominations the Indian school question got its start in the hope that such institutions would bridge the gap between stone-age wanderers and sedentary farmers. Like so many of the ideas imposed on the Indians by well-intentioned white folk, the Indian schools probably did more good than harm but unfortunately fell far short of being an adequate solution to the problem which in retrospect seems more difficult to us than it did at the time. Nevertheless, some expedients had to be tried and when others despaired and gave up, Father Lacombe tried and tried again.

If on a small scale at his Dunbow School Father Lacombe was having difficulties, other problems of which he was acutely aware were disturbing his bishop and the governors of the Northwest Territories as well as the Ottawa government. All over the West the Indians and Métis were naturally bitter. The complete disappearance of the buffalo and the resultant starvation, combined with the political patronage in appointing Indian agents, had made Cree and Blackfoot, Sarcee and Stoney ready to listen to the exhortations of the more trigger-happy Métis.

Not long after Father Lacombe had enjoyed the hospitality of George Stephen's private railway car, the recalcitrant Cree Chief Big Bear had sent a messenger to Crowfoot to see if plans could not be hatched to tear up the railway, whack the white man over the head with it and make him return to whatever greedy land he came from. Participation by the Blackfoot was vital to his scheme but Crowfoot, holding the reins, decided not to act.

For years he had been an outstanding chief, a fact which was confirmed at the signing of Treaty No. 7. Since then, because he was the one chief whom the white officials respected above all others save perhaps Red Crow of the Bloods, his power over his people increased. All of them depended on the government for food and because of his influence with the officials his compatriots all looked to him as the supreme arbiter of their problems. He was a dignified man, taciturn at times, but an impressive orator when moved, and his sincerity and sense of justice brought out a favourable response in white breasts. At the same time his only concern was for the good of his people and if in his opinion he could best serve them by agreeing to some unpopular course suggested by the white officials, he did so. But he was never what in derision his people called a "government Indian" — one who for value received danced to the white man's tune.

By 1884 his friendship with the mounted police had soured and so had much of his faith in the white man. Nevertheless, he still trusted five or six of them, including Colonel Macleod, Edgar Dewdney, Father Lacombe, John McDougall and Cecil Denny, the ex-policeman. Strangely enough too and in spite of the man's eccentricity he still held Jean L'Heureux in high esteem and let him live with his band. It was only natural, of course, that under the circumstances and despite hereditary hatreds, he had a soft spot in his heart for several of the Cree chiefs, including his adopted son Poundmaker, whose people were suffering like his own.

During the summer of 1884 Lieutenant-Governor Dewdney, worried about the influence that hostile Métis and Crees were gaining with the Blackfoot chief, decided to try to offset it by taking Crowfoot and two or three of his prominent associate chiefs on a railway trip to Winnipeg. There, with his rock-hard face as immutable as ever, Crowfoot saw the brick houses, streets and multitudes in a white man's city, and for the first time realized that though he and his abused colleagues could easily wipe out the shack town villages of Alberta, doing so would avail them nothing in their conflict with the white man's might.

With opposing forces pulling him many different ways and finally with Dewdney confronting him with a picture more striking than words, Crowfoot faced an unenviable dilemma. But no one, neither the white police whom he now regarded coolly, nor the Métis whom he found hard to tolerate, nor Big Bear and his Crees — none knew which way he might jump.

Neither did Louis Riel who reappeared on the Canadian scene that summer of 1884 to become a thorn in the side of the Ottawa government and to present Archbishop Taché with another major headache. After he had been unable to take his seat in the House of Commons following the 1874 election, he had been detained in an insane asylum for two years before going to live in Montana in 1879. Remaining there for five years during which he continued to incite any Canadian Métis who travelled into his area, he accepted an invitation from them to return to the prairies as their leader and spokesman.

Once Father Lacombe heard that he had crossed into Canada the priest's visits to Crowfoot became more frequent. Up at St. Albert Bishop Grandin worried about Riel's presence in the Fort Carlton area and paid the Saskatchewan Métis a visit. He knew as well as Riel that the Métis had grievances which needed attention and he had consistently pressed Ottawa to remedy these. In September 1884 he made a further effort to alert the federal government to the danger by writing Sir John A. Macdonald. While at Prince Albert he had discovered what to him was a serious indication that the Métis were getting out of hand — they were not taking the priests into their confidence and were reported as believing that the priests had been "sold to the Canadian government."

In his letter he declared:

"I blame the Métis and I have not spared them reproaches. But I will permit myself to say to Your Honour with all possible respect, that the Canadian Government is itself not free of blame. . . ."

Writing to Sir Hector Langevin about the same time he said:

"Once pushed to the limit, neither pastor nor bishop can make them listen to reason, and they may proceed to acts of extreme violence. I beg you then to instantly employ all your influence to secure for them whatever is just in their demands."

But, as usual, nothing was done.

Indian agents, government officials, mounted police and missionaries all worried their way through the winter. Compared to some five thousand white folk in the arable portions of Alberta, there were about eight thousand Indians, as well as nearly fifteen hundred Métis who were mainly located near the North Saskatchewan River. Those at Lac Ste. Anne, St. Albert and Lac La Biche were thought to be sufficiently under the thumb of the Catholic missionaries that in the event of trouble they would probably stay clear of it. The one-time settlement around Buffalo Lake had pretty well dispersed, but its place had been taken by a relatively new Métis colony along the Battle River. Although Father Beillevaire had built his Duhamel church in its midst, its people were quite closely tied with their relations to whom Riel was preaching near Fort Carlton and were apt to throw in their lot with them.

The Indians were more scattered up and down the province. One concentration of their reserves was clustered around Edmonton. Another grouping of two or three straddled the Calgary-Edmonton Trail on either side of the Battle River, while not far from Calgary other reservations contained hundreds of plains Indians as disgruntled as their relations on the large reserve tributary to Fort Macleod and Lethbridge.

This, then, was the state of affairs when on March 27, 1885, the telegraph keys at Edmonton and Calgary tapped out the terse message, "Métis attacked at Duck Lake yesterday, ten police killed. Louis Riel and Gabriel Dumont victorious." The North-West Rebellion had been touched off.

At all of Bishop Grandin's missions his priests were in the difficult position of being sympathetic to the Métis and yet of having to do all they could to prevent them from taking up arms and of condemning them when they did so. At St. Albert the bishop's influence was so great that the Métis never molested them; at Fort Pitt, Father Fafard and Father Marchand were watched with suspicion; at Batoche, right under Louis Riel's nose, Father Vegreville made no secret of his hostility to the rebels who had him arrested and forced him and Fathers Fourmond and Touze to sign a pledge of neutrality. The Métis did not molest Father André at Prince Albert and, of course, Father Lacombe and his priests in southern Alberta, being reasonably remote from direct Métis action, had little to fear from them.

At Calgary the news of the fighting at Duck Lake created considerable alarm. Even though that town had the protection of the railway, it nevertheless could not forget that it had some five hundred Sarcee Indians at its back door and several times that many Blackfoot fifty miles down the river. It was these warriors under Chief Crowfoot that worried all southern Albertans and all Canadian officials and politicians. As Father Lacombe wrote,

> "The Blackfeet were well armed with rifles and they had plenty of cartridges. Among the Indians of the North-West there was a kind of general feeling, with the old and the young, that the time was at hand to finish with the white policy. Many influential Indians were at the time fomenting the fire of rebellion."

With respect to the Indians, then, the key figure was Crowfoot, a prickly cactus whom everyone from John A. Macdonald down handled gingerly. These included Cecil Denny, Dewdney and Father Lacombe, who were kept running back and forth.

A day or so after receipt of the news of the Duck Lake battle, when it was rumoured that Crowfoot and the Blackfoot were about to attack their town, Calgarians sent to the Dunbow School for Father Lacombe. Putting a special train at his disposal, they sped the blackrobe to the reserve. There he wandered around sizing up matters and concluded that for the time being Crowfoot was on the side of the government. On March 30 he sent a telegram to the prime minister.

> "I have seen Crowfoot and all the Blackfeet. All quiet. Promised me to be loyal no matter how the things may turn elsewhere."

In fact Father Lacombe was never certain that Crowfoot would refrain from joining the Métis side of the fight. In public he let on that he felt certain that the Blackfoot chief would stand by his white friends but in his correspondence he exposed his real opinion, saying,

"For my own part, what I have seen of the Blackfeet and their kindred since last Spring makes me believe that if they have been quiet and have made loyal promises during the Cree rebellion, it was purely out of self-interest in order to get more and more out of the Department."

This, of course, was a correct judgment. White men thought of each Indian as being loyal or disloyal to the only side they could see — the white side. They had not realized that there might be another loyalty, not to some abstraction but to a concrete conception of the best interests of an Indian tribe. Crowfoot was all the greater man because he did not allow baubles or fine words to divert him from seeking the best good for his people. The best good was not glory or revenge but peaceable possession of the lands still left to them and food enough to carry his people through crises. And that good could only be obtained from the white man, who must inevitably win the war. If he had thought that in the long run the lot of the Blackfoot would have been improved by fighting with the Métis he would have jumped into the fray on that side.

On April 2, Big Bear's Crees wiped out the hamlet of Frog Lake in northern Alberta and killed and mutilated nine men, including two priests. One of them, Father Fafard, a friend of Father Lacombe's, was a man of several years' experience in the country, a priest who had served at Buffalo Lake and more likely than not a man known to Crowfoot.

With all this on their minds, the men who were able to influence Crowfoot arranged to confer with him and his fellow chiefs. Their meeting on April 11 got off to a good start when, as they stepped down from their train at Cluny station, he and 150 of his mounted followers met Dewdney, agent Denny and Father Lacombe and escorted them to the Catholic mission. Before the day was over Crowfoot dictated a carefully worded telegram, which included a reference to Father Lacombe, for transmission to Sir John A. Macdonald, assuring him of his tribe's loyalty. Amongst other things, it said,

"We are agreed and determined to remain loyal . . . we leave our future in your hands. We have asked for nothing but the governor has given us a lot of presents of tea and tobacco."

It was a greatly relieved prime minister who read that telegram to his cabinet and let it be broadcast over the land.

As soon as that meeting was over Father Lacombe rushed north to the reserves near the Battle River where Father Scollen had reported that the Crees had pillaged a store and a stopping house. His journey to Edmonton paralleled that taken by the Reverend John McDougall who carried messages north for General Strange and at the same time helped to pacify such Indian chiefs as Samson and Ermineskin. Both missionaries had headed north before April 15, when the troops began their march to Edmonton. Father Lacombe's hurried trip included a three-day visit to Bishop Grandin at St. Albert.

When making his way along the St. Albert Trail he stopped at the Harnois farm (corner of 156 Street and the St. Albert Trail and immediately south of today's St. Joseph's Seminary Newman College) to see how his sister Christine was faring and found the family deep in the tragedy of diphtheria. One of the five children was already dead. All the rest showed the dread symptoms of its onset. Unfortunately he had to hurry away to perform his other duties, so that it was not until a couple of weeks after he had returned to Calgary that he heard that all the children had died. As the Edmonton *Bulletin* reported: "Four children in seven days and the remaining one has since died."

On a far more cheerful level was Father Lacombe's meeting with some of his Quebec compatriots, the Carabiniers Mount Royal commanded by Lieutenant-Colonel J. A. Ouimet, and the 9th Voltigeurs de Quebec commanded by Lieutenant-Colonel Amyot, and his appreciation of how loyally they had jumped in to help the government. Moreover, although he had no direct hand in it, he was proud later on of the part the people of St. Albert, Métis and white, played in cooling off the troubles.

He was pleased, too, that the Quebec soldiers were seeing the country and that in their long march to Edmonton the Mount Royal Regiment had the task of guarding the army's line of communication. In doing so they built three blockhouses on the way and named these after some of their officers: Forts Normandeau (Red Deer), Ostell (Ponoka), and Ethier, near Wetaskiwin. Being stationed at these strongholds, even for a short while, gave them a chance to see how rich were the soils of the area.

Rich soil he knew would attract French farm boys and although he was busy with so many things, he never forgot his hope of seeing these farms settled by colonies from Quebec and in his mind's eye could conjure up French pioneers making the trek north to Edmonton.

As usual he hurried from one duty to another and by May 1 was back in Calgary where he could keep his eye on his industrial school of which during his absence Jean L'Heureux had been more or less in charge.

News of Louis Riel's complete defeat and capture at Batoche came less than two weeks after Father Lacombe's return to Calgary. Inevitably at the battle of Batoche the Métis nation, which for some seventy years had maintained a desultory identity, was irretrievably broken. It had been born with their participation in the Battle of Seven Oaks with Cuthbert Grant. Their great moments had been the Sayer trial of 1849, the battle with the Sioux when Father Lacombe had been along on their hunt, and the Red River uprising. Now, sadly, Batoche saw their end as a coherent community. Their line would persist, but it would lead a marginal and submerged existence for years to come.

If, however, the North-West Rebellion had been disastrous to the Métis, it had raised Father Lacombe's fame to the topmost rung. Others may have played large parts in quelling the rebellion but in one way or another all these men had enemies who were glad to nip at their heels and decry their contributions. Father Lacombe appeared to have no enemies; his determined, weather-beaten, open face, his courage, his sacrifice and his wisdom had caught the eye of the press and all Canada knew that it had a new hero.

As such, in many ways and in several important circles, he was honoured and thanked by letter and in person. In a backlash of public relief, so, of course, was Crowfoot, the chief whom he was thought to have kept docile. By combining his own powers of persuasion with the advantages he could gain by using Crowfoot as a stage prop, Father Lacombe obtained valuable gifts and concessions for his missions and for his Indians. And he was able to use his influence to help obtain leniency for the Cree leaders who had been sent to prison for their role in the rebellion.

Crowfoot's adopted son Poundmaker, whose camp had been attacked at Cut Knife Hill, was one of the prisoners. Consequently Crowfoot's voice was added to those of Cecil Denny, Lieutenant-Governor Dewdney, Father Lacombe, Archbishop Taché and the Reverend John McDougall, who all appealed for the confined chiefs. Early in March, after having served six months of their three-year sentences, the least culpable, including Poundmaker, were released. Father Lacombe carried the news from Ottawa to the Stony Mountain penitentiary at Winnipeg.

Once Poundmaker got back to his reserve he rested for several weeks and then set off to visit Crowfoot at Blackfoot Crossing. To what straits he had been reduced is shown by this once great chief's entourage as in the middle of May 1886 he started the two-hundred-mile trek across the rippling prairies he had ruled so recently. For nine days, Poundmaker, his wife and a young nephew headed south with only one horse to assist them and a couple of dogs to run at its heels. Unfortunately, after spending a few brief weeks with Crowfoot, he died.

In January 1886, at the same time that Sir John A. Macdonald had talked with Father Lacombe about releasing the prisoners, he sounded out the father about the advisability of bringing Crowfoot and some of the other leading chiefs east as a reward for their loyalty. For some reason, probably because he felt that Crowfoot's loyalty had not been of such whole cloth as he had let on, Father Lacombe was opposed to his being so honoured. As Sir John wrote Lieutenant-Governor Dewdney, "he is very much opposed to Crowfoot's coming east, for what reason I don't know."

When, however, his opinion was overruled and Crowfoot, Red Crow of the Bloods, North Axe of the Piegans, four Cree chiefs and a couple of others were asked to take part in the trip, he jumped on the bandwagon. Thenceforth, for those men with whom at times he had camped in their vast, grassy empire of parkland and prairie, he tried to make the excursion an impressive experience. Securing permission from Dewdney to take Crowfoot and Three Bulls, as well as interpreter Jean L'Heureux, on ahead of the others, he made certain that they saw as much of Catholic cathedrals and ceremonies as they could.

Whisking them about, now to the Parliament Buildings and

Rideau Hall and then to the archbishop's palace in Montreal, Father Lacombe made sure that they met most of the important people, bishops, cabinet ministers and CPR executives. During this trip Van Horne gave Crowfoot a perpetual pass on the railway line which he had allowed to disturb his reserve. Everywhere everyone was friendly, and curious crowds came to stare. With his striking garb, rugged features and commanding presence, Crowfoot made a deep impression. On several occasions he told of his people's high regard for Father Lacombe. "Here is one of the greatest friends of our nation. When we rejoice, he rejoices; when we are sad and in mourning, he is sad and sorrowful with us."

Courteous gentleman that he was, he said what his hosts expected him to say. Nevertheless, his remarks bore the stamp of truth and sincerity. Brave man that he was, with so much of his own to weep about, he had the courtesy to praise his friend of twenty years' standing. His own people's course was finished, his tribe's race was run and he was within four years of his own death, but he had the grace to realize the inevitable and the fortitude to face the anguish that was bound to fill the days ahead.

Having been the objects of much tiring attention, Father Lacombe and Crowfoot were glad to board the train and be off west. On their long journey home after the train pulled out of Winnipeg and they began their two-day, nine-hundred-mile trip across the plains, what thoughts must have filled the minds of these friends who for so long had known this region so well? Fingering their railway passes, the symbols of the present, what emotions rose unbidden in their breasts as these two men not yet old remembered the symbols of the past. Sweeping down this valley or over yonder ridge both could recall so clearly the wild freedom of four decades ago, when they had been young men and when the pass to the prairies was a sound horse and a brave heart.

Somewhere out in these endless, rolling ridges Crowfoot had been born and amongst them he had grown to manhood. In those days a few white men had been around to wheedle for furs but the Blackfoot were the masters of the plains and no man dare gainsay them. A few missionaries had come in talking of their god, warning that the buffalo were decreasing and hinting that the people should start tilling the soil. How utterly ridiculous. Even up to the time of the battle of Three Ponds, when he had found Father Lacombe running around waving his crucifix in a snowstorm, Crowfoot's people were still lords of the magnificent plains.

Then *apixosin*, the smallpox, had struck them and in rapid succession the whisky traders had arrived and then the mounted police and then the treaties. From the smallpox to the treaties had taken a mere seven years and after them they were no longer masters of the prairies. Another seven years had finished them; the buffalo had died out, starvation had followed and then confinement to the reserves, and now they were barely masters of their own souls. Finally the completion of this railway had paved an easy way by which thousands upon thousands of white men would soon come in. They had not reached the Bow River country yet but they would as they had done already for the first two hundred miles out of Winnipeg, where small towns, some with a thousand white men, were springing up like mushrooms.

As the train carried the two friends across the river at Medicine Hat and swept them northwest, Crowfoot found his thoughts grey like the bare October prairies outside the windows. Soon they would reach Cluny station and Blackfoot Crossing and even now, though the ridge was not visible from it, the train was paralleling the Great Sand Hills on their right, that bleak land in which all warriors, including Crowfoot, finally found peace.

Crowfoot had been born in the prairies and naturally loved them. His friend the priest had chosen to come to live in these prairies and parklands and his choice had developed into a loyalty nearly as deep as that of the chief. Like Crowfoot, he too could remember the Indians' great days and the subsequent tragedies leading to the present.

But there the resemblance between the two men ended. Since he had first set foot in the parkland Father Lacombe had known that the day of the railway would come and with it a million white settlers who would enjoy tilling the soil. For decades he had tried to prepare the Indians for their catastrophe but had failed. However, now that the day had come, though he was tormented by regret and nostalgia, those pains were eased by his anticipation of the future. For he was a white man and had a future. Crowfoot was a red man; his lot was to get off the train at Cluny and quietly try to help his people endure life on their reserve. Father Lacombe's was to return to Calgary to embark on three more decades of work assisting white immigrants to take their first halting steps towards a bright future in a white man's land and to have his reputation glow all the more brightly with the passage of each decade.

Although Father Lacombe was never to lose his interest in the Indians or to cease his efforts to relieve their suffering, for all intents and purposes, the conclusion of this trip marked the end of his major involvement with his native friends.

CHAPTER SEVENTEEN

The Separate School Question
1887–97

When Father Lacombe returned from his triumphal tour with Crowfoot, he was nearing his sixtieth birthday. With thirty-seven years of varied experiences tucked under his sash he was by far the most versatile of all the ordinary priests in the archdiocese. Although lacking the full measure of long-headedness possessed by a bishop such as Monsignor Taché, he was nevertheless the best public relations man vis-à-vis Protestant officials that the church had. When any concession had to be obtained or any new or old cause advocated or pleaded again, he was always the man judged most likely to emerge from the political maelstrom bearing the prize for which he had contended.

Since he was an actor who could play many parts, Bishops Grandin and Taché assigned him to various stations from which he could be withdrawn at a moment's notice and sent to Ottawa. While in general Father Lacombe thought of himself as a missionary to the Indians and undoubtedly enjoyed the psychological reward of helping them, the church's role in the West left him less and less time to pursue that work. Indeed, since in the main the Indians had been converted or had settled on reserves and in effect had become stationary parishioners much like any other congregation, the distinctiveness of that work had lessened.

The pitifully small supply of new priests to work the western field helped little to relieve the pressure on the ranks of the old guard. Even then the need for their services in new settlements imposed a heavy burden on everyone. The miners at Lethbridge, the other non-French but Catholic groups which were coming in as labourers and the new parishes which were springing up in new villages where Catholics were in a minority, all called for priestly services. The influx of white people had begun and, even if until about 1895 the stream of migration remained a gentle trickle as compared to the flood it was to become, it imposed a heavy load. To carry that load kept the priests of the St. Albert diocese scurrying all over the vast district which since 1882 had been known as Alberta.

And none enjoyed the pace more than Father Lacombe, whose itchy feet kept him ever on the move and whose personality and reputation made him welcome everywhere. After his return with Crowfoot he had been attached to Calgary's St. Mary's parish but as often as he could went out to work with the Blackfoot and Piegans. He kept up his interest in his Dunbow School, continued to badger the authorities until he won a hospital for the northern Blackfoot and persisted until he obtained some nursing sisters to run it.

In the midst of all this work he suffered many interruptions — pleasant ones to the extent that they involved travelling and unpleasant when they included soliciting for funds. In the spring of 1887, successfully twisting the CPR's willing arm for free transportation, he conducted a tour to the Pacific coast headed by Archbishops Fabre and Taché. Included in the group was his old confrere from St. Albert days, Father Maisonneuve, stooped now and frail.

A few weeks later he and Bishop Grandin commenced a circuit of French Canadian parishes in the eastern states begging again and beating up colonists for western Canada. Though they came back with a definite impression that their "holy audacity" had been distinctly unwelcome, Father Lacombe was able to bring $6,000 to spread sparingly over the diocese's many needs. Nevertheless, "these are terrible journeys for my strength, physical and mental."

Whether or not while he was on that trip he was able to be in Quebec when his mother died at the age of eighty-seven is not apparent, but that year saw the snapping of the fond link between the mother who had hoped for so much for her son and the boy who had become nationally famous. If, however, her demise severed the last link with his old farm home, it did not break off all family ties, for his sister Christine Harnois, who had suffered so by the onset of diphtheria, was still helping her husband farm on the St. Albert Trail. Moreover, living in Edmonton by this time was his niece Georgiana, whom he had brought out to teach school but who in 1885 had married John Edmund Kelly. He was a steam engineer, and the couple and their eldest son, Edmund, were living in a spacious new home at the edge of the cluster of houses that made up the tiny hamlet of Edmonton.

Father Lacombe had no sooner returned to what he regarded as his real work at Calgary than Bishop Grandin called him away to St. Boniface on another jaunt. There in July 1889 these two attended the first Provincial Council of Western Catholic Clergy. At the same time the gathering celebrated the seventy-first anniversary of the arrival of the church in the prairies and parklands when Fathers Provencher and Dumoulin had come to the Red River Settlement. And a solemn and prideful occasion it was too, when as a mark of the progress made in that rugged three-quarters of a century the church's ordained personnel alone had swelled from two priests to one archbishop, five bishops, and 126 priests. Perhaps even more notable was the fact that in all that time the St. Boniface diocese had been ruled by only two bishops, and they great ones, the venerable Provencher until 1853 and his successor, the still vigorous Archbishop Taché. Well might the older priests at the conference be proud of the part they had played — those, as Father Lacombe was to write, "who in sowing the divine seed, had paved the way and beaten the roads which today belong to the church of St. Albert. They have sown in tears; and today, do we not still sow in tears? But we are consoled by the thought that those who will follow us, will reap in joy."

About the time Father Lacombe returned from the conference he began writing his memoirs. He was sixty-three and undoubtedly felt that if he were to leave a record of his unparalleled forty years of experience in the West he had better start to do it. They are in the form of letters addressed to his benefactors, Mons. and Madame Forest, in his old college town of L'Assomption and extend to some two hundred pages. As the reader will be able to tell from the number of quotations from his memoirs used in this book, they are an invaluable record of some of the father's experiences. At the same time they have to be read with caution; they lack the clarity of arrangement that in 1890 Father Lacombe was still capable of commanding when preparing some brief or other for any cause he espoused.

While he was working on them he heard that Crowfoot had died on April 25, 1890. The chief, in his early sixties, had been more or less confined to his couch all winter and his death came as no surprise to his followers. Soon after, in the course of sorrowing over his friend, Father Lacombe wrote an article for the Fort Macleod *Gazette* telling some of the warrior's history. In it he pointed out that since Father Doucet had taken part in the funeral and recited prayers over the grave, the old chief had died a Catholic. In a technical sense he did, because, much to the priest's relief, the records of the church at Cluny indicate that "he was baptized on the 23rd day of April 1890, according to the Rites of the Roman Catholic Church. . . ."

For all practical purposes, however, it is hard to disagree with the opinion expressed by the Anglican, the Reverend J. W. Tims: "He died as he had lived, in the faith of his fathers. His favorite horse was shot at his death, so that he might ride it in the 'happy hunting grounds.'"

It may well be that thinking of Crowfoot's death prompted the aging missionary to record his disappointment at his failure to impress the Blackfoot. Referring to that tribe in general, he wrote that they were a pitiable people.

"All we have been able to do so far is prepare a few adults for death, and sow the seed of Christianity which Divine Grace will have germinate in God's good time. Polygamy, contact with the white man whose vices they adopt are the principal obstacles preventing our making much progress in christianizing the Indians. We wonder what the results will be from these schools which we set up with so much sacrifice, to try and civilize the children at least. I am still far from ready to state that such is or will be a success."

His feeling of failure, however, was not confined to full-blooded Indians; the Métis, too, from whom he had expected much more, also disappointed him.

"Poor Métis! They are ever the same! What can one do to change them? For over fifty years the priests have been sacrificing themselves for them. . . . These bands of Métis, who were formerly well established, today drag about and are looked down upon and miserable near new cities. Having neither the necessary energy nor the required perseverance, they have lost the chances and advantages this country could offer, to become the servants, or rather, the slaves of the newcomers. They have lost everything, except the faith, which, in many, though considerably weakened, remains intact and is easily aroused."

Such were the sentiments of the clergy and of the day. But a pastor must be an optimist, ever looking forward to success in the work which lies ahead. If with the Indians Father Lacombe and his brethren had achieved little but converting them to nominal Catholics, at least that was something. Certainly they had been spared the errors of Protestantism. Perhaps by using that achievement as a base the priests could build on it and by extreme patience and determination slowly improve the Indians' opportunities and outlook. In the meantime, the flow of white immigrants was increasing and attending to their needs as well as those of the Indians kept the priests on the jump.

So far most of the settlement on the prairies and parklands had taken place in Manitoba and southern Saskatchewan and up to 1890 relatively few people had come in to try conclusions with Alberta's soil and climate. In anticipation of a wave of immigrants the CPR was already building branch railway lines. As far as Father Lacombe was concerned, the two most important of these were the line from Regina to Prince Albert and the other extending north and south out of Calgary to Edmonton and Fort Macleod.

It was mainly in reference to these that on December 22, 1889, Van Horne wrote Father Lacombe a jocular letter at the time he sent him his new pass for the coming year and said,

"We are still following you wherever we go, with our rails and locomotives, and it is possible that you will hear our whistle at Macleod before the end of the coming year.

"I send you herewith a little charm against railway conductors, which you may find useful since you cannot get beyond their reach."

In his official as well as in his purely personal capacity anything that happened anywhere on the prairies concerned him. Being more intimately familiar with every acre of the valleys of the Red Deer, Battle and North Saskatchewan rivers, he was eager to see their rich soils become the home of thousands of settlers. As to the type of settlers, of course, he had certain definite priorities. He wanted all the lands settled but in his heart he listed prospective immigrants in a decreasing order of desirability: French Catholics, other Catholics, French and others. Like his associates, he knew that if the French fact in the West were to survive, it would need transfusions from Quebec.

Although his residence was in Alberta, he pricked up his ears at the new railway which reached Prince Albert in 1890. It passed near the old Batoche Métis colony and would undoubtedly open up much land which, if his hopes should be fulfilled, would become the home of a French-speaking colony. That year, anxious as ever to ensure that the French of Quebec or their New England relatives had an opportunity to share in the prairies' bounty and eagerly supported by the archbishop, he spent months in the East drumming up settlers for the future Saskatchewan and Alberta.

From his previous experience Father Lacombe knew, of course, that his hopes of seeing the prairies settled by at least an equal number of French folk had little chance of fulfilment. This he revealed in his memoirs when writing of a journey he made from Calgary to Edmonton about this time.

> "That which most grieves the heart of the priest and the missionary as he covers this distance of 212 miles from Calgary to Edmonton, is to see this beautiful fertile country already occupied by the English Protestant element, among which our Catholic families are but a small minority. In mentioning this fact here, I can but repeat anew that which we have already so often said and deplored. What will you, — the English, at home and in the colonies, have more means, and are more organized, and, I would dare say, are more tenacious and perseverant in overcoming difficulties and the hardships of displacement and the beginnings of starting

anew. Isolated and far from their neighbours, they more easily accept their lot, in awaiting that neighbours come closer. Our people, that is to say, especially our French Canadians, submit with difficulty, for some time, of being deprived of the church, their friends, and the consolation of parish life."

Everywhere he looked the proportion of Roman Catholics in the mix of immigrants to Alberta was declining. Despite that, he rejoiced as he watched more and more tendrils of settlement creeping farther and farther into the valleys he had so recently trod with his Cree and Blackfoot friends. Although he was away the day his friend Lieutenant-Governor Dewdney turned the first sod of the Calgary-Edmonton line in July 1890, the expansion of the CPR along Alberta's main axis from Fort Macleod to Edmonton made accessible a land he knew so well. He could now look forward to making rapid trips to Edmonton — without charge thanks to his pass.

It was during these months that the tactful Van Horne once more demonstrated his affection for the priest by asking him to suggest names for the railway stations along the new Calgary-Edmonton line. Before the line had been laid out it was only natural, of course, that the reconnaissance engineers would have discussed its proposed route with Father Lacombe and consequently, as Van Horne, perhaps being overly generous, wrote to Katherine Hughes, they then knew just where to locate it. Now that the line was practically finished and the time had come to give names to the various sidings which so far were merely designated by numbers, Van Horne turned to his old friend. As a result, the father suggested such names as Wetaskiwin, Otaskawan, Ponoka and Nisku. At the same time, Van Horne, by assigning three names which he had chosen himself, took the opportunity to honour a painter whose work he admired, one of Father Lacombe's confreres, and the silvery-haired priest himself — Hobbema, Leduc and Lacombe.

Before that, however, Father Lacombe had tried out the new marvel, the train to Edmonton, which left Calgary on Mondays and Thursdays. Waving his pass at the conductor who knew him anyway, he could settle into a soft seat and in twelve hours be in Edmonton. How simple it was now to cross the Red

Deer River, the Blindman or the Battle. How swiftly the train flashed by some spot where he and Alexis had lain supperless in their snow banked camp. How unheeding were the sparks from the locomotive that set fire to the woods south of Leduc where in 1870 he had come upon the victims fleeing from the Fort Edmonton Crees.

Then, arriving at South Edmonton station, how simple it was to cross the river now on the ferry and to drive past the Hudson's Bay Company's greying, bullet-spattered log buildings on the way to the new St. Joachim church. Only some minor sheds remained of all the buildings that had stood in doughty old John Rowand's time; the rest had all been replaced. Now that one could go to Winnipeg by train and come back, all within a week, what a contrast that was to the Red River cart days of 1857 with their return trip of 145 days. Now, however, by an occasional wink or nudge or indeed a stern scowl from the holder of that pass, many an assistant — even bishops, and sometimes more than one — could flit about the country. To Father Lacombe and his church Van Horne's pass was a godsend; to others it was sometimes a matter of levity. Such it was to one of the conductors who stood fingering this pass, which permitted "Father Lacombe and an assistant" to travel free, and frowning down at the two black-gowned sisters who presented it.

"Dear Sisters," he asked, "which one of you is Father Lacombe?"

A pass which allowed nuns and others to travel was only one of the concessions Father Lacombe was able to exact from a willing CPR. Because the company wanted freight to haul, it was necessary to fill the West with settlers who would generate it. To do that it was willing to help all colonizers such as Father Lacombe, who seemed likely to attract such settlers. As a result, in 1890 we find the father writing Bishop Grandin about his hopes for reduced rates for his colonists and their goods. At the same time, he was preparing to embark on another colonization campaign in the East.

While he went canvassing and kept his fingers on the general policy, he left the detailed work of setting up the main Alberta colony to Father J. B. Morin. Under his capable hands in March 1891, the first of this group of French colonists and one of the first of many such colonies passed through Edmonton.

The convoy consisted of twelve wagons bringing sixty-five immigrants of all ages, who had detrained at Calgary and been met by willing Catholic colleagues who had come from St. Albert to bring them back to land which the good father had reserved for them.

These, of course, were only the advance guard of a much larger migration which, under the auspices of the church, came to settle: habitants from Quebec, fellow celebrants from France and Belgium, and repatriated French from the United States coming once more under the protective cloak of the church. Year by year as they slashed new fields out of the timber they extended their parishes: Vegreville, sixty miles east of Edmonton; Beaumont, twenty miles south, and Morinville, Villeneuve, Riviere Qui Barre, Legal, Vimy and Picardville to the north. Year by year, living in the primitive simplicity of all pioneers, these laughter loving, sociable people progressed up the scale of material well-being, cutting out roads, and building schools and churches.

Father Lacombe's activities were not concerned with Alberta alone and many smaller groups of compatriots found homesteads in Saskatchewan. Most of them were sent to areas previously well-known to the priests because of their having at one time or other established missions for Métis in them. South of Prince Albert, the French colonists settled an area embracing Duck Lake, St. Louis and Domremy. Other colonies started south of Moose Jaw or in the vicinity of Wood Mountain. Others, such as at St. Paul des Métis, Alberta, and in the Peace River country, were to come in a decade or two later. For his efforts in colonization alone the prairies from Manitoba to the mountains owe a great debt to Father Lacombe whose driving force exerted over a long period of time initially directed these doughty French-speaking group-settlers to the West.

Of course the travelling necessary to do this was made possible by the pass Van Horne had given him. So long as his superiors approved, it allowed him to run back and forth from Alberta to Ottawa and Montreal on almost any slight pretext. During those trips, however, on which as he said he was "encumbered with business and commissions," and complained that "I have need of a frame of iron," he enjoyed himself. He found relaxation in the warm welcomes extended to him by major businessmen and politicians, as well as by Rideau Hall where Lord and Lady Aberdeen had come to consider him both a likeable friend and a man of some importance. It is doubtful if Father Lacombe had ever relished his combination of work and relaxation so much as during this era.

Typical of the sort of entertainment that came his way was an evening in Van Horne's home in 1892 of which he wrote:

> "Last Saturday I dined with my good friend Van Horne in company with several *'gros bonnets.'* The evening was a veritable triumph of refinement and amiability."

To a man who similarly dined at the homes of prime ministers and various cabinet ministers, perhaps his reference to *'gros bonnets'* — big shots — was a bit of dissembling. On one occasion Bishop Grandin chided him quietly for what he may have regarded as a false modesty which smacked of boasting. The bishop wrote: "You make me laugh with your reference to your fear of speaking before the Ottawa big shots . . . you who speaks and corresponds with princes and emperors, you would experience certain emotions when speaking before Canadian ministers, but those *'gros bonnets'* are only little boys to a Father Lacombe. All joking aside, dear Father Lacombe, I admire you and congratulate you on your zeal and energy."

To counterbalance all this strenuous social-cum-business activity in the East, Father Lacombe often cast his thoughts back to the silences and the solitude of the far West. A spot on the hill above Pincher Creek appealed to him. There when he (and perhaps some of his confreres) hoped that he was about to retire, he built a shack which he called his hermitage, "Ermitage de Saint-Michel." There in May 1893, as he thought or pretended, he settled down to seclusion. "Alone on top of the hill with my dog and my cat. . . ."

But his seclusion lasted only a few weeks and thereafter was to be interrupted many times as the good father was dragged away to the political turmoil of Ottawa to take on one of the most difficult of all his assignments. For between French-Catholics and English-Protestants hostility had broken out again. English-speaking settlers had poured into Manitoba so much more vigorously than the French that by this time the Catholics were a minority of 20,000 in a total population of 150,000. The new settlers expected English culture and the Protestant religion to predominate. But they collided with the Catholic bishops who felt charged with the defence of their French faith. This particular battle began in the field of education.

The ruckus had really broken out before John A. Macdonald's death, when the Manitoba government decided to revise its educational system. In the Manitoba Act of 1870, and due largely to the insistence of Father Lacombe's college friend, Father Ritchot, French had been made an official language. The province controlled its own educational policy but there was a proviso to ensure that Roman Catholic separate schools would be supported by public funds. Thus the province had started with a sectarian system. In 1890 the provincial Liberal government of Thomas Greenway did away with these sectarian privileges. In 1891 the administration of the Northwest Territories took similar action.

With tooth and nail Archbishop Taché and all his associates fought these legislative steps. With his usual wisdom John A. Macdonald, seeing that the resulting fury was liable to wreck his newly assembled Canada, backed away from it and stalled. His suggestion that the issue be passed along to the courts was an attempt to give the excitement some time to cool. His death in June 1891, however, dropped the matter into less tactful hands. Meanwhile, Father Lacombe was kept in close touch with the discouraging problem. His intervention only became apparent in 1893 when the furor yanked him out of his Pincher Creek hermitage.

By that time various tribunals had been dealing with the matter and on January 21, 1893, the governor-in-council sat to hear arguments. The Toronto *Empire* of January 22 indicated the importance of this court hearing:

"Every leading newspaper in the Dominion had its representative present, while about a dozen gentlemen represented the great Canadian public. Among the more notable outsiders present were Rev. Father Lacombe, the famous N.W. missionary...."

From this hearing Father Lacombe went back to his hermitage only to be recalled in August when the hot potato was passed to further courts and his respected mentor, Archbishop Taché, needed his more active help. For by that time Taché, a weary old man, was ready to turn the whole problem over to him. In the meantime, the court, grinding away methodically, had decided that Manitoba's legislation had been within its powers. As a safety valve to keep Canada from blowing apart, the Privy Council held out the possibility that the Dominion government could pass "remedial legislation" overruling Manitoba.

Here indeed was a pretty kettle of fish. A Conservative prime minister, Mackenzie Bowell, a former grand master of the Orange order, with his political support coming from Protestant Ontario, was being asked to coerce a Protestant Manitoba to enable its small Catholic minority to retain its sectarian schools. Waiting in the corridors of the House of Commons was his enemy, a Liberal French Catholic, ready to back the Protestants of Manitoba against the Catholic hierarchy — Wilfrid Laurier, leader of the Opposition. Was ever any other prime minister suspended over a pit like that? For Laurier was beginning to rise to statesmanship and Bowell, like many a lesser man, was destined to fall before him.

Wilfrid Laurier, like Father Lacombe, was a French Canadian farm boy and, of course, a Roman Catholic. Like him too, but some fourteen years later, he had been born within fifteen miles of L'Assomption and had been moulded by the teachings of L'Assomption College. From that point the two men's careers had diverged until Lacombe became a priest and Laurier a Liberal member of parliament speaking out against many of the policies of the bishops. With such differing ideologies it was inevitable that if their paths ever crossed one of them would get hurt.

Meanwhile, building up towards its climax the school fight dragged on with Father Lacombe shuttling between Ottawa and Montreal. Early in 1894 he took Archbishop Taché's "Memorial on the Schools Question" to Montreal for publication. By April he was writing to tell Father Legal that he had "thousands of copies printed in French and English. . . . It is causing a sensation. It is a thunderbolt to the Government. . . ."

His next move was to carry around a petition to which he obtained the signatures of all thirty Catholic bishops of Canada. On May 16, for the last time, Archbishop Taché wrote to Bishop Grandin commending Father Lacombe: "Our dear hermit . . .

has done a good piece of work . . . all the bishops of Canada have signed our petition." Six weeks later the great archbishop was dead.

His death, though not unexpected, was a hard blow to all his colleagues and particularly to Father Lacombe. Since 1852, over forty years previously, when the West was in a most primitive state, the two had been intimately associated. It was Bishop Taché who allowed Father Lacombe to build St. Albert when and where he had wanted to. It was Bishop Taché, the patrician, who all these years had encouraged him, chided him, educated him and favoured him. Of all the Canadian bishops he was the one Father Lacombe loved most. He was also preeminent among the bishops that Canadians would look back upon as great men and statesmen.

Yet the sixty-seven-year-old Father Lacombe had too much to crowd into the years that remained to him to mourn too long. Within a month he found himself officially transferred from his hermitage at Pincher Creek to Edmonton. In July 1894 he was made pastor of the parish of St. Joachim — a position he had occupied some forty years earlier when, to please him, Chief Factor Christie had had its first chapel built. Other than the bonds created by his long-time association with Edmonton, he found little to arouse his enthusiasm in the slowly growing town of one thousand people. "Parish priest," he wrote, "what a post for my grey hair!"

Every day, of course, he ran into somebody who brought back vivid memories of the early years at Lac Ste. Anne. One of these was his old associate and teacher from the days of his noviciate, Father Rémas, spending his last days at St. Albert. With his usual drollery Father Lacombe wrote, "Father Rémas is in absolute retirement at St. Albert like a rat in a cheese."

Perhaps it is some indication of the calibre of Father Lacombe that in spite of the friction between himself and Father Rémas in 1863, he could refer to his old tutor with such obvious fondness. Time had softened the old hurt and by 1890, when he came to write his memoirs, it had vanished and he had been able to say, "I will never forget this friend of my heart, this devoted father who was not always understood."

In October, while he was stationed at Edmonton, his friends Governor General Lord Aberdeen and Lady Aberdeen came through on their visit to the West. Before this trip, of course, both had met Father Lacombe in Ottawa and had come to enjoy his company and to regard him as one of the leading men from the West. Of the two, Lady Aberdeen seems to have been the more perspicacious and it is a pleasure to see her high regard for the silver-haired priest reflected in her *Journal*. On this occasion Father Lacombe accompanied the vice-regal party to St. Albert. "And gradually we got him to talk of the old days, when he first came to this part of the country as a young missionary priest, forty-seven years ago. . . . He is enthusiastic over the Cree & its power of expression. 'Ah! How one could preach in that language!' "

While Lord and Lady Aberdeen toured the West their pair of problem politicians, Bowell and Laurier, glared at each other in Ottawa. The question of "remedial legislation" had to be dealt with but as the year 1894 closed Bowell was still passing its hot potato from one hand to the other. The question of when he might drop it, and where, worried everyone including Lady Aberdeen. On February 22, 1895, she and her husband met Father Lacombe in Ottawa and drove him to Lord Aberdeen's office "where we all had a talk about Manitoba Schools etc. He is very clear that the Government will be hopelessly defeated if they do not settle the question before going to the country."

It was indeed an explosive question and as Wilfrid Laurier wrote to Premier Fielding of Nova Scotia, it was one which "may break the Opposition, or break the government, or break both the Opposition and the government."

By that time the new archbishop of St. Boniface, L. P. Adélard Langevin, had sent Father Lacombe back to Ottawa to shoulder the load of the school question again. As someone said, his rushing back into the fray began "the most extraordinary obedience in the life of a most extraordinary missionary." His prolonged session at Ottawa occupied him with some of the most delicate and difficult negotiations of his whole career.

On March 21, 1895, Prime Minister Bowell took the fatal step of issuing an order instructing Manitoba to restore separate schools. Manitoba refused to obey and in June said so officially. Mackenzie Bowell gave the province until January 1896 to reconsider or suffer the consequences. Premier Greenway countered the move by calling a provincial election on the issue and thereby strengthening his position with a resounding electoral victory. Now the ball was in Bowell's court and Opposition leader Laurier stood leering at him across the net.

All Canada stood watching. Ranked shoulder to shoulder on the one side stood the Catholics of Manitoba and their allies, the hierarchy of Quebec, which Dr. W. G. Hardy has described as "always more Roman Catholic than the pope." On the other, ranked no less stubbornly, were the Ontario Protestants. Intervening on his church's side and battling eighteen hours a day, Father Lacombe flew from pillar to post.

He found himself in the situation of trying to bolster the position of Bowell, the Orangeman, against that of an alumnus of his old L'Assomption school, Wilfrid Laurier, a fellow French Canadian and a Catholic. Bowell was having trouble holding his Conservative party and his cabinet together. One resignation he regarded ruefully was that of his minister of Agriculture, Auguste R. Angers, who broke with him because he would not move fast enough in forcing Manitoba's hand. At this point in Canada's history the parish priest from faraway Fort Edmonton, this confidant of governors general, prime ministers and cabinet ministers, played his unusual role. Following Angers's resignation, Bowell asked Father Lacombe to be his agent or intermediary who in effect would select one from the stable of contenders to fill the gap in his cabinet. Father Lacombe's choice fell on Alphonse Desjardins, who entered the cabinet in January 1896 "on the condition that a remedial bill which met the approval of Father Lacombe" be introduced.

After enlisting Desjardins in the cause, Father Lacombe watched with growing apprehension as Mackenzie Bowell tried to maintain his balance on the high wire. On January 29 he went to dinner at Government House and afterwards Lady Aberdeen confided the following sage comments to her diary.

> "Father Lacombe very full of the School Question. He acts in great measure as the emissary of the Bishops to the leaders of the different parties. Unfortunately he sees only the present & not a possible future. If this Bill is passed by the vote of the French Members from Quebec of both parties, the cry against French ascendancy will become a yell & then what hope will they have for their schools in the other English provinces."

At the time she must have been unaware of a letter he had written about a week before. Even though his efforts may have saved the unity of Prime Minister Bowell's cabinet and thus assured that a remedial bill would be presented to the House, he felt that he must keep on fighting to ensure its passage. That fight involved him in an almost unprecedented step and one he was ever to regret. He prepared another thunderbolt; unfortunately, it turned into a boomerang.

He wrote a letter to Wilfrid Laurier, a most extraordinary letter which he claimed to be "in the name of our Bishops, of the Hierarchy and of Canadian Catholics." In it he demanded such action which, had he been a better judge of great men, he would have known was a course which Laurier could not take. He asked him to help settle this prickly question by voting with the government on the remedial bill. But he didn't stop there; he issued an ultimatum, saying,

> "If, which may God not grant, you do not believe it to be your duty to accede to our just demands, and if the government which is anxious to give us the promised law should be beaten and overthrown while keeping firm to the end of the struggle, I must regretfully inform you that the Episcopacy and the clergy, united as one man, will rise to support those who may have fallen to defend us."

Strong language indeed. Father Lacombe's recent successes in helping to remake Bowell's cabinet must have gone to his head. But Wilfrid Laurier was neither Métis nor Cree to be cowed by a wag of the priest's finger. For Laurier, objecting to priestly interference in matters political, refused to let the church dictate to him. Nevertheless, he did complain to Archbishop Bégin and it appears that as a result Father Lacombe came in for at least a minor tongue lashing.

However severe it may have been, it was based not on any lack of faith in the necessity for the remedial bill but on his indiscreet threat — he had committed the crime of getting caught. Regardless of that, as the liaison between the government and the bishops, he had to take one more step for the bill's sake. On behalf of the Bowell government he had to twist Archbishop Langevin's arm to make him agree to the only salvage measure now possible — a remedial bill. Thus acting at times as an aid to the government and at others as a spokesman of the church, he had to run back and forth between the two, whittling bits off the desires of each till he could make them fit into an effective compromise.

Working with Lord Aberdeen, his old friend Donald A. Smith of Winnipeg and CPR days, Archbishop Langevin and Premier Greenway and writing a barrage of letters, he finally assisted the concerned parties to come up with a poor bill but one which they could accept. All this he had accomplished by February 22, 1896. The next step was to see it through the House of Commons before Bowell fell off his high wire.

Finally in March the bill came up for consideration in the House. At that point Father Lacombe could only sit and listen and hope. Wilfrid Laurier, however, could talk, and talk he did. After referring to Lacombe's threatening letter, he pointed out that as leader of the Liberal party, he represented "not Roman Catholics alone but Protestants as well." Finally, concluding a brilliant speech which had lasted an hour and a half, he moved a six months' hoist to the bill — a motion equivalent to killing it.

Poor Father Lacombe sitting listening suffered intensely. He was so convinced of the righteousness of his cause that it hurt him to hear a compatriot and a fellow Catholic take such an opposite stand. His inability to understand how a cultured man like Wilfrid Laurier could possibly believe what he said or how, if he didn't believe it, he could pretend to do so made Father Lacombe declare that his heart bled for the mistaken man. Writing to Archbishop Langevin the next day he said that he had "listened to a speech given in our favour by a Protestant, Sir Charles Tupper, and another by a Catholic Mr. Laurier against us." Continuing, he said that Laurier in an eloquent address had "condemned us, the bishops, the clergy and of course myself. In spite of his protestations of being a Catholic and of his attachment to his mother the church, it is the end, he has committed suicide yesterday in front of his country and his church. My God, how sad and regrettable it was to hear such magnificent eloquence used to defend such a bad cause! . . . He has finished himself."

But once again Father Lacombe had misjudged Wilfrid Laurier. Having by this means put the remedial bill out of the way, Laurier went on to destroy the Conservative government. In the ensuing election in July 1896 Laurier's Liberals carried the day and Father Lacombe's friend, the Orange prime minister, took the remedial bill down to defeat with him.

Its demise, however, did not mean that the Catholics of Manitoba were to be thrown completely to the Orange wolves. For Laurier, besides being a great man in many others ways, was also concerned with the injustice done the French Canadians in Manitoba. Consequently he went to their aid and achieved much that Bowell had tried to do, not by frontal attack but by slipping around to the back door. Being a Liberal prime minister and dealing with a Liberal government in Manitoba, he persuaded the province to pass legislation amending what had gone before. The new act still deprived the Roman Catholics of some of the privileges they had enjoyed previously but did take considerable notice of their desires. The Liberals found that it was possible to dispose of the matter in this way. Despite Father Lacombe's efforts, relatively few French Canadians had settled in Manitoba and when this crunch came there was no strong French Canadian political voice — no votes — to raise an uproar. A strong, religious voice remained but that too Wilfrid Laurier toned down.

The verdict of history has declared Wilfrid Laurier to be a far greater statesman than Father Lacombe. When the kindly white-haired priest sat listening to him make his speech, Laurier was proving his greatness. He was handling the Manitoba school question as a Canadian first and as a Roman Catholic second. Father Lacombe, seizing the problem, had reversed his priorities.

The religious voice in Manitoba was not so easy for Laurier to overlook as the political one and working with the bishops of Quebec, Bishop Langevin kept the issue alive with a persistence the new prime minister considered vindictive. Finally Laurier the politician appealed to the political wisdom of the Vatican. As a result, a papal envoy was sent to size up the situation in Canada. In the end, after pointing out that though the new legislation was far from satisfactory, it might have been or might even yet get worse, the envoy recommended that the Canadian bishops should muffle their outcry.

Long before the papal envoy arrived, Father Lacombe, sturdy and loyal, wished that he had never been involved in the fight. His long struggle at Ottawa had taught him a thing or two about political manoeuvring. He must have regretted that the valiant struggle he had put up during the peak years of his service to his church should have ended as had so many of his other worthy efforts — in defeat.

Never one to cry too long over spilled milk, however, he returned to his Edmonton St. Joachim parish and settled down to rest with audible grunts of relief. During all the wearying months of the separate school campaign he had been forced to neglect his Edmonton parish. Even at that, he had gone to considerable effort to keep abreast of the changes that swept over the town during the first few years after the completion of the Calgary-Edmonton railway. The church, of course, was making its own changes and at St. Joachim was having a new rectory built. A block or so away — Edmontonians had progressed so far as to measure distances in blocks — the bricks of the Grey Nuns' General Hospital were being hoisted into place. Once it was completed it was to become a godsend to the hundreds of homesteading families which were beginning to flock into the Edmonton district. Not only did it have a large clientele from the growing town but it was a haven for all the ill amongst the new settlers: the large French colony which was expanding north out of St. Albert and scores of immigrants of assorted languages and faiths who were taking up land all around Edmonton, including the Slavic community which was putting down roots beyond Fort Saskatchewan.

The influx of new settlers had been so encouraging that Edmonton's businessmen had started both a telephone system and an electric light plant. St. Joachim rectory had become so effete that it was making use of both of these services. With a brick hospital, telephones and electric street lights, the parish was a far cry from the days when Father Lacombe, stumbling around Fort Edmonton in the dark, had called to the trigger-happy Blackfoot.

In a personal way things had also progressed for Father Lacombe. His niece Georgiana, whom he had brought west in 1884, had liked the country and by 1896 had been married for over ten years to J. E. Kelly, the engineer and part owner of the electric light company. In 1894, her husband had purchased the Harnois farm out on the St. Albert Trail.

Because Father Lacombe was a man of national repute, everyone with a cause which needed an advocate came seeking

him. As soon as the populations of Edmonton and Calgary began to grow, both places felt the need for bridges over their
rivers. On their behalf Father Lacombe accompanied delega-
tions to Ottawa to use his influence there in securing help for
such local improvements.

On May 13, 1897, his good friend of many years and his
one-time companion at Blackfoot Crossing, Father Legal, was
appointed coadjutor bishop of St. Albert. The following June,
Lacombe's superiors allowed him to leave the St. Joachim parish
in the hands of another old friend, Father Leduc, and the
seventy-year-old priest was able to write that at last he was
"freed from this Edmonton."

CHAPTER EIGHTEEN

St. Paul des Métis
1898–99

Once more in 1897 the white-haired, gentle-faced old man with the steady eyes sought the silences of the foothills. It was time to turn over the affairs of the West to younger men and to guide from the sidelines.

Such a move was logical but in his heart sentiment always outdistanced logic. No one could make him listen to logic when human need or suffering demanded his attention. It had been sentiment that had sent him out to Lac Ste. Anne in 1852, that had prompted him to try to teach farming at St. Paul des Cris in 1865 and that had carried him from one smallpox camp to another in 1870. All of his associates knew that sentiment would remain the driving force which, until the end of his days, would prompt the soft-hearted and yet often overbearing old man to prod others into carrying out the schemes he conjured up. They also knew his tendency to lose his enthusiasm for a project after he had initiated it and then turn it over to others while he went to champion some new cause. They knew too that it was his utterly unselfish sentimentality that had pushed him into the position of patriarch of the West whose fame and footsteps were being followed by an ever growing throng of admirers amongst both believers and unbelievers.

It is in this light shining on a kindly but domineering old man that we must view the declining decades of his long and eventful life. Even when nearing seventy at his hermitage at Pincher Creek many achievements still lay ahead of him — many achievements and many more honours.

With some justice, his fellow priests were inclined to feel that in the popular mind Father Lacombe's fame was considerably overrated. Since that fame contributed to the causes they all supported, they never made an issue of the matter. To a keen observer such as Lady Aberdeen, however, their feelings were obvious as when on her visit to St. Albert during Father Lacombe's absence in the fall of 1895 she commented in her diary:

> "There is a wee bit of jealousy amongst these good fathers as to the popularity of Father Lacombe with the outer world. In truth, for one who has heard Bishop Grandin's name, a hundred have heard of Father Lacombe & of his influence over the Indians & of the way he exerts it."

Nevertheless, the saintly Bishop Grandin found him to be both a useful helper and a problem child who persisted until he had his own way. The bishop could put him to any task demanding effort and energy and, while his interest remained aroused, he would work wonders with it. His stubbornness is perhaps best illustrated by the persistence and wishful thinking with which, against the advice of his bishop and of many of his associates, he brought into being the St. Paul des Métis colony.

It was not only a venture to which he had devoted a great deal of effort during the years when he was fighting the school battle at Ottawa but one which had simmered in his mind for years. Decade after decade he had watched the Métis decline from an independent, reckless people to hangers-on at the fringes of white society where they were exposed to liquor, vice and the corruption of idleness. He kept hoping that someone, somehow, would find a method of helping them to help themselves.

In 1890 he estimated that there were some twelve thousand Métis in western Canada. Writing of them before white men had demoralized them, he said they were "courteous and generous in rendering service to their fellowmen." On another occasion he said, "The Métis are doomed. They have sold their lands for a song; they are children and they have been reduced to poverty."

Nevertheless, Father Lacombe was determined to help them. One of their virtues never overlooked by the sympathetic French priest was that after all the Métis were mainly of French descent and spoke that language and in a land where that race was, or felt it was, an abused minority, it behooved the priests to assist them. Moreover, at times, and particularly to Father Adeodat Thérien, it appeared possible that the priests might be able to use the Métis as a nucleus in the formation of a new Quebec on the prairies.

As far back as 1894, in spite of Bishop Grandin's coolness towards his project, Father Lacombe, taking advantage of the influence he had acquired under varying circumstances with the government and the CPR, began a round of visits to Ottawa and Montreal offices. By April 1895, he had talked a number of important people, including his friends the governor general and his wife, around to his point of view and some funds started rolling in. Amongst other offers tendered to him was the CPR's promise to carry free of charge all freight destined for his proposed St. Paul des Métis mission — a significant contribution. In the process of soliciting, Father Lacombe pelted his friends with all the ammunition at his command, including a pamphlet he had written called "A Philanthropic Plan to Redeem the Halfbreeds of Manitoba and the North-West Territories."

Amongst its many suggestions was a proposal to set aside a tract of land as a Métis colony. In this colony, which was to be administered by the Oblate order, half-breeds from all over were to be induced, by persuasion and not by force, to settle. In it they would be provided with seed grain and implements and then expected to buckle down to a sedentary farming existence and thenceforth to make their own living by tilling the soil and raising cattle. While such a Métis was to be allowed to select an eighty-acre parcel of land and could farm it during the lifetime of the colony, he was never to be given title to it and therefore could not sell it as nearly all the half-breeds had done with the land they had received after 1885. The administration was to provide a school and other facilities.

During 1895 Father Lacombe managed to have Father Thérien, an enthusiastic priest half his own age, seconded to what his associates called his Métis utopia. While the idea of a Métis colony was germinating, Father Lacombe had thought that it should be located on the shore of Buffalo Lake. By 1895, however, he had changed his mind and in June that year Father Thérien and Father Morin, the successful colonizer of the large

Morinville area, went out to inspect another location. Travelling down the Saskatchewan River as far as the ruins of St. Paul des Cris, they struck across to the old Carlton Trail and on June 18 camped on the site of today's St. Paul. The land they traversed enchanted them, fertile plains, shady thickets, forests, pearly lakes full of fish and creek bottoms and ravines full of wild game. *"Vrai Eden pour les Métis déshérités."*

Soon after Father Thérien had satisfied himself that the land was fertile, four townships (144 square miles) north of the North Saskatchewan River were set aside. In December 1895 they were covered by an order-in-council from Ottawa and by that time Father Lacombe had already visualized a mission and a village which should be located along the old Carlton Trail and should bear the name of St. Paul des Métis. For was it not the lineal successor of his nearby St. Paul des Cris of 1865 now reorganized and re-oriented?

The announcement of its creation set off a howl of opposition. Many correspondents and newspaper editors saw in it a Roman Catholic plot aimed at increasing the church's power in the West. Others saw it as a waste of effort which the Métis would not appreciate. In a letter to the Calgary *Daily Herald* John McDougall, the Methodist, was of the opinion that the government had already been generous enough with the Métis. Amongst other things, he said,

"I very much admire the zeal of the promoter of this scheme and, from a purely ecclesiastical standpoint it looks wise, but I humbly think the reverend gentleman is away off in 'social economy,' therefore as a citizen of this commonwealth I beg to record my firm protest against any such disposition of any part of this fair domain."

Despite this opposition, Father Thérien went ahead and, accompanied by Fathers Legoff and Comire, reached the site of the colony's headquarters on July 15, 1896. There, beside three Métis huts, they put up their tents and went to work on their mission house. That fall a few Métis moved to the new colony but within two years only thirty-two Métis families had been wheedled into coming to try their luck at farming in the area. If Father Lacombe had expected a rush to his Métis colony, he was to be disappointed. In some ways its experience was a repetition of that of his industrial school. Once more he had led a horse to water but could not make it drink. It was to be many a month, however, before he began to admit that the scheme might possibly fail. Meanwhile, in a desperate search for colonists, he travelled all over the West and as a last resort was prepared to grant concessions to the Montana Métis if only they would come to his St. Paul colony.

Indeed, in his enthusiasm and his sympathy for them in their urgent distress, he was inclined to promise them anything if only they would move to the colony. For as Father E. Drouin has said, he was an inveterate optimist who could always assure himself that regardless of what kind of individuals he had to work with he could coax them into a rosy future. Father Thérien, on the other hand, had adopted a firm policy of not giving anything to any Métis unless he had earned it. Perhaps it was well for Father Thérien's discipline that Father Lacombe seldom saw his colony and only visited it for three brief periods.

But if he rarely wandered as far from his hermitage as the new St. Paul, few weeks went by without the old voyageur turning up in Fort Macleod or Calgary or going to say mass for some group of frontier Catholics who otherwise would have gone spiritually hungry.

The following December as his seventy-second birthday was approaching, he was to write a friend:

"Just a word to tell you that it is very cold — and still colder. My kidney trouble seems a little better, but to offset that I have a frenzied cold in my head which torments me cruelly — Look you, I am old."

For nearly twenty years now the rugged life he had led had made him susceptible to various disorders. At times he felt like turning down some of the work imposed by a new country filling with new settlers. But he had to help relieve the drastic shortage of priests under which his bishop laboured. The work had to go on. For decades he had hoped this west land would receive its proper share of catechumens and now that on railway construction and in the busy coal mines it was obtaining them, he could scarcely refuse to do his utmost.

Moreover, no day ever went by that he did not pray for his

Métis and worry about them. At St. Paul des Métis Father Thérien was performing a difficult task and his difficulties were compounded by a lack of cash needed for a residence and a boarding school, a flour-cum-sawmill and for farm machinery and cattle. When on behalf of the federal government A. A. Ruttan reported on the state of the colony, he had nothing but praise for the work Father Thérien had done. Commenting on January 8, 1899, he was optimistic enough to hope that within ten or fifteen years the Métis in the colony would find their outlook tremendously improved. At the time of writing, however, he felt that they were "a weakness to Canada by reason of their ignorance and consequent helplessness; they will, however, when suitably educated, be a strength in the national life. . . . These People are much more unfortunate than the Indians; they were too ignorant to realize the meaning of enfranchisement and it is perhaps doubtful whether Canada really got rid of its obligations to these former wards by allowing them to withdraw from Treaty (whose obligations and privileges they did not understand) to a freedom of the perils of which they were certainly most sublimely ignorant."

While Ruttan was penning that report, Father Lacombe was away in the East trying to collect enough money to keep the colony going. On this visit he tapped the purses of all his close acquaintances, the CPR officials, cabinet ministers and others. He missed his good friends the Aberdeens, whose term of office had ended, but came to know their successors, Lord and Lady Minto. By the spring of 1899 he was able to remit a sizeable amount to Bishop Grandin, almost all of it from these rich friends in the East. From the ordinary public his collections were negligible — less than a thousand dollars — because in such quarters no one had much sympathy for the Métis.

At the same time, however, having some sympathy for the woods Indians north of the Athabasca River, the government had decided that it was now necessary to pay attention to their desire to obtain the security a treaty would give them. Unlike the plains Indians who found their livelihood cut off when the buffalo had been swept from the prairies, the Indians in the north had experienced little change in their food supply or way of life until the last decade of the nineteenth century. As early as 1888, Bishop Young of the Anglican church and others wrote to the minister of the Interior suggesting that a treaty should be signed with them. He said, "Owing to the strong competition in the fur trade, and other causes, the Indians cannot look to the Hudson's Bay Company for help as they used to do." The implication was that if an agreement was reached with the Indians, then in times of scarcity the government, complying with treaty provisions, would feed them.

For some years no action had been taken but during the 1897–98 rush to the Yukon many of the Klondikers aroused the wrath of the Crees and Beavers and once more various men in responsible positions advocated the conclusion of a treaty. As a result, late in May 1899, a party made up of two sets of commissioners started north from Edmonton. One group, headed by the Honourable David Laird, was to treat with the Indians, while the other headed by Major James Walker, an ex-NWMP officer, was to lay to rest the half-breeds' claims to the land by an issue of scrip certificates similar to that which their relatives in Manitoba had received previously.

The committee in charge of assembling the treaty party recommended that because Father Lacombe had "been so long in the country" and possessed the natives' confidence, he should accompany the party in an advisory capacity. Thereupon, but not without misgivings, the Honourable Clifford Sifton, the minister of the Interior, girded up his loins and called upon the calm-faced father. The fact that on the school question two or three years earlier he had been one of the old priest's most active opponents was no help in making his visit an easy one.

Father Lacombe felt it to be a high compliment that he should be asked to serve his country and his natives once more, but at first he demurred.

> "I am too old to travel hundreds of miles in little boats, and I will only bother your people to take care of me if I fall sick. Try to find somebody else."

And yet, even as he turned down the offer, the call of the canoe routes to the North was strong and he half hoped that they would keep trying to talk him into going. If they did, he would go. It was nearly thirty years since he had seen the mighty Peace River and many a year since he had stepped from a canoe. He could visualize paddling along the great northern lakes where the wall of the north woods came down to meet the shores and where, keeping well clear of the craft, an inevitable pair of loons talked back and forth.

Finally on May 11, Father Lacombe wrote to Bishop Legal. "It is finished. I have decided to accept the offer of the commission. There is no repose for me."

Thus it came about that on May 29, climbing into the sturdy wagon of the stage line taking the party to Athabasca Landing, Father Lacombe set out once more for the Peace River country. With the official party went eleven mounted policemen, as well as Bishop Grouard who was returning to Fort Chipewyan and would join the group at Athabasca Landing. It took them the best part of four rainy days to reach the landing.

From there two scows, a York boat and some fifty souls had to track or be tracked against the swift current of the Athabasca. The party's first short spell away from the landing took them a mere seven miles to the mouth of Baptiste Creek where Father Lacombe found a camp of several of his Métis acquaintances. They then went on through a day of pouring rain while the trackers, putting up a brave front, slipped and slithered about on the muddy shore, bringing back vivid recollections of the priest's first trip up the Saskatchewan with the great John Rowand forty-seven years earlier.

Finally the entourage left the broad Athabasca River and started its difficult ascent of the swiftly flowing portion of Lesser Slave Lake River. Two days of pulling the craft around the never-ending sweeps and loops of the little river brought the party to a delightful camping place at the point where the Saulteaux River poured its placid waters into the larger stream. There Father Lacombe was surprised to find that the party chief had ordered camp to be made much earlier in the day than usual.

Without giving the matter much thought, the seventy-two-year-old priest strolled off far enough to be out of the way of the commotion of putting up the tents and preparing supper. For a while as he sat on a log watching the waters of the stream coming in from the west eddy and whirl and mix with those at his feet, he wondered how long it had been since this river had first borne the name of those Saulteaux Indians whose blood flowed in his own veins. What wanderers they had been, those Saulteaux, over a land nearly three thousand miles wide from Montreal to the nearby Swan Hills.

For that matter, he chuckled, what a wanderer he himself had been since that evening fifty years ago to the very day when in the old college of St. Hyacinthe sixty priests had stood in line to bless him, to lay their hands on his head, to salute him and to raise him to the priesthood. Fifty years ago he had been raised to his high calling. And now, just as the waters of the Saulteaux River kept tumbling steadily towards him, so had the years flown, fifty of them flowing steadily until half a century had swept past. Had he achieved any of the high promise those at the ceremony had held before him?

Musing thus and enjoying the magic of a summer evening in this forest-locked spot, he noticed that his tent had been erected and went over and entered it. Even there, however, the quiet gurgling of the flowing water entranced him and he sat gazing upon the streams. Then, as he described it, "Suddenly the Governor, he came to my tent and asked to come in. . . ."

Behind him in happy array came the whole party to stand in respect as Mr. Laird read him a congratulatory address appropriately inscribed on birchbark and signed by every member of the group. Along with it they read a poem composed by J. A. Coté and also written on birchbark. After a touching impromptu reply from the bemused priest, many hands spread a special banquet on the grassy ground.

Recalling that happy event, Charles Mair, secretary of the commission, wrote:

"Many of us were not of the worthy Father's communion, yet there was but one feeling, that of deep respect for the labours of this celebrated missionary, whose life had been a continuous effort to help the unbefriended Indian into the new but inevitable paths of self-support, and to shield him from the rapacity of the cold incoming world now surging around him. . . ."

On June 19 the party arrived at the community of Lesser Slave Lake which lay a short distance south of the St. Bernard mission which on his last visit twenty-nine years earlier Father Lacombe had started to build. After a day or so of discussion, during which the old priest urged the assembled Indians to sign the treaty, they did so. Its signing paved the way for the negotiations which led to about a hundred Métis families taking scrip in settlement of their general claim to the land in question.

The government and the commissioners intended that each Métis would be given scrip entitling him to claim and settle any 240 acres he chose. These authorities did not want any repetition of the forlorn experiences of the other Métis who had been given scrip after the Red River troubles and the North-West Rebellion and had more or less immediately sold it to traders for a piddling amount of cash and in some cases for a quart of whisky. Their intention had been to make this treaty's scrip non-transferable, so as to save its recipients from the speculators. None was more aware of the dangers of the Métis selling their scrip right away than Father Lacombe whose St. Paul des Métis colony was an attempt to help salvage similar natives from their own recent and identical follies.

Yet, in spite of his ardent and impressive speech counselling them to accept non-negotiable scrip which they could not sell to the lurking traders, the traders won. The Métis, whom they had egged on, insisted that they had a right to sell their scrip if they chose to do so. In a last ditch attempt to avert a repetition of previous scrip tragedies, the commissioners adjourned the meeting till the next day. That night the treaty party and Father Lacombe reluctantly faced the painful decision to let the Métis have their own way and the next day the scrip was issued on a negotiable basis. As Charles Mair wrote:

"Whether the half-breeds were wise or foolish it is needless to say. One thing was plain, they had made up their minds. Under the circumstances it was impossible to gainsay their assertion that they were the best judges of their own needs."

Some months later when the Opposition at Ottawa was questioning Sir Wilfrid Laurier about why these Métis had been allowed to barter away their birthright the prime minister explained:

"There is no man who has taken a stronger view than Father Lacombe against the excesses resulting from issuing scrip or who saw less benefit in its results to the half-breed. But in view of the determined attitude of the half-breeds. . . ."

On June 25 the father accompanied the others on their ninety-mile trip to Peace River Crossing. "Terrible road, continual rain through an immense forest, mudholes without number . . . the creeks and little coulees are torrents. Camped in the rain." On the 28th when crossing the Harmon River he was to write: "I am on the point of being carried away with the wagon in a river where the horses had to swim. The road is more and more frightful and the mosquitoes a torment." The next day, however, the mighty Peace River burst into his view and he finds it "grand and majestic." Pausing at the St. Augustine mission, he takes time out to write to Bishop Legal to assure him that he is enjoying being a voyageur again. He is so delighted that he would not trade his place on the trip for all the feasts he has had amongst the *gros bonnets*. Now towards the end of his days his place, he states, is still to be with the Indians and the Métis. "It is so my destiny is written."

Then once more he and the party set out down the river in open scows, "current very rapid and we travelled all night, warm weather and a good trip indeed — with the help of oars we descended with a remarkable swiftness." All this stretch of the river was new to him and night after night he lay awake for hours "watching the mountains, the trees and the river. To me they are like phantoms." Stopping at such places as Carcajou, Fort Vermilion and Vermilion Chutes, his barge reached the Quatre Fourches at the outlet of Lake Athabasca on July 14, whence a short pull took them to Fort Chipewyan. There at the Nativity mission he received a warm welcome from Bishop Grouard's people.

"It was witching that night, when we reached the mission at eleven o'clock."

The mission, however, held an even greater fascination for him because the very first mass to be said there in 1847 — forty-two years previously — had been performed by his dear departed friend Bishop Taché.

His tour of the northeastern corner of Alberta filled Father Lacombe with a deeply satisfying return to the wilds as he had known them so many years earlier. On it, too, he had travelled two of the province's most majestic rivers by varied conveyances and now here at Fort Chipewyan he boarded the Hudson's Bay

Company's sternwheeler, the *Grahame,* which took his party up the 120-mile stretch of the Athabasca to Fort McMurray. While his diary exclaims over the scenery, Fort McMurray, whose fortunes were then at their lowest ebb, elicited the comment *"Quelle triste place dans le bois. Rien — Rien."*

The first third of the 250 miles up the river to Athabasca Landing involved ascending rapids so turbulent that a steamboat could not navigate as far up as the Grand Rapids. Any goods or passengers taken upstream had to be tracked up and Father Lacombe had to leave the comfort of the *Grahame* for the inconveniences of a tracked scow. Although he had never travelled this section of the river, he knew it by repute and he also knew that in 1856 his friend Bishop Taché had investigated the feasibility of opening a transport route from Lac La Biche to the far North by taking a canoe through the Grand Rapids. Later on, following in his wake, the church had worked out a system of scow transport down this dangerous portion of the river.

It was, therefore, with more than usual interest that Father Lacombe set out to ascend this rough water and the entries in his diary reflect that interest. A day or so after leaving Fort McMurray the first note reads:

"But those rapids, which appear like white hills before us. How dangerous for us! Poor men who pull the lines!"

Next day the notation is:

"All day we go through new waterfalls, which seem to want to swallow us up. It is as if we hardly seem to advance but a few inches against that terrible current."

A couple of days later when they came to the river's major hurdle, the Grand Rapids, he comments:

"The river is just nearly a continual waterfall. See that 'army of white sheep' — they are huge torrents coming towards us. With great labour our party has trouble advancing only a few inches."

The scowmen's struggles failed to get them through to the head of the rapids before dark. Next day,

"We continue to fight our way against the rapids and the rising water. The middle of the day is generally very warm — nights are humid. The mosquitoes inhabit this part of the country and they welcome our visit."

For the next week after overcoming the barrier of the Grand Rapids the trip was more or less uneventful and on August 27 Father Lacombe reached Athabasca Landing. From there, huddling from the rain in the stage wagon for the best part of three days, he was finally landed at St. Albert. His entire circuit of northeastern Alberta had taken ninety days for which the government had paid him, or his church, $10 per day — a welcome addition to the funds of the diocese. They had been pretty strenuous days for a man of his age but his zest for travelling had counteracted any hardships he had experienced. While occasionally he did complain or at times pretended that he had only undertaken the trip under duress, in fact, he would have been sorely disappointed if anyone had taken him at his word and suggested that he turn back. So it was that when he returned to St. Albert he was able to rejoice, "They cannot kill me — neither bishops nor Governments."

At St. Albert Father Lacombe found that his comrades of the cloth had been awaiting his return to celebrate with him on his having reached the golden jubilee of his accession to the priesthood. Accordingly, on September 25 the mission of St. Albert spared nothing in holding a celebration worthy of the old man who forty-seven years earlier had come to minister at Lac Ste. Anne and thirty-eight years ago had started the mission which now acclaimed him. Archbishop Langevin and Bishop Dontenwill from New Westminster, B.C., together with priests from every part of the diocese all came to pay homage to the silver-haired missionary. Indian friends and Métis had been alerted and gladly camped around the grounds as they had years ago so that during his hour of triumph they could rejoice with their old friend.

Solemn religious services were followed by a banquet and that by a display of fireworks. Bishop Grandin recalled how so many decades ago Father Lacombe had laid the foundations of this prosperous mission which by now was an episcopal see.

He pointed out that their honoured guest had not only worked for the diocese but for the whole ecclesiastical province of St. Boniface. If, he said, within that province anyone needed an intermediary to deal with the Hudson's Bay Company, the government or the CPR, or for any other unusual job, they asked him to lend them Father Lacombe. Raising the question so many had wondered about, he said, "How is it that Father Lacombe is not a bishop?"

Then, answering himself, he pointed out that if all who were worthy had been made bishops, all his priests would hold that office. "The creator," he said, "forms special men for special missions. A bishop is charged with the administration of a particular diocese. Father Lacombe, however, is the universal man." He went on to say:

> "God, who directs all with wisdom, has willed that he should be free, that he should lend himself to all and for all."

Finally the speeches were over and the sturdy old missionary, weary of so much adulation, was left to himself, perhaps to wander to the brink of the hill to look across the pleasant valley and to recall the days of his strength when with axe and saw he had felled the trees for his first church.

CHAPTER NINETEEN

The Lacombe Home
1900 – 16

The days of our years, Moses said, are threescore years and ten; and if by reason of strength they be fourscore years, yet is their strength labour and sorrow.

Father Lacombe's fiftieth jubilee marked a major turning on the austere highway he had chosen to follow. Though he was now threescore and twelve and had noticed some decline of his capabilities, physical and mental, he was far from being a doddering old man. Nevertheless, his superiors, while still using him as a collector, seeking his valuable advice and utilizing his incomparable skill in maintaining good public relations, allowed him to spend longer intervals relaxing at his Pincher Creek hermitage.

But such a man as he could never retire. He could never lose interest in what went on in the field and consequently, year after year, he was called out of retirement to fill in at the parishes of Calgary and Fort Macleod, to go collecting in Quebec and even to make two trips to Europe. And to every request he responded, grumbling, of course, as an old man does when called upon to do something which he would not miss for all the world.

That part of his life which had been so closely bound up with the opening of the West — his years of extreme hardship and adventure — was over. He had run his last rapid; he had hung up his snowshoes. The tasks to which he now turned were tiring enough for a man of his age, but while performing them he slept in beds with springs and sheets and dined amidst linen and silver. His final progress to such luxuries was small repayment for the debts society owed him. The increasing honours heaped on him by a grateful public, Roman Catholic and Protestant, were a source of great pleasure to him. As his later years slipped by we have less reason to follow his movements in detail. We can watch, however, as the legends continue to build up around the white-haired old man, the Man of the Good Heart — no longer only to Cree and Blackfoot and not only to Catholics and Protestants but to all Canadians.

By this time the rush of settlement to the West and to Alberta was in full swing. By 1901, Alberta with its total population of 73,022 was ready to step into a future bright with rich resources and the promise of thousands of new settlers. Alberta's era had dawned, its prospects were rosy.

Over three thousand Mormons had come to the area south of Lethbridge. Along the Calgary and Edmonton Railway hundreds of settlers of northern European extraction were starting on their homesteads. In northern Alberta, radiating out of St. Albert, hundreds of Father Morin's settlers had made deep furrows in digging themselves into their new land. South of them, on the Stony Plain and out Fort Saskatchewan way, scores of German families were hewing their way into the forest. East of them much of the valley of Beaverhills Creek had begun to fill up with Anglo-Saxons from Parry Sound, Ontario. And beyond them to the northeast hundreds of Ukrainian families from the Austrian provinces of Galicia and Bukowina were thatching their first Canadian roofs.

These Ukrainians, whom Father Lacombe called Ruthenians, found on their arrival that neither of their two main ancestral churches had become established in Canada and that some Protestant bodies and the Roman Catholic church had stepped in to try to fill the gap left in their lives by the absence of their own pastors. As well as being inspired by the immigrants' need, the various Protestant churches considered all the Ukrainians' religions to be some form of Catholicism and, therefore, in their crusade against that faith were delighted when they won any converts amongst these Slavic newcomers. Father Lacombe's church, realizing that the Ukrainians were divided into Eastern rite and Roman rite Catholics and that once they got to Canada many of them hoped to break away from the Roman rite and revert to their Eastern liturgy, did what they could to bring all the Canadian Ukrainians into the Roman Catholic fold and tuck them into the ecclesiastical province of St. Boniface.

Bishop Legal and his associates felt that they could help by trying to interest the Austrian authorities in sending out Ukrainian Catholic priests to minister to them. In Canada, of course, these priests were to be placed under the authority of the Roman Catholic church. Once it had been decided to send an ambassador to Europe it took but a moment's thought to select the man for this rather delicate task — Father Lacombe. So in the third month of the twentieth century he found himself called from his hermitage and sent overseas to wander through Italy, France, Germany, Austria, Galicia and Belgium.

On June 28 he obtained a private audience with the pope. "That was a beautiful day, my audience at the Vatican. . . . How good and lovable is the Pope. . . . We talked about the Ruthenian question. . . ."

He spent most of the summer travelling in Europe, sometimes on religious matters and sometimes drumming up colonists for Canada, for which the government paid his expenses. In a report of his trip written in Paris in October he pointed out some of the difficulties the priests were having with the Ukrainians who had migrated to the prairies.

"These people were antipathetic towards the Latin clergy, whom they thought wanted to Latinize them. This poor population, ignorant of the language and the customs of the country in which they were arriving, found themselves demoralized and exploited by the schismatics, by heretics and certain socialists who took advantage of their isolation to separate them even more from the Catholic faith."

One of the fruits of his trip to Europe was the fact that he persuaded the nuns of the order of the Franciscan Sisters and Missionaries of Marie to come to St. Boniface where they worked exclusively with Ukrainian and Polish people. Moreover, when he went to Galicia one Austrian and one Polish sister went with him as interpreters.

On September 4, according to his report,

"Accompanied by the Mother Superior's secretary and two postulants, I leave for Vienna, by way of Cologne, where we sleep. The next day I go to the famous Cathedral where I say Mass at the altar of the Three Wise Men. In fact, as I have heard it told so often, what a beautiful monument erected to the glory of the Catholic religion! What a mass of columns, which support that aerial arch! And those stained-glass windows which would take days or rather weeks to study! It is very difficult to image such structures without having seen them and studied them closely.

"We continue our route by railroad, following the captivating shore of the Rhine, and it was a beautiful day. See those two railway lines, on each side of the river, richly bordered with greenery, with villas, with castles. From time to time one notices on the mountain tops, those old fortified fortresses of the middle-ages. One glances with pleasure and admiration on the immense wineyards [sic] which blanket the sides of the hills, at the bottom of which are situated lovely little villages with their Catholic or Protestant churches. But what seemed to draw mostly one's attention, were the numerous steam boats, large and small, which cross each other with such dexterity and play in the middle of the rapid current."

Like any ordinary tourist Father Lacombe was overawed by the majesty of Cologne Cathedral and enchanted by the scenery along the Rhine. The river's beauty, its history and its busy commerce were such marked contrasts to anything Father Lacombe's magnificent untamed western rivers could show.

The Austrian officials not only allowed him to visit Galicia but paid his party's expenses while he went to Lemberg, Stanislawow and Pryzenyls where the Ukrainian churchmen received him cordially. Finally he returned to Vienna where, by the influence of the highly-placed friends he could always make under any circumstances, he soon had an appointment with the aging emperor, Franz Joseph. His audacity could only be matched by his ability and his deep anxiety for the souls of his Ukrainians.

While waiting for arrangements to be confirmed he was the guest of the Countess Melanie Zichy (neé Metternich). She explained that the emperor was a man weighted down by tragedy and sorrow and cautioned Father Lacombe not to expect too much. When the great day, September 24, arrived, she tidied up the old priest's garments, made him as presentable as she could and explained the proper etiquette for the occasion. Realizing what a great man the priest must be in Canada, she said, "Father, where are your decorations? You must wear them to impress the emperor."

Never having thought of decorations in all his life, Father Lacombe was set back for a moment or two until, recovering himself and opening his coat, he displayed his large crucifix.

"Fifty years ago," he said, "I was decorated with this. It is the only decoration I have — the only decoration I need."

The carriage sent for him rattled through the streets of Vienna and in due course he was admitted to the palace. This turned out to be the most magnificent lay building he had ever entered — rich with a splendour he felt should only be lavished upon a house of God. "I was able to admire the riches and the splendours of the rooms which I had to pass through in order to get to his Majesty who is 70 years old. . . . I had been told that this monarch never laughs any more and talks very little."

The emperor, though polite, was cold and preoccupied but he did assure Father Lacombe "that his Government would do something to help his former subjects." But the emperor let the conversation lapse and the priest, sorry for the old man and disappointed in what he had hoped to accomplish, bowed himself out. "It was thus that I left. I was forgetting that I wanted to thank him for having been good enough to receive me, but, he hurried to say that: 'It is not up to you to thank me, but it is up to me to do it, for the very charitable concern you have for those poor Galicians.'"

Before leaving for Canada Father Lacombe enjoyed a visit of a few days in London where George Stephen, now Lord Mountstephen, and some of his other friends entertained him. Among these was Lady Aberdeen, now back in England after her husband's tour of duty in Canada. One and all loaded him with presents, mainly for his missions but some which they hoped he would use himself. Gratefully he accepted them and blessed his benefactors, but at the same time could hardly wait till he could get back home to distribute all of them to those whom he felt needed them more than he.

Our language has a glib expression to the effect that a person can be so generous as to "give away the very shirt off his back." Fortunately many people are like that, but none was ever more so than Father Lacombe, who, as far as his person was concerned, was utterly unselfish. On scores of occasions people observed his frayed cassock and gave him articles of clothing which, as soon as their backs were turned, he gave away to the first person in need who came along. The late Ed Kelly, a long-time friend of the author and the son of Father Lacombe's niece Georgiana, witnessed one instance of such generosity when late in 1900 the old priest returned from Austria with a fur coat.

The donor was the aging emperor who may have been non-committal but was nevertheless observant. Noticing the priest's threadbare apparel and perhaps aware too that such obvious poverty was partly a stage prop, he made no comment about his visitor's garments during the interview. Father Lacombe had not left the Countess Zichy's home, however, before a costly and warm overcoat was delivered for her guest. For the remainder of his trip the priest wore it on chilly days and then found it a wonderful protection against Calgary's December weather. His young nephew, when he came to examine the coat, admired it and felt envious of his uncle's luck. If he had any hopes that the old priest would give it to him he never admitted them, but he did tell me of his shock when he watched it given away. While he was visiting the old father, three Blackfoot came in to call. Considering the state of his clothes it was with some justice that, rather incidentally, one of them complained of the cold. Father Lacombe looked at him as if to size up his need and then, taking the coat from its nail, handed it over to a man whose want was greater than his own.

In the fall of 1900 he was glad to seek the seclusion of his hermitage and there in the chinook belt he spent most of the winter. Now, he thought, permanent retirement had finally come his way. But for a man who had reservations about being tucked away out of sight, retirement was to be a will-o'-the-wisp. In the spring of 1901 he was sent to serve in the parish of Macleod. He went, but wrote: "I am not so enthusiastic about it. . . . So once again I find myself obliged to leave my fireside and pick up my bundle."

But then without consulting his enthusiasm his superiors found it necessary to send him collecting again. Unless it had a significant increase in funds at its disposal, the diocese of St. Albert simply could not keep afloat and try to provide the services necessary to the influx of settlers. Moreover, Father Lacombe's St. Paul des Métis colony was proving a much heavier financial load than anyone had imagined. So, at the age of seventy-four, he went once more to beg. Within a year he was able to return to St. Albert and account for $21,000 of tribute he had exacted from the East. But it was with slow steps that he ascended the hill at St. Albert for in June 1902 during his absence Bishop Grandin had died.

One by one his links with the past were snapping. One by one his old comrades of the pioneer decades were dropping off. Around him swirled a new generation of westerners who called themselves pioneers, but the real old-timers, the men who had walked back and forth from Fort Edmonton to Winnipeg, were fading away. The latest of his friends to go was Father Scollen who had died in November 1902. Shortly after his death Father Lebret died in Calgary in Father Lacombe's presence.

As good news alternated with bad, his life was becoming a patchwork of sun and shadow. During 1903 he received word that his visit to Emperor Franz Joseph had brought some results after all and that the Austrian authorities had sent four Ruthenian Catholic priests to Manitoba and promised that others would follow and come to Alberta.

If a small glimmer of success seemed to be shining in that quarter, the shadow of failure dipped low over his St. Paul des Métis colony. Writing to Father Thérien in February 1903 he admitted to being "heartsick of this problem." Remembering how so many of both his colleagues and his critics had forecast failure for his scheme, he feared that they would say,

" 'We spoke wisely in declaring Father Lacombe's plans were only Utopian.' And I, hanging my head will have to say: *'Bonum est quia humiliasti me. . . .'* "

His deep dejection set his pen to greater activity and he wrote many of his friends in the East pleading for further financial support. He got it, too, because his friends were far more than mere fair weather allies who would use the priest when it suited them. In spite of his continual importunities their bond of mutual respect was to continue to the end of their lives and, time and time again, they responded to his requests. Typical of the sort of response was the letter Lord Mountstephen wrote in March 1903 when he enclosed a cheque for $2,000.

> "I had not forgotten you and the old days of which you remind me. . . . I think your efforts to train the young half-breeds to industrial habits so that they may be able to gain their own living, is an excellent thing to do and a truly religious work. . . ."

Father Lacombe had barely sent that cheque on its way north when a vicarial council in St. Albert decided that at last the seventy-six-year-old man would be permitted to retire permanently to his hermitage. Immediately he took steps to tie up his small bundle preparatory to holding his farewell service at Calgary's St. Mary's church on May 3, 1903. There he was to be succeeded by an Irish priest, Father Fitzpatrick, and Father Lacombe pointed out that the time had come when in St. Mary's parish at least a priest would be far more suitable if he came from English-speaking stock. That afternoon a few of the congregation came to the presbytery to wish the old priest well and to give him a small token of their esteem.

The Calgary which he was leaving once more had made nearly incredible strides since twenty years ago he had first been appointed pastor of St. Mary's church. Then it had been a hamlet of shacks, saloons, tents and flop joints. Now in 1903 it had become a modern city of over ten thousand busy people. Now the area which was soon to become the province of Alberta held well over a hundred thousand white folk busily wresting a living from coal, cattle, soil or timber.

Whenever Father Lacombe got an opportunity to wander aside from the beaten track extending from Lethbridge to Edmonton, he found farmers assiduously claiming new quarters and clearing new acres. Sometimes on the very creek bank where he had buried the victims of smallpox or along the shore of a pond where he had held his crucifix before eyes closing in the last gasps of scarlet fever, they built their shacks. Few of them paid any heed to what the priest could tell them. For these were a new people, a conquering people, ignorant of the past, intolerant of the Indians and impatient with old-time missionaries, particularly if they were French and Catholic.

In any event, as soon as he was released from Calgary, Father Lacombe hurried south to the new green grass of the rolling Pincher Creek country. A day or so later, brimming over with satisfaction, he wrote Bishop Legal.

> "At last! I have arrived at this dear Hermitage — the goal of my desires for a long time, as you know. . . . Yesterday morning at six o'clock I went up the hill. I knelt there in the silence of the dawn at the feet of the statue of my dear St. Michael. . . . You know this was a solemn moment for your old pioneer! I went up to the Altar in the pretty church, where the morning sun came in through those splendid windows dazzling me. And then in the organ was the voice of St. Michael revealing himself to welcome me . . . !"

For a while he rejoiced in his freedom, his entire freedom to do what he liked, his freedom to meditate, to pray or just to look at the mountains. But it soon palled. So long as there had been some obstacle to his retiring he was eager for its removal. Now that he had been turned out to pasture, however, it was not long before he was looking over the fence at the busy world that seemed to be doing well enough without him. Soon he was writing, "So the dear Father Vegreville is dead. . . . Ha, the old ones are going! It is for this I made my retreat. One must be ready for all possibilities."

Ready he may have been but at the moment there were too many interesting developments taking place in the world and too many problems still to be solved, and, retired or not, he had to see them or have a hand in them. One of these was mentioned in Bob Edwards's High River *Eye Opener* on August 8, 1903. "Billy Cochrane of High River has introduced the first automobile to Alberta." Undoubtedly Father Lacombe had seen other cars on his visit to the coast or on his trips to Montreal, but to one who had first seen the valley of the Bow River several decades earlier this car was a never to be forgotten miracle. For some thirty years he had walked behind his missions' Red River carts hauling supplies. Then twenty years ago the CPR had crossed the prairies and now these curious little self-propelled carriages had started to try conclusions with prairie trails. Progress had followed in his steps — progress for the white man.

Hand in hand with that progress, however, came regress for the native folk, the Indians and the Métis, and even in his retirement his self-imposed Métis problem gave him no rest. During the fall of 1903 worries over it pulled him away from his hermitage again. As he had done long ago, he rafted down the North Saskatchewan River as far as his old St. Paul des Cris, abandoned a third of a century earlier, and got a ride from there in a wagon.

His on-site inspection did little to cheer him. True enough Father Thérien and his associates had much to show for the money which Father Lacombe and the St. Albert diocese had provided. Though they had done a great deal, much remained to be done and it was obvious to Father Lacombe that the whole scheme was in danger of collapsing. Hoping against hope that he was too pessimistic, he decided to try to succour it once more. Maybe his efforts would turn out to be merely pouring good money after bad, but with characteristic determination he decided to go east once more to collect.

Early in 1904 he set out again. When he stopped in St. Paul, Minnesota, Archbishop Ireland welcomed him warmly. There he met an old friend whose magic with railways had made him a millionaire, J. J. Hill of the Northern Pacific Railway. Before he left St. Paul, Hill gave him a cheque for $5,000 for his colony. A round of his friends in New York and Montreal resulted in similar large gifts from men like Sir Thomas Shaughnessy of CPR fame. Once more by an effort which no one but he could have carried through, he rescued St. Paul des Métis.

Not all the interruptions to his solitary hermitage life made the same wearying demands that his St. Paul des Métis did. His next major trip was arranged by Archbishop Langevin as a reward for a lifetime of devotion and the old priest found it an exhilarating pleasure. For, leaving in the spring of 1904, with his expenses defrayed by lay friends and in Archbishop Langevin's company, he visited the Holy Land. Sailing from New York and crossing France to the port of Marseille, the small Canadian party joined a pilgrimage of scholarly French Catholics.

To while away the time on their Mediterranean crossing and to get acquainted, the group organized a series of lectures and someone persuaded Father Lacombe to give a talk on his experiences with the Indians. He held his audience spellbound. From an insignificant white-haired old missionary exuding a whiff of smoked buckskin he became a celebrity.

Unfortunately the acclaim went to his head and when within a day or so he was asked for another speech he chose to talk not on his life with the Indians but on a more scholarly topic. An Abbé Loisy had recently published a dissertation on Modernism about which scholars in the upper echelons of religious philosophy held divided opinions. Of all the unfortunate topics for a man not noted for his scholarly attainments to wade into, he picked that one. Within minutes, to the anguish of his Canadian friends, and the obvious boredom and impatience of his learned audience, he found himself floundering in a morass of his own making. The one-time tactful politician was showing signs of his age.

His suffering on that occasion was completely washed away when a few days later on May 18 he wrote to Bishop Legal.

> "Jerusalem! Yes, Jerusalem — the Holy City — where we arrived last night. . . . Is it possible that I, a poor old Indian, am today in the country where our Saviour died? Is it possible that this morning at three o'clock I offered the Holy Sacrifice in the magnificent basilica of the Holy Sepulchre on the tomb of the Great Arisen! It is a favour which was spontaneously accorded to the old chief of the Northwest. . . ."

A few weeks later other satisfactions beyond the power of words to express were added unto the aging man who knelt in front of his commending pope.

The next step in his successful and far ranging peregrinations took him back to revisit Emperor Franz Joseph on behalf of the Ukrainians who had come to Canada. This time, in spite of the fact that he had to interrupt the niceties of the chit-chat his bishop and the emperor were exchanging, the visit bore more fruit. The emperor made a token donation and promised that more priests would be sent to Canada.

The rest of his European tour consisted of visits hither and yon so that it was autumn before he started back towards Canada. Unfortunately on a train some distance outside of Frankfurt he discovered that his Oblate crucifix was missing — his sole decoration — the crucifix which for fifty-five years he had carried back and forth across Indian battlegrounds and through the mazes of Ottawa's political barren grounds. By November he was back in his hermitage feeling more fulfilled than ever and more ready for the call which would end his earthly pilgrimage.

Fortunately it was a long time coming and many another call was yet to intrude upon his solemn reflections. Some were gratifying; one was heart-breaking.

It concerned his Métis people, the descendants of some of the hunters who had befriended him fifty-six years earlier when he had first laid eyes on the prairies and the buffalo and when they had taken him to their hearts. For their sakes he had conceived of St. Paul des Métis and by his energetic collecting had poured thousands of dollars into it until at last many buildings marked the solid core of the new Métis community. For their sakes the new church for which he had recently obtained $5,000 from Senator R. Forget saw the celebration of its first mass on December 25, 1904. Nearby stood the recently erected three-storey boarding school, its spruce lumber still sticky with gum, but already accommodating some eighty-five Métis children. It was this school which was to strike the knell of Father Lacombe's colony. And it did so on January 14, 1905, when some of its nearly adult students maliciously set the fire which consumed it.

For a year or two Father Lacombe had realized that the Métis were failing to respond to the opportunities he held out to them and that his whole idea was on the point of failure and needed but some incident to expose it to all the world as a blunder. The burning of the school was that incident. For all practical purposes it marked the end of his active involvement in the affairs at St. Paul des Métis. He did publish an appeal for continued help in Quebec and at other times chipped in to use his influence here and there. But otherwise, having a mortal blow dealt to his dream, he dropped it.

The diocese and the Oblate fathers could not get out from under it so easily. They kept plugging away and by September 1908 had built a smaller school which they found to be attended by some thirty students, not all of whom were Métis. The smaller registration at the school was but an indication of the flight of the Métis from the colony. Many had already moved away to try to find a life of their former freedom or to hang about the outskirts of the prairie cities in poverty. It was becoming obvious that it would be better to abandon the whole idea and to let the land they had spurned be given to homesteaders who were already clamouring to occupy it.

Because this was the way the wind was blowing, discouragement enveloped the aging missionary who, looking back over his life, often thought that he could see more failures written in his record than successes. One of these failures which still rankled was his defeat in the battle over the school question. Amidst other complications which came to the surface in 1905 when the two provinces of Alberta and Saskatchewan were created, the problem of separate schools bobbed up again. Trying to influence its progress stood the church. Fortunately Father Lacombe at seventy-eight years of age was considered too old to take part in the special pleadings and thereby was spared the bitterness of another personal defeat. He could not help but regret, however, that once more the bishops' wishes had been foiled.

Nevertheless, when the two provinces of Alberta and Saskatchewan were set up and self-government came to his old prairies, Father Lacombe, like all other westerners, was well satisfied. Of the two provinces, he found his interest more heavily vested in the westerly one. Aside from such of his years which had been passed in Manitoba, practically all of his working life on the prairies had been spent in Alberta — mainly near Fort Edmonton, Fort Calgary, Fort Macleod and at Pincher Creek.

It was, therefore, with an intimate knowledge of its history and geography and a great pride in its beauty and its resources that the benign old missionary noted its elevation to provincial status. Few things pleased him more than that the province's white population was nearing the 180,000 mark.

For some months after the first Alberta legislature had finished its inaugural session in 1906, Father Lacombe divided his time between his hermitage, Medicine Hat, Lethbridge and other points in the south of the province. In January 1907, during a visit to Edmonton he went out to Beaumont, one of his French Canadian settlements. He had been largely instrumental in inducing its pioneers to come west and when word got around the community that the *fameux Père Lacombe* was coming they flocked to hear him. At the conclusion of a thrilling sermon he advised them to stick with their colony and to persevere. "Courage and tenacity," he said, "these form the secret of success." A month later, flitting across the continent by the grace of his CPR pass, he became a guest in Archbishop Bruchesi's palace in Montreal. There at a banquet in his honour he celebrated his eightieth birthday.

Father Lacombe soon returned to his hermitage where with only an occasional side trip, he spent the next several months. By 1908 the affairs of his St. Paul des Métis had come to such a pass that Father Lacombe, the trustee of the colony who had held out the longest, gave in and signed the documents which in effect wound it up. A few of the more staunch of the Métis remained and took the opportunity of obtaining title to the lands on which they lived. The rest had flown to the cities or to the woods and lakes far back from civilization.

Prior to that, however, an influx of settlers from Quebec had been directed to vacant land surrounding St. Paul des Métis for miles on all sides. By the end of 1908 the foundations of the parishes of Bonnyville, St. Edouard, Lafond and St. Vincent had been laid. To the satisfaction of Father Lacombe's colleagues the area for miles north and east of St. Paul des Métis had been claimed as a new Quebec. But now that in the centre of this large French settlement the Métis colony had dispersed and left a nearly empty rectangle with a well-stocked Oblate mission at its centre, what was to become of it? One of these days it would be thrown open for settlement and immigrants of all nationalities and faiths would rush in to claim it. Such a multicultural mixture in the heart of an otherwise French Canadian colony might present problems that the good fathers of St. Paul des Métis resolved to head off.

That they were in a good position to do. Between them and Frank Oliver, the minister of the Interior, had flown a reciprocal stream of benefits: concessions for them, votes for him. In 1904, for instance, he had needed votes badly and in the St. Paul area all but a handful of the 134 eligible voters were Métis. When the polling had taken place the returning officer reported: for Oliver, 134; for Secord, 0. When the fathers delivered votes they delivered all of them.

Now that the fathers needed assistance, surely Oliver could help them. If the old Métis colony were to be thrown open for settlement on a day announced well in advance, a multilingual mob would storm the land office and "pouf" would go most of the best land in the heart of the French settlement. If, however, the date were kept secret from the world at large and disclosed only in the most discreet circles, the French folk surrounding the old colony could assemble all the uncles, brothers and cousins and just happen to have them go to Edmonton so that on the morning of April 10, 1909, they could form a line waiting for the land office doors to open. Greater miracles had happened. But that one was great enough and on the appointed day, with only one thought in mind, nearly five hundred men from the St. Paul region filed on homesteads. So ended the St. Paul des Métis colony. In that fashion one of the province's good farming areas came into the hands of a group well prepared to develop it.

The final loss of his Métis colony severed another of the ties that bound the aged priest to the busy world. It was to be expected, of course, that a man of fourscore years should find the world passing him by while it laid its never ending problems on younger shoulders. Less and less frequently visitors came to consult the benign old gentleman whose memories of the West went back far beyond the year in which they had been born. Whenever a visitor or a suppliant came, he met with a cordial reception and went away richer by his contact with the old priest's warm and witty wisdom. Since he spent most of his time at the hermitage he was somewhat outside the mainstream of visitors.

But to offset that, he was frequently invited to preach here and to speak there, and to attend ecclesiastical councils. November 1908 saw him in Chicago where he was acclaimed when he attended such sessions and sat through the lectures. Much of their meaning passed over his head for his ears were ringing with dreams of a new charitable venture. On his return to the West he opened the year 1909 with an announcement of his new campaign.

For years now white civilization had found itself seated firmly in the saddle of the West. With it had come many good things, schools, hospitals and churches. With it also had come the old, infirm or helpless ones, who in Blackfoot culture would have been cared for but who all too often found their white confreres unseeing, arrogant and passing them by. It was to them that the old missionary now directed his not inconsiderable talents. From then on the charitable institution which he planned to build at Midnapore occupied all but the few of his waking hours spent attending meetings at which everyone deferred to his white locks and honoured him in various ways.

In Quebec he coupled a collecting campaign with a great gathering when in August 1909 he attended the first Plenary Council of the Church in Canada. A month later he was back in the West when he heard that the new University of Alberta was to bestow an honorary degree upon his old friend Lord Strathcona. Moreover, both of the cities which faced each other across the Saskatchewan River, Edmonton and the recently incorporated Strathcona, which had been named after him, had decided to honour the ninety-year-old statesman who came on his own CPR special train. On September 7, 1909, driving him around each of the cities by automobile, the officials let him greet welcoming crowds which stood amidst the bonfires and the Chinese lanterns. From four to six in the afternoon he was to be entertained at Government House, which was then on the corner of Edmonton's 100 Avenue and 103 Street.

Though Father Lacombe had not been included in the official party, he hurried over to the reception, and finding Lord Strathcona there ahead of time, greeted him affectionately. Escaping from the gathering crowd the two old veterans seated themselves on a rustic bench and there, oblivious of the others, chatted about the days when they had first met and of their association while the CPR was being built.

Of the pair an Edmonton *Bulletin* reporter wrote: "There, seated side by side, were Lord Strathcona and Father Lacombe, chatting with a hand on each other's shoulder and talking over the old days in the west country, which each knew so well. Both men had spent nearly three-quarters of a century in Western Canada and their animated conversation showed that they had many a memory and probably a secret or two in common. . . ."

Father Lacombe could not let the occasion slip away without a request for a *"petit souvenir"* for his home for the poor. Listening, the one great man, the millionaire, studied the other perhaps greater one, the missionary and the acknowledged chief of the West whose claim to fame lay in his greatness of heart.

As the two were forced to separate to talk to other guests, Father Lacombe's parting words were: "My Home shall be my last piece of work."

A few days later he received a *petit souvenir* for two thousand dollars.

The day following the reception at Government House the old priest moved over to St. Albert to take part in a combined ceremony honouring him and the Grey Nuns. For him it was the sixty years he had served as a priest; for the sisters it marked the fiftieth anniversary of their predecessors' arrival at the little mission of Lac Ste. Anne. To honour both, but perhaps mainly the vivid old priest, clergy and laymen, as well as nuns of many orders and garbs, had come from near and far. Mingling with them all were the remainder of the old guard of the Oblates. Oldest perhaps in years of service was Father Tissier, who recalled Father Lacombe's visit to Dunvegan thirty-nine years previously; Father Leduc, pock-marked by the 1870 smallpox, and Father Blanchet, who had tended him. Father Doucet, who in 1874 had first seen the Bow River, was there, as well as Father Lestanc and Father Legoff. And present in spirit were all those others who had gone before: Fathers Thibault, Rémas, André, Vegreville, Bishop Grandin and the great Archbishop Taché, for all of them had known hardship and shared it with Albert Lacombe. Present too was Gaspard Lacombe, the foot-loose wanderer who had long since settled down to farm, as well as Father Lacombe's niece Georgiana, with some of her nearly grown children. Already her eldest son, Edmund, had tasted of Father Lacombe's benevolence by having spent a year or so at St. Boniface College. But he was grown up now and was working towards becoming a locomotive engineer on the old priest's CPR and on the line which ran from Calgary to Macleod.

It was on this run that week after week Ed Kelly was able to watch the progress of Father Lacombe's new home for which the old priest had many a step to take. One of the first was to discuss the matter with Calgary's first millionaire, Pat Burns, the one-time Irish Catholic boy who, seizing every opportunity, had contracted to supply meat to the CPR construction gangs as they worked their way west from Winnipeg to Calgary. By the time the rails reached the Bow River he was a rich man who, while still contracting, had started ranching and made Calgary his headquarters. As Father Lacombe looked upon him, he felt his rich friend to be doubly blessed; he had money, endless piles of it, and he owned land a few miles south of the new city, endless acres of it. Being so blessed he fell a ready and willing victim to the campaigning priest who extracted from him a large sum of money and two hundred acres of land. That was just a start. For the next year or so he collected from rich and poor in Alberta, in the West and even on a trip through Quebec. By 1910, well after Lord Strathcona's *petit souvenir* had been added to his fund and, when he found that he had collected $30,000, he let a contract to some builders to erect his brick home for a figure close to $60,000.

From then on, every time Ed Kelly drove his locomotive through Midnapore he noted continuing progress on the red brick building until, as the snow started to fall, it was finished. Then in a ceremony on November 9, 1910, the Lacombe Home for the Poor was declared open and some of the West's destitute, red and white, had a haven. Almost unaided, the determined old missionary had raised some $60,000, a sum equivalent to half a million of today's dollars.

During all the months of the home's construction Father Lacombe, as enthusiastic as he had been when half a century earlier he had built St. Albert, lived in a hut on the site. On its completion he moved into his home, the most personal of all his lifetime of works. For the next few years, cared for by the Sisters of Providence, he lived amongst the latest in his decades-long line of protégés. From his eyrie on the home's south-facing porch he watched all of the world that could be seen from his now limited outlook. And ever as he sat with the days and the weeks clinging tediously, the years nevertheless sped rapidly.

To relieve their tedium many local and Calgary friends came to call and once in a while some great figure from the outside world would come to renew a vivid acquaintance of decades earlier. Such a figure was Sir Thomas Shaughnessy, then president of the CPR, who, whenever he could, made a point of visiting the mellowing old man on his birthday. When he came in person he brought a unique present; when he could not come he sent it, and Father Lacombe never tired of its sameness. For each year the bag which he handed the priest contained gold coins, one for each year of his life. When 1913 rolled around Shaughnessy appeared again, saying,

"Well, Father, it is about that time of year again. So here once more is your annual gift — one piece of gold for each year."

For a few minutes the two men toyed with this pleasantry which had grown up between them and Father Lacombe counted the coins. "One, two, three . . . thirty . . . sixty . . . eighty-five, eighty-six — yes, they are all here. I am starting to fetch a good price."

"Yes," replied Shaughnessy, "but, my friend, I hope and pray that we shall pay it for many a year to come."

Shortly after Shaughnessy's visit Father Lacombe made one of his very infrequent excursions beyond the borders of the home's grounds. In March 1913 he allowed himself to be taken the few miles into Calgary where at St. Mary's church he gave his last public address. There, bent by the burden of his years and leaning heavily on his cane, he pleaded for more funds for his home. His silvery hair touching his shoulders framed the deep furrows of his face, which at times streamed with tears of emotion and gratitude as he looked out upon the large auditorium packed by men and women of several creeds. Fortunately a *Family Herald* reporter caught the spirit of the occasion when he wrote:

"As the black figure, leaning on a cane, stood at the altar and waved for silence, a thrill of admiration passed over the audience. There was something melodramatic about the hush that followed in the wake of the uplifted arm. The bent figure silently gazed at the sea of faces before him and the gaze was returned by thousands of eyes and so profound was the silence that even breathing seemed a sacrilege.

"A sob, audible in every part of the church, came from the grizzled Father. . . . The profound truth that this appeal might be his last in public, seemed to dawn on the aged man and his audience at the same time, and there was another lull until the realization of the fact had sunk deep into the hearts of everyone present.

"But the figure at the altar stiffened, the withered lips moved, and . . . in simple words, but a direct manner, clear and deliberate, audible to the farthest corner of the church, he pleaded the cause of the Indian. He remained standing with the support of his cane, until shaken with emotion, and overcome with the efforts of his task, he was forced to sit down and in that position finished his plea. At the conclusion of his remarks there was hardly a dry eye in the audience."

It was indeed a stirring sermon and he concluded with these words:

"A man of eighty-six cannot expect to do very much. . . . Many years ago I stood here on this piece of ground and pictured to myself the time when a great cathedral would stand here. . . .

"I shall not be with you very long now. I want to plead with you for the poor and the needy and the destitute. God bless you all, both now and in your day of need and suffering. God bless you for your kindness to those needy ones at Midnapore. God bless you, people of Calgary, God bless you!"

It was his last public appearance. For three more years, in full possession of his faculties, he made his way amongst the poor and the aged in his home. Aside from that, nothing was left to him but to remember and dream of the sixty-odd years he had spent in the prairies and parklands of the West — the great days.

At times in memory he galloped again over the hills of North Dakota to the rescue of Métis under the attack of the Sioux or relived that grey, snowy morning when in the Battle River valley he had been grazed by a bullet. Sometimes as he closed his eyes he saw his thousand Crees crossing the broad river at St. Paul des Cris, sometimes he saw the view from the Neutral Hills when for miles below the country was black with buffalo, and many a time he sat by any one of a thousand creeks boiling his kettle in a Cree or Blackfoot camp.

But on December 11, 1916, the dreams ceased and his spirit became forever free to roam the wilderness wonderland of his youth — to roam from Fort Chipewyan to Fort Benton, from Fort Garry to Fort Edmonton. Men said the old priest was dead.

CHAPTER TWENTY

Epilogue

As word spread from church to church, from Indian reserve to Métis cabin, from province to province and from the mountains to the Gaspé, sorrow filled the land. All the West paused to acknowledge the passing of one of its greatest pioneers. For two or three days the floodgates of memory and sentiment ran unabashed as the West anticipated or heard of Father Lacombe's funeral and as tributes poured in to a bereaved bishop and diocese. Sir Thomas Shaughnessy:

> "In our annals there is none more deserving of the admiration and undying memory of his fellow countrymen than that good man, Père Lacombe."

The Calgary *Albertan*:

> "A life given devotedly to the interest of suffering humanity . . . evidence of his life work will long endure and bear witness to his unselfish and unstinted devotion and service to the people of the new West."

The Lethbridge *Herald*:

> "His death . . . crowns a life spent solely in the interests of suffering humanity."

When on December 14 his first funeral mass was celebrated in Calgary, the Right Reverend J. T. McNally, bishop of Calgary, could look out upon the lieutenant-governor of Alberta, as well as members of the provincial cabinet, representatives of the CPR and civic officials from Fort Macleod, Lethbridge and Calgary.

From the church the solemn procession led by the mounted police, and composed of various religious, civic and Indian societies, as well as most of the leading men of the southern part of the province, made its way to the CPR station through blocks lined with sorrowing, respectful crowds. From there the great railway corporation paid further respect to its one-time "president." Though his friend Sir William Van Horne had predeceased him by a year, the CPR felt privileged to provide a special train to bear his body northward to be buried at the mission he had started so long ago. This time there was no pass to be tendered by an old man and no conductor to wave it aside smilingly.

Instead, at the throttle of the specially assigned, sombrely draped locomotive stood the old missionary's nephew, Ed Kelly, son of his niece Georgiana. And as he urged his train north over the rise of land near Crossfield whence the old buffalo pasturing prairies swept around nearly a full circle to the horizon forty miles away, Kelly and his crew wondered how often on foot, horse or more recently by train the great missionary had made his way across these vast flats. Swinging around the curves along Waskasu Creek and rocking down to cross the Red Deer River and then rolling on to the bridges over the Blindman and Battle rivers, each of the priests in the mournful procession wondered in how many places their train wheels were actually pounding over the site of some happy or sorrowful camp wherein decades ago their old comrade had played his part. Boring on into the north, whistling mournfully when crossing roads leading to the farms of some of Father Lacombe's colonists, the locomotive finally rattled over the switches until it slowed to cross Edmonton's magnificent new high level bridge.

As the train crawled over it, its passengers peered out the windows of its right side. Far below them at the water's edge was the now unused landing onto which sixty-four years previously the young Father Lacombe had stepped to begin his work in the West. Higher up the bank, mere ridges in the snow outlined the spot where John Rowand's old Fort Edmonton had stood before it had been torn down in 1915. For a hundred years it had been a landmark in this nearly empty land. Now its place had been taken by a building to mark the years ahead — a magnificent stone domed Legislative Building. And as Ed

Kelly allowed the locomotive to coast into the new CPR station the funeral train rolled past the relatively new church of St. Joachim, the descendant of the log edifice William Christie had built for the eager missionary fifty-seven years ago.

It was to this church that on the morrow the hearse was conducted by a long cortege which included the 233rd Battalion with its French Canadian band. It was there in the presence of sorrowing Edmontonians, led by the Honourable Frank Oliver, that Bishop Grouard celebrated a requiem mass. Finally on December 16 the old missionary's body was taken up his "dear hill" where in the St. Albert mission started so long ago by a fresh-faced, vigorous young priest, his last ceremony, conducted by Archbishop Legal of Edmonton, a long-time comrade, came to a close. At its conclusion his mortal remains, except for his heart, were laid reverently in the crypt of the church beside his bishop, the saintly Grandin. By his request, his heart had been left out on the prairies of his Blackfoot people in his last great work, the Lacombe Home for the Poor.

For a profit-oriented society scrambling for the rewards which were accruing to it partly because of the toil of pioneers such as the old father, it would have been easy after that to have forgotten all about him. His goodness had run too deeply, however, and his humility had touched so many hearts that even such a society could not forget. The passing years instead of shrinking his reputation had swelled it until as western Canada's foremost legendary figure the fame of the French farm boy from St. Sulpice had come to tower above all others. Ten years after his death, in a large celebration, a West already effete marked the hundredth anniversary of his birth. Arising out of that came a move to follow in his mendicant's steps and to collect money for a statue to be erected in his memory.

As a result, on July 21, 1929, in a village with a population of but a few hundred, some five thousand people attended the unveiling of a statue of the pioneer. Cast in bronze, this life-size likeness with outstretched arms and raised crucifix appears as the old missionary must so often have appeared to welcoming Indian camps. Placed in a choice setting on the brink of the hill, the bronze figure faces out towards the trail which still leads to the site of Fort Edmonton and on toward his old prairies and parklands. Two paces from the statue is the spot where some sixty years earlier Bishop Taché had stuck his staff and around which Father Lacombe had built the St. Albert mission.

But the statue is not all of this memorial dedicated to the memory of the past. So as to preserve it for future generations, the good father's friends also built a brick structure around his old church. The aging building itself, a crude cabin hewn by his own and his Métis' hands, speaks of his triumphs as one by one its logs went up, the door was hung on leather hinges and the little openings left in the walls were filled with parchment. We can imagine his final satisfaction in assembling the crude altar and saying its first mass.

Having preserved the sagging log structure as a museum, they filled it with pictures and souvenirs of its builder and of his associates. Outstanding among them are the successor to his first Oblate cross, a few books in Cree and Blackfoot, his Catholic ladder, pictures of various episodes in his life and on a wall one of the many dozen pairs of snowshoes he wore during the days of his tireless struggles against snowstorms, fatigue and famine.

Such memorials are due him for no one did more for the early West than he. It is well, too, that these relics of the early Oblates have been preserved, for to no priests are we so indebted as to the Oblates of Mary Immaculate. And of all who fought in their ranks no one was more deservedly acclaimed than Albert Lacombe, O.M.I.

Well may we apply to him words he used in reference to others. "They have sown in tears . . . those who follow will reap in joy."

Picture Credits

Index

Two Hills, town of, 141, 185.

Van Horne, W. C., 245, 259, 262, 268, 280, 287-292, 338.
Vegreville, Rev. Father Valentin, 81, 190, 192, 248, 274, 325, 333.
Vegreville, town of, 185, 291.
Vermilion River, 144.
Viau, Rev. Father, 17, 19, 21-26.
Victoria mission, 130, 137, 153, 154, 179, 193, 205, 208, 251.
Villeneuve, hamlet of, 291.
Vimy, village of, 291.

Walker, Major James, 309.

Ward, George, 100.
West, Rev. John, 31.
Wetaskiwin, city of, 96, 269, 289.
Whitefish Lake, 78, 111, 117, 124, 137, 208.
White Horse Plain, 32, 42, 44, 47.
Whitford Lake, 141.
Winnipeg, city of, 27, 180, 224, 225, 230, 232, 234, 237-245, 248, 261-264, 272, 279, 280, 290.
Woolsey, Rev. Thomas, 89, 90, 93, 102, 106, 117, 118, 123, 127, 129.

Young, Harrison, 201.